Pekka Kujamäki / Leena Kolehmainen / Esa Penttilä / Hannu Kemppanen (eds.)
Beyond Borders – Translations Moving Languages, Literatures and Cultures

Hartwig Kalverkämper/Larisa Schippel (Hg.)
TRANSÜD.
Arbeiten zur Theorie und Praxis des Übersetzens und Dolmetschens
Band 39

Pekka Kujamäki/Leena Kolehmainen/Esa Penttilä/
Hannu Kemppanen (eds.)

Beyond Borders – Translations Moving Languages, Literatures and Cultures

Verlag für wissenschaftliche Literatur

Umschlagabbildung: Kasinoinseln in Savonlinna, Finnland, © Pekka Kujamäki

ISBN 978-3-86596-356-7
ISSN 1438-2636

© Frank & Timme GmbH Verlag für wissenschaftliche Literatur
Berlin 2011. Alle Rechte vorbehalten.

Das Werk einschließlich aller Teile ist urheberrechtlich geschützt.
Jede Verwertung außerhalb der engen Grenzen des Urheberrechts-
gesetzes ist ohne Zustimmung des Verlags unzulässig und strafbar.
Das gilt insbesondere für Vervielfältigungen, Übersetzungen,
Mikroverfilmungen und die Einspeicherung und Verarbeitung in
elektronischen Systemen.

Herstellung durch das atelier eilenberger, Taucha bei Leipzig.
Printed in Germany.
Gedruckt auf säurefreiem, alterungsbeständigem Papier.

www.frank-timme.de

Contents

Foreword ... 7

TRANSLATIONS AS REACTIONS TO POLITICS

CARMEN CAMUS CAMUS *(Santander, Spain)*
Tracing the Voyage of Arthur Penn's Little Big Man into the Spanish Culture: Reception of the Film and Censorship Constraints ... 13

CHAPMAN CHEN *(Joensuu, Finland)*
Postcolonial Hong Kong Drama Translation ... 39

SOCIO-CULTURAL FACTORS AFFECTING TRANSLATION STRATEGIES

KATARÍNA NEMČOKOVÁ *(Zlín, Czech Republic)*
Translating Slogans: Advertising Campaigns Across Languages ... 59

MINNA RUOKONEN *(Turku, Finland)*
Target Readers' Expectations and Reality: Conformity or Conflict? ... 73

PIET VAN POUCKE *(Ghent, Belgium)*
Translation and Linguistic Innovation: The Rise and Fall of Russian Loanwords in Literary Translation into Dutch ... 101

DISCOVERING THE ROLE OF TRANSLATIONS

MARIEKE DELAHAYE *(Brussels/Leuven, Belgium)*
Intertextuality and Historiography: The New World Popularized, or the Encyclopaedic Language of Historical Discourse ... 121

HANNU KEMPPANEN *(Joensuu, Finland)*
Pamphlet or Scholarly Work? Book Reviews and Determining the Place of a Translation ... 145

ANALYZING TRANSLATIONAL SHIFTS

RITVA LEPPIHALME *(Helsinki, Finland)*
The Taming of a Translation: Microlevel Choices Leading to Macrolevel
Thematic Shifts   163

MAURIZIO VIEZZI *(Trieste, Italy)*
The Translation of Book Titles: Theoretical and Practical Aspects   183

TRANSLATION SHAPING THE TARGET LANGUAGE

JOSEP MARCO *(Castelló, Spain)*
Some Insights into the Factors Underlying the Translation of
Phraseology in the COVALT Corpus   197

LEENA KOLEHMAINEN *(Joensuu, Finland)*
Source Language Influence Without the Effect of "Shining Through":
Over-Representation of Generic Person Reference in Translations   215

ESA PENTTILÄ & PIRKKO MUIKKU-WERNER *(Joensuu, Finland)*
English Gatecrashers in Finnish: Directly Translated English Idioms as
Novelties of Finnish   247

Foreword

The present volume is a collection of articles presented at the conference on Translation Studies, December 10–12 2009 in Joensuu, Finland. The conference was organized to mark the end of the three-year transition period in which the former Savonlinna School of Translation Studies, University of Joensuu, was being relocated to the university main campus in Joensuu. With the conference we wished to relocate us on the map of Translation Studies and invite our international colleagues to discuss current and future orientations in the field. Hence the conference title *Translation Studies: Moving In – Moving On*. As structural changes are characteristic of the contemporary Finnish academic life, we need to add for the sake of clarification that at the same time with our moving to Joensuu, the Universities of Joensuu and Kuopio were joining their forces and merging into the University of Eastern Finland. This means that, by the time of writing this foreword, the training of translators and interpreters, which started in Savonlinna in 1968, and the conjoined research into translation and interpreting are carried out on the Joensuu Campus of the University of Eastern Finland, Philosophical Faculty, School of Humanities.

The conference *Translation Studies: Moving In – Moving On* focused on topics that represent the three central research areas of Translation Studies in Joensuu, namely, (1) translation process research, (2) research on translated language, and (3) the sociology of translation. The invited plenary speakers, Professor emerita Sonja Tirkkonen-Condit (University of Eastern Finland), Professor Arnt Lykke Jakobsen (Copenhagen Business School) and Professor Anthony Pym (Universitat Rovira i Virgili), each represent research excellence in one of these areas. The present proceedings contain papers selected from presentations in the last two thematic areas, whereas presentations on translation and interpreting processes will be published as a thematic issue of *Across Languages and Cultures* in 2011 (working title: Towards professionalism, edited by Riitta Jääskeläinen, Pekka Kujamäki and Jukka Mäkisalo).

The title *Beyond Borders – Translations Moving Languages, Literatures and Cultures* implies a twofold descriptive research question common to all papers in this volume: First, all contributions relate to the question of how translation moves, i.e. *transfers*, literature, cultural scripts, or products, and linguistic features beyond borders. What changes are involved in or even necessarily caused by this transfer? What changes do translators deem necessary and why? How do target cultural factors impinge on their translation strategies? Secondly, the papers frequently discuss the question of how translation and translations move, i.e. *influence, try to influence* or *are allowed to influence* target languages, literatures and cultures. For example: What kind of traces does translation as a process leave in the translated language? How do these traces live on in the target culture? What functions are given to the translated text before or after translation – apart from the fact that it is represented as another text from the source culture. In other words, looking from the target culture perspective, the papers deal with the question of how and under what circumstances target cultures accept or reject linguistic features, concepts or ideas that cross cultural and linguistic borders through translation. These questions are approached through different empirical data including advertisements, audiovisual translations, encyclopedia as well as translations of literary prose, drama and history texts. Moreover, as the multiplicity of the questions above already imply, a variety of methodologies are needed to answer them; the methods used in this work vary from corpus-linguistic methods to analysis of paratexts, and from cross-linguistic analysis of source and target texts to contextualization of target texts in their respective target cultures. The languages dealt with in these articles include Catalan, Czech, Chinese, Dutch, English, Finnish, French, German, Italian, Russian and Spanish.

The volume opens up with two papers discussing translations as reactions to political circumstances of the target culture. **Carmen Camus Camus** describes the passage of Arthur Penn's movie *Little Big Man* into the Spanish culture focusing on the effects of Franco's censorship on micro- or macrostructural changes introduced by the translator or by the distribution company. The article shows how the shifts relate to an aim of adapting the film to the predominant values of Franco's era. **Chapman Chen** provides a critical account of mainstream postcolonial (translation) theories and their applicability to the Western drama in Hong Kong translation. According to Chen's study, postcolonial drama translation in Hong Kong reflects – in the translators' manipulations as well as in the re-readings by the directors and audiences – a clear nostalgia for the British colonial rule and, at the same time, a critical attitude towards China as the second colonizer. In this context, the translation is not used for the deconstruction of Western colonialism but for interrogations with the new colonial power.

The second chapter discusses translation norms and strategies changing with the socio-cultural factors of the target side. **Katarína Nemčoková** offers a case study of advertising campaigns moving together with the (global) products into Czech and Slovak Republics in the last 20 years. She observes a change of advertising and translation strategies reflecting the global status of the Czech and Slovak markets, the assumed status of the target language, consumers' and advertisers' attitudes as well as the translational practice in the target culture. **Minna Ruokonen** discusses literary translators' attitudes towards the target readers' expectations, using the Finnish translations of Dorothy L. Sayer's detective novels translated in the 1940s and 1980s as her case in point. This case study into the Finnish translation history shows that as the readers' expectations have remained fairly constant in the course of time, the translators' response to them have experienced a real change from conflict to conformity. Ruokonen argues that this change is linked to translators' working conditions, SL competence and to the target culture status of the translated genre. **Piet Van Poucke** provides a diachronic analysis of the use of Russian loanwords in Dutch translations of Russian literary texts. The study of 20 translations spread over the period of forty years (1970–2009) reveals a move away from foreignizing translation strategies and use of Russian loanwords of the 1970s and 1980s towards domesticating translation strategies as indicated by the decreasing number of Russian loanwords in the data. Explanations for these observations are sought in the Dutch readers' changing interest in Russian literature, in the translators' changing ideas of what is acceptable for Dutch readers as well as in the dominance of Anglo-American (domesticating) translation norms.

The role and place of translations in the target culture discourse is dealt with in two papers. **Marieke Delahaye** analyses traces of translation in the discourse on the "discovery" and "conquest" of the "New World" by the Spaniards. With a corpus of three European encyclopaedias, Delahaye shows how translation and other discursive techniques contribute to the hybrid and seemingly monolingual character of this discourse and shape the world views carried by the encyclopaedic articles in question. In order to study the acceptance of foreign (and translated) contributions in the domestic discourse, **Hannu Kemppanen** uses book reviews of one Russian book on Finnish political history translated into Finnish in 1974. He divides the reception in two discourses, into the discourses of rejection and acceptance, both of which reveal different attitudes towards the contribution of the reviewed translation in the discourse as well as towards translation and its cultural place in general.

Ritva Leppihalme and Maurizio Viezzi approach translation as a problem that calls for conscious strategic considerations. In **Leppihalme's** study, the translator is challenged to creativity by micro-level translation problems such as malapropisms, rhymes and palindromes that possess – in addition to their micro-level playfulness – macro-level thematic and characterizing functions in the postcolonial novel *The Poisonwood Bible* by Barbara Kingsolver. Leppihalme shows how the Finnish translators have to a great extent leveled-out these micro-level features of the source text. She elaborates the thematic shifts prompted on the macro-level, and discusses the potential reasons for these translational deviations. On a somewhat more general level, **Maurizio Viezzi** looks at translation of book titles from a practical as well as from a theoretical perspective. The formulation – or the translation – of a title for the target text, Viezzi argues, is influenced first and foremost by its distinctive function in the target culture, which may lead to titles that deviate strongly from the corresponding source text titles. For the description of the relationships between such translations and their source titles, Viezzi proposes the concept of *translemic equivalence* coined in 1991 by Rabadan.

The last three studies focus on features of translated language and on translation shaping the target language. Starting from the observation that Catalan translations of English literature seem to be more phraseological than their corresponding source texts, **Josep Marco** reports on a survey of translators' views on translation of phraseology in literary texts. The translators' answers indicate that stylistic motivation and translators' expertise are important factors behind the observed phenomenon, but, at the same time, they suggest that a multitude of other factors also has an effect on the translators' choices. **Leena Kolehmainen** contributes to the study of translation universals with a corpus-based investigation into the over-representation of generic person reference in German translations from Finnish. Kolehmainen shows how cross-linguistic differences in grammatical devices for person reference are reflected in German translations from Finnish. Her results support previous observations of conspicuous correlation between over-representation and source language stimuli. However, the source language stimuli do not "shine through" as deviating use of target language items that imitate the source language practice, but they rather cause untypical frequencies of items that are already used in the texts anyway – an observation to be added to the discussion of translation universals. The volume is closed by **Esa Penttilä** and **Pirkko Muikku-Werner**. They introduce another case of source language influence in the target language, namely, the phenomenon of word-for-word translations of English idiomatic expressions into Finnish. The writers provide a classification of these imported expressions according to their transparency for the actual users, look for possible reasons for their seemingly increased use and discuss their capacity to enrich the Finnish idiom repertoire.

Beyond Borders – Translations Moving Languages, Literatures and Cultures is a collection of papers selected through an anonymous peer review procedure. We would like to express our deepest gratitude to all our 14 anonymous international peers for their valuable contribution to this project, and especially for their constructive and clear comments that helped the writers to develop their papers further.

Joensuu December 21, 2010

Hannu Kemppanen   Leena Kolehmainen   Pekka Kujamäki   Esa Penttilä

Tracing the Voyage of Arthur Penn's *Little Big Man* into the Spanish Culture: Reception of the Film and Censorship Constraints

Carmen Camus Camus
University of Cantabria, Santander, Spain

Abstract

This paper provides a case study of the incidence and effects of Franco's censorship on the passage of Arthur Penn's *Little Big Man* into the Spanish culture. The film is studied with a three-stage method: preliminary analysis of the reception of the film and of the censorship data; analysis of the suppressions and modifications made to scenes at the macrotextual level; and a comparison of selected fragments of original and dubbed dialogues to identify the formal microtextual changes introduced due to (self)censorship, and their resultant semantic shifts and pragmatic effects. The analysis shows that, despite mixed reviews in the USA, the film was generally well received in Spain. At the macrotextual level, the distribution company suppressed one scene before presenting the dubbed version to the censorship board for authorisation, and altered a further five scenes in their negotiation with the board after the initial resolution. The predominant translation techniques applied to the dialogues studied were commutation of meanings and refocalisation, which were aimed at accommodating the discourse to the postulates of the regime, the main concern being sexual morality but also involved safeguarding the image of institutions such as the Church and the military.

1 Introduction

Within the ideological context of the Franco regime (1939–1975), the *Western* genre experienced an unparalleled increase in popularity both in narrative and film. At the height of its popularity, the genre accounted for almost 80 percent of the censorship files for popular narrative (Rabadán 2000: 261). This study forms part of a broader research project on the incidence and effects of official state censorship and self-censorship on the English-Spanish translation of *Westerns* and their cultural influence on the Spanish polysystem. During Franco's dictatorship all works in Spain had to be submitted to the official Board of Censorship to obtain authorisation prior to publication or exhibition. The files opened for each individual work are kept at the Administration's General Archive (AGA), a procedure that has left enough traces to allow the reconstruction of the translation and censorship process to which works were submitted. This paper offers a case study of the incidence of both official censorship and self-censorship on the translation of the script dialogues of Arthur Penn's film version of Thomas Berger's novel *Little Big Man*.

2 Film censorship during the Franco regime

Although censorship was implemented in the areas controlled by Franco's "National" troops even before the end of the civil war, official censorship was made compulsory for the whole country after Franco's victory by a Ministerial Order passed on July 15th, 1939, (BOE [Spanish Official Bulletin] 30/07/1939). These regulations, with certain modifications, remained in force for nearly forty years until the new Spanish Constitution was enacted in 1978. In the censorial macrostructure created to this end, film censorship was just one of five branches which controlled all cultural activity in the country. However, for film censorship they continued to apply almost the same censorial procedure established in 1938 (BOE 23/04/1938) and kept in force until 1963, when the long-awaited Film Censorship Norms were passed (BOE 08/03/1963). These norms represented the first set of detailed rules that codified "what was prohibited", with the novelty of establishing and regulating criteria that producers and distributors had to follow. Although the new criteria brought about little change in actual censorial practice, which continued to be applied in an arbitrary manner, they served as a general guide for film production and distribution companies in their strategic use of self-censorship and negotiation in the censorship process. These norms remained in force until they were replaced by new Film Censorship Norms in 1975 (BOE 01/03/1975).

The censorship boards responsible for the task were composed of members of the military, representatives of the Catholic Church, ideologues of the *Falange* (the regime's political wing) and cinema experts aligned with the regime. However, the composition and balance of the boards varied during the dictatorship in the same way that the censorial filter was adapted to the changing socio-economic and political climate over the forty-year period (Camus 2010: 43).

3 Materials and methods

3.1 Selection criteria

The voyage of *Little Big Man* into the Spanish culture took place during Sánchez Bella's term at the Ministry of Information and Tourism (1970–1973), a period when the popularity of the Western genre began to decline, but which also saw a return to stricter censorship practices. This pair of intersemiotically coupled parallel texts was chosen in accordance with the criteria set for the TRACEciO corpus (Camus 2009): (1) the film was based on a narrative work, and not on an original film script; (2) both the film and the narrative work had suffered some kind of censorship; (3) the different coupled parallel texts were representative of the prolonged time span of the Dictatorship (1939–1975), thus reflecting changes in censorship in relation to significant changes in the socio-economic and political context; (4) the text material was readily available for analysis.

In the case of *Little Big Man* (*LBM*), Arthur Penn's film (1970) is based on the homonymous novel by Thomas Berger (1964). When the Spanish translation of the novel was submitted to the censorship board for authorisation, the only change documented was to the title. Although, unfortunately, the censorship files and documentation for the film could not be located at the AGA, we know from a previous study (González Ballesteros 1981) that the Spanish version of the film *Pequeño Gran Hombre* (*PGH*) had been generously pruned by the official censorship procedure. The film *LBM*, first shown in the USA in December 1970, was released after the Hays Code was abolished.[1] In Spain, *PGH* was released on the 27th of November, 1971, during the final period of Franco's regime (1970–1975), when the Spanish Film Censorship Norms passed in 1963 were still in force.

---

[1] Motion Picture Producers and Distributors of America, directed by Will H. Hays, introduced an ethical code whose main aim was to self-regulate the film industry. The code, which came into effect on 1st July, 1934, specified what could or could not be shown in American cinemas in accordance with basic principles of "good taste" and the requirement that "no picture shall be produced which will lower the standard of those who see it". The code remained in force until 1966, when pressure for social change and greater freedom of expression led to it being replaced in 1968 by a new age-based classification, the Code and Rating Administration System.

The analysis of the film version of *LBM/PGH* is aimed at revealing the extent to which the Spanish censorship system adapted to the cascade of changes in the regulation of films in the USA and how this was reflected in the visual and textual modes in the Spanish version.

3.2 Method of text analysis

The study is framed within the Descriptive Translation Studies paradigm as its epistemological foundation (Toury 1995), and adopts the postulates of the TRACE Project for its methodological basis (Merino 2005).

Textual analysis proceeds in three phases: preliminary, macrotextual and microtextual. The preliminary analysis focuses on the reception given to the works in the sociocultural context in both the source and the target culture. The latter covers not only an analysis of the paratexts (e.g., film reviews, critical studies) but also a study of the censorship data available in document form. The macrotextual analysis examines suppressions and other modifications made to extensive segments of the film (scenes) in terms of the censorship criteria in force at any given time, which for *LBM/PGH* were the 1963 film censorship norms. The microtextual analysis identifies the shifts of meaning in the coupled pairs of translation units (Toury 1995: 79). The translation unit (TU) used varies in extension and consists of "replacing" and "replaced" elements so that the "replacing" element constitutes the solution to a translation problem in the "replaced" element.[2] This definition admits a zero "replacing" element (suppression of a word or larger unit) as the solution to a translation problem in the source text. The changes are first classified formally as total or partial *suppression*, total or partial *addition*, or *modification*. These formal changes are subsequently analysed in terms of their semantic shifts. Total and partial *suppressions* always represent a semantic reduction while total and partial *additions* represent either an explicitation of content already present in the co-text or an intensification of the meaning through the introduction of new matter. *Modifications* can be either *commutations* or *neutralisations*.

---

[2] Toury defines the "replacing" element as follows: "a segment of the target text, for which it would be possible to claim that – beyond its boundaries – there are no leftovers of the solution to the translation problem which is represented by one of the source text's segments, whether similar or different in scope (Toury 1995: 79).

Commutations consist of an exchange of semantic concepts, which can intensify meaning, attenuate it, or maintain a similar semantic effect. *Neutralisations* attenuate meaning in a number of ways: *semantic reduction* by means of paraphrase, *stylistic elevation*, usually achieved through euphemism, or *refocalisation*, whereby the semantic content is reoriented and presented from a different perspective, thereby eliminating undesirable effects. Finally, the semantic shifts are analysed and explained pragmatically in relation to general censorship criteria (Gutiérrez Lanza 2000: 420) or are deemed to have no effect in this regard:

1. To favour the postulates of the regime
2. To reduce suggestive, morbid, erotic content
3. To improve the image of one of the characters
4. To limit the form of expression

This three-phase approach aims to uncover the norms that underlie the translation process and to establish whether the translator favoured adequacy (adherence to the source text and culture) or acceptability (adaptation to target culture requirements) (Toury 1995).

4 Results

4.1 Preliminary analysis

In the USA the film *LBM* received mixed reviews. For some, Penn's film was a grotesque satirical caricature of American society that successfully reproduces Berger's "social criticism, bizarre fantasy and modern humor" (French 1971: 103), and boldly deals with thorny themes such as homosexuality and genocide, drawing a parallel between the massacre of the Indians and that carried out by the American army in Vietnam. In contrast, others considered that the film lacked a unitary vision of the events portrayed (Braudy 1971), used the ills of society to no clear purpose (Murphy 1971), and saw in Jack the archetypal liberal American capable of recognising and understanding the two sides of a problem but incapable of taking action (Braudy 1971).

In Spain reception of *LBM/PGH* from the critics was generally favourable. The review published in the magazine *Fotogramas* predicted an important box-office success, giving the film a four-star rating out of a maximum of five. The writer compared the characterisation of General Custer in the film with the style of the occupants of the Pentagon, with the Cheyenne viewed as the North Vietnamese and the Pawnees as the South Vietnamese. The review published in *Arriba* praises the accurate translation of the title of the film and the ferocious and lucid way Penn attacks what he sees as the ills of his country. Although *Cine Asesor*, the official specialised publication on the film industry, gave the film a moral classification of 3 (4 being the maximum) and gave the film the merit of being an entertaining adventure Western, they highlighted only the most innocuous aspects of the story, focusing on the massacre of Custer's troops, but omitting to mention the cruel slaughter of the native Indians before Little Big Horn. In addition, in the technical details *Cine Asesor* gave a running time of 137 minutes, surprisingly only two minutes less than that published in *Films & Filming* (Gow 1970). The length of films released in Spain at that time was always a topic of considerable debate among film reviewers as they took for granted that all films were shortened or modified by censorship to some degree. The reviewer in *El Alcázar* expressed delight at the two and a quarter hours of *LBM*, but implied that it had been cut from an original three hours.

As mentioned, the search for the censorship file for the film *LBM/PGH* at the AGA proved fruitless so that we are unable to detail the difficulties that the distribution company Filmax had to overcome to get the film through the censorship filter. In the absence of that information, our study will draw on the data provided by González Ballesteros (1981: 320), who claims that *PGH* was censored on the grounds of "its amorous and sexual content" and who documented the cuts shown in Table 1.[3]

Table 1. Scenes censored according to González Ballesteros (1981).

Reel no.	Indication from the Censorship Board to the Film Distributor
Reel 3	Begin the bath scene after the husband's entry.
Reel 4	Cut when, after they are discovered in the cellar, the laughter and panting becomes audible.
Reel 7	Replace the sentence "Does she show pleasant enthusiasm when you mount her?" and the expression "It was a great copulation".
Reel 9	Replace the words of the homosexual Indian "And I will be your wife".

---

[3] All Spanish-English translations and backtranslations in this article are mine.

Reel 10	Cut when Jack enters the tepee of the three Indian women and takes off his shirt. Fade to black and start with Jack's Indian wife presenting him with his son.
Reel 11	Kill the wife and the child with a single shot, and do not show the child's bloodied face.
Reel 15	Suppress the allusion that the wife copulates with gentlemen.

4.2 Macrotextual analysis

In addition to the information in Table 1, the macrotextual analysis is based on a printed copy of the draft of the original film script[4] and the dialogues and subtitles in the original and dubbed versions of the film available in DVD.[5] These were contrasted with the suppressions effected on the film in its passage through the official censorship system as documented by González Ballesteros (1981). The macrotextual changes not documented by this author we have attributed to self-censorship carried out by the distribution company before submitting the film for authorisation to the censorship board. Viewing the DVD film with the dialogues in the original version and the subtitles in Spanish and vice versa proved an effective way to locate both the suppressed fragments and the modifications made to the dialogues.

Since the cuts and modifications to the dialogues and scenes observed in the DVD employed for the analysis correspond to those indicated by González Ballesteros, it can be deduced that they were the same dialogues as in the dubbed version of the film authorised at the time by the censorship board. The DVD is a universal copy and not subject to zone constraints. Thus, the cuts introduced in the dialogues become evident when the film is viewed in the original version with Spanish subtitles.

---

[4] The draft of the original production script is the property of Stockbridge Production, the only available copy of which is located in the Southeastern Library of Massachusetts and which I was able to consult thanks to the diligence and efficiency of the library staff at the University of Cantabria central library.

[5] The DVD used for the comparative analysis belongs to the Widescreen Collection and was distributed in Spain by Paramount Entertainment S. L.

4.2.1 Self-censorship

The comparative procedure outlined above revealed the suppression of one scene, which was attributed to self-censorship by the distribution company Filmax. The 28-second scene shows General Custer talking openly with his officers about a personal and intimate issue (Table 2).

Table 2. Scene and dialogue suppressed by Filmax through self-censorship.

153,26"–153,54"	Original Dialogue
Custer signals a halt. Custer, the Major, and the captain dismount.	
Custer (solemnly explains the gargling)	Poison from the goo-nads
Skeptical Captain	Poison from what, sir?
Custer (with utter gravity)	The goo-nads. That's the medical terminology.
Harried Major (not interested in science; his eyes are anxiously slewing toward the coulee)	General, it is my duty as your subordinate--
Custer (spits, and to Captain, ignoring Major)	Oo-goo-goo-goo-oogle-oggle-oggle-ARGLE-ARG! The poison rises from the goo-nads to the throat and seeps down into various muscles.
(Takes another swallow and gargles)	Ooo-goo-goo-oogle-argle-argle-argle...

Besides improving the image of Custer, who is parodied relentlessly throughout the film, the suppression of this scene aims to preserve the image of the army, since section 2 of norm 14 prohibits "anything that in any way causes harm or offense to our institutions and ceremonies". The petulant attitude shown by Custer in the scene and the familiar tone in which he talks to his subordinates could also be considered to violate "the elementary norms of good taste" (norm 13).[6]

4.2.2 External censorship

After viewing the scenes selected for analysis with the English dialogues and the Spanish subtitles, and vice versa, the following suppressions were found.

Suppression 1

The first suppression corresponds to a scene that takes place in Mr Kane's store, where Mrs Pendrake has taken Jack for a rest and a soda after a stroll. On the

---

[6] Norm 13: "Colloquial expressions and scenes and shots of an intimate nature that violate the most elementary norms of good taste shall be prohibited." (Ministerial Order 09/02/1963, BOE 08/03/1963: 3929–30).

pretext of having to do some more shopping, Mrs Pendrake abandons the establishment leaving Jack behind, who suddenly feels an inquisitive urge that takes him down to the cellar, where he hears Mrs Pendrake emitting cries of pleasure, pleading for help and referring to the person she is with as a devil. However, peeping through a window, Jack realises that she is in no need of his help. In this scene only Mrs Pendrake's voice is heard and all that is seen is her boots and Mr Kane's shoes in such a way that leaves no doubt as to what was happening. According to González Ballesteros (1981), the scene was suppressed. However, the existence of Spanish dialogues for this scene, in contrast to the other scenes for which there are no dialogues even in the current commercialised version, suggests that Filmax negotiated with the censorship board and that the latter acceded to their requests to maintain this scene at the expense of introducing certain slight cuts in Mrs Pendrake's cries of pleasure (Table 3). Thus, some of the utterances of encouragement, such as "Oh yeah", "Yeah, please", and the final "I'm dying, I'm dying" were eliminated from the dubbed version. The rest of the sounds emitted by Mrs Pendrake are retained, so that we suggest that the scene was permitted with the introduction of these partial suppressions. The pragmatic effect of the suppressions is to reduce the suggestive, morbid and erotic content of the scene and to harmonise the "distorted" female figure of Mrs Pendrake with the passive image promoted for women by the regime.

Table 3. External suppression 1: modified dialogue.

31,51"–32,39"	Original Dialogue	Dubbed Dialogue	Backtranslation
Mrs Pendrake	Don't. Don't. No, don't Oh, yeah. No, don't Yeah, Please. No don't Pagan, beast, Help You devil. You filthy, dirty devil. Heathen. No, no. Yeah, yeah. No. Help! Help! Help! I'm dying! I'm dying!	No cariño, no! No, No. Oh No, pagano, bestia. Socorro. Socorro. Eres un demonio, un malvado demonio, eres un demonio. Socorro. Socorro.	No darling, no! No, No. Oh no, pagan, beast. Help. Help. You're a devil, an evil devil, you're a devil. Help. Help

Suppression 2

The second cut was made in a scene filmed in Old Lodge Skins' tepee, where Jack is conversing with his Indian father and informs him that he has a white wife. The Indian chief is very surprised at this revelation and enquires about her aptitudes especially with regard to her sexual response. When Jack provides positive replies to all his queries, the chief expresses his astonishment, confessing that in his one attempt with a white woman, she remained totally impassive to his attentions. In this scene, in addition to the suppression of some shots, there is a modification to the dialogue (Table 4).

Table 4. External suppression 2: modified dialogue.

59,39"–59,49"	Original Dialogue	Dubbed Dialogue	Censored Dialogue	Backtranslation
Old Lodge Skins	You do? That's interesting. Does she cook and work hard?	¿De veras? ¡Que interesante! ¿Sabe cocinar? ¿Trabaja?		Really? How interesting! Can she cook? Does she work?
Jack Crabb	Yes, grandfather.	Sí, abuelo.		Yes, grandfather.
Old Lodge Skins	Does she show pleasant enthusiasm when you mount her?		¿Muestra una alegría entusiasta cuando la montas?	Does she show enthusiastic joy when you mount her?
Jack Crabb	Well, sure, grandfather.			
Old Lodge Skins	That surprises me even more. I tried one of them once, but she didn't show any enthusiasm at all.	Eso me sorprende. Una vez lo intenté con una de ellas, pero no mostró entusiasmo de ninguna clase.		That surprises me. I once tried it with one of them, but she didn't show any enthusiasm at all.
Jack Crabb	Well, grandfather... all the whites aren't crazy.			

When Old Lodge Skins asks "Does she show pleasant enthusiasm when you mount her?" the Spanish subtitles read "*Eso me sorprende. Una vez lo intenté con una de ellas, pero no mostró entusiasmo de ninguna clase*" 'That surprises me. I once tried it with one of them, but she didn't show any enthusiasm at all'. The dialogue that follows can be heard in the original version, but no subtitles are shown. In the dubbed version, the lack of synchronisation passes unnoticed because the suppressed dialogue occurs in a shot when Old Lodge Skins has his back turned to the camera.

This suppression is justified by norm 13 relating to scenes of an intimate nature and to good taste. In accordance with the general censorship criteria proposed for our analysis, the suppression introduced reduces the suggestive, morbid and erotic content of the dialogue and, as in the previous cut, is consistent with the submissive role promoted by the regime for women, especially in the sexual sphere.

Suppression 3

The third suppression corresponds to a scene that lasts about 3 minutes (Table 5). It takes place inside Jack's tepee where he vigorously responds to the insistent pleading of his Indian wife, Sunshine, that, in accordance with Cheyenne customs, he attend to the sexual needs of her three husbandless sisters. Suppression of this scene is again justified by norm 13 and the pragmatic effect is to reduce the suggestive, morbid and erotic content of the film and also to maintain the image of women within the moral boundaries of the dictatorship.

Table 5. External suppression 3: original dialogue of eliminated scene.

122,22"–125,12"	Original Dialogue
Jack Crabb	Who wants to be first?
Jack Crabb	Who's this here?
Little Elk	It's me.
Jack Crabb	All right, I guess you'll do as well as any.
Old Jack Crabb	I figured she was the littlest one and would be easy … but Lord help us, them young girls is deadly.
Old Jack Crabb	However, the Great Spirit was with me, and I survived. Only thing was, just as I was about to drift off real peaceful.
Little Elk	No… you stay. Not yet.
Jack Crabb	Maybe I can get back later
Old Jack Crabb	Idle boastin', I assure you.
Jack Crabb	Who's this here?
Digging Bear	It's me, Digging Bear!
Old Jack Crabb	Well, she wasn't called Digging Bear for nothing. I can tell you that.
Digging Bear	Stay here. Corn Woman is too tired.
Jack Crabb	She don't sound tired to me
Digging Bear	That's not her, that's Little Elk.

Jack Crabb	That's both of 'em. Little Elk, you go on to sleep. You, too. Digging Bear.
Jack Crabb	Corn Woman, where are you?
Old Jack Crabb	I was lucky I came across her last.

Suppression 4

For the suppression corresponding to reel 11 (see Table 1), the lack of dialogue makes it difficult to ascertain the extent of the cut. In the suppressed scene, Jack's Indian wife and her son are brutally killed at the hands of an American soldier, who disobeying strict orders not to open fire on women and children, shoots them both at point blank range. Suppression of this scene is aimed at improving the image of the army and the cut is justified by the application of norm 12 concerning images of cruelty.[7]

Suppression 5

The final suppression corresponds to reel 15 and, according to González Ballesteros, to the elimination of the allusion to the wife copulating with gentlemen. This scene occurs at the end of the film when Old Lodge Skins, accompanied by Jack, leaves the hill he had climbed to meet with his destiny, after realising that his "magic" sometimes fails to work. Returning to his tepee, he invites Jack to eat with him and tells him that he has a new wife, a Snake woman who cooks dog very well.

Table 6. External suppression 5: modified dialogue.

211,26"– 211,44"	Original Dialogue	Dubbed Dialogue	Backtranslation
Old Lodge Skins	The only trouble with Snake women is they copulate with horses, which makes them strange to me. She says she doesn't. That's why I call her Doesn't Like Horses.	*El único inconveniente es que tiene gran afición a los caballos, lo que me parece muy singular. Ella me dice que no pero, por supuesto, miente.*	The only drawback is that she is very fond of horses, which seems odd to me. She tells me she isn't, but, of course, she's lying.
Jack Crabb		*Por supuesto, abuelo.*	Of course, grandfather.

---

[7] Norm 12: "Images and scenes of brutality, of cruelty towards persons and animals, and of terror, that are presented in a morbid manner and unjustified in relation to the plot and corresponding cinematographic genre, and, in general, those that offend the dignity of humans shall be prohibited" (idem 1963).

| Old Lodge Skins | But, of course, she's lying. | | |
| Jack Crabb | Of course, grandfather. | | |

According to the data of González Ballesteros (1981), the translator replaced the term "horses" (*caballos*) with "gentlemen" (*caballeros*) in the dialogues presented to the censorship board. However, in the dubbed version, it is the term "copulate" that suffers a semantic shift to "*tiene gran afición a*", that is, 'she is very fond of' horses. The reference to the wife's nickname is also eliminated to maintain the coherence of the discourse. In the subtitled version, the subtitles disappear as the old chief's and Jack's voices continue the dialogue, producing a lack of synchronisation, as shown in Table 6. The justification (norm 13) and pragmatic effect of reducing the suggestive, morbid and erotic content are similar to previous examples.

4.3 Microtextual analysis

For the microtextual analysis the four dialogues selected were those modified in some way as they passed through the censorship procedure. The first dialogue corresponds to the bath scene in which Mrs Pendrake, the Reverend Pendrake's wife, lovingly baths her newly adopted son, Jack Crabb. The second occurs in front of Old Lodge Skins' tepee, where the Indian chief tells Jack that he dreamt that he saw him frolicking with his Indian wives, which bemuses Jack since the Cheyenne only have one wife. The third modified dialogue occurs when Jack, who at the time is on the side of the American army, engages during battle in a fight with his Indian brother, Shadow, who is shot dead by a soldier. The final altered dialogue occurs in the Cheyenne camp between Jack and a homosexual Indian called Little Horse. Three of the four dialogues, therefore, belong to scenes which were indicated for censorship (González Ballesteros 1981) but were retained because of the skilful manipulation of the dialogues, and are thus particularly suitable for analysis at the microtextual level to determine what kind of techniques were applied to avoid more radical measures.

The bath scene, the longest of the dialogues, consists of 26 TUs both in the original and the dubbed version (Table 7).[8] Of these 10 (38%) were considered to be conceptually equivalent in the original and dubbed versions while the remaining 16 showed some kind of alteration. The predominant formal changes were modifications, 7 commutations and 6 neutralisations, with only 2 partial suppressions and one partial addition.

Table 7. Fragment 1: comparison of original and dubbed dialogues.

TU	25,06"	Original Dialogue	Dubbed Dialogue	Backtranslation	Comparison
1	Mrs Pendrake	You do realise, don't you, dear Jack, that the reverend Pendrake is not altogether wrong.	¿Te das cuenta verdad, querido Jack, de que mi hermano no está del todo equivocado?	You do realise, don't you, dear Jack, that my brother is not altogether wrong.	MC: PR
2	Jack Crabb	Huh? I mean…What, ma'am?	No, ¿cómo dice señora?	No, what did you say, ma'am?	=
3	Mrs Pendrake	Well, Jesus is your savior.	Bueno, él será tu protector.	Well, he will be your protector.	MRF: PR
4		You do realize that, don't you?	Te das cuenta, ¿verdad, querido Jack?	You do realize, don't you, dear Jack?	PA: E
5	Jack Crabb	Oh-h-h, Lordy yes, Miz Pendrake!	Oh, sí señora Pendrake.	Oh, yes Mrs Pendrake.	PS: PR
6	Mrs Pendrake	Are you thinking of Jesus, Jack?	Estás pensando en mi hermano ¿verdad, Jack?	You're thinking of my brother, aren't you, Jack?	MRF: PR
7	Jack Crabb	Yes'm, yes ma'am	Sí señora, sí señora, sí señora.	Yes, ma'am, yes, ma'am, yes, ma'am.	=

---

[8] In the tables for the microtextual analysis, the right-hand column indicates the result of the comparison of the original and dubbed dialogues for each translation unit (TU). Units considered to be semantically identical are marked with the symbol (=). The letters before the colon indicate the formal and semantic categories: total addition (TA), partial addition (PA), total suppression (TS), partial suppression (PS), and modification (M), this formal change having the semantic subcategories of elevation of style (ES), refocalisation (RF), and semantic reduction (SR). The letters after the colon indicate the pragmatic effects: reduce erotic content (E), promote postulates of the regime (PR), limit form of expression (LF), improve the image of one of the characters (I), or no effect (NE).

8	Mrs Pendrake	You mustn't fib to me, you know.	Bueno, no debes decir mentiras ¿sabes?	You mustn't tell lies, you know.	PS: NE
9	Jack Crabb	Oh, no ma'am. I love…Jesus, and Moses, and all of 'em.	De veras, pensaba en su hermano, se lo aseguro.	Really, I was thinking of your brother, I assure you.	MRF: PR
10	Mrs Pendrake	Well, there is quite a difference, dear.	No es tan severo como aparenta.	He's not so severe as he seems.	MRF: PR
11		Moses was a Hebrew, but Jesus was a gentile like you and me.	Aunque parezca brusco más de una vez, en el fondo es muy comprensivo tanto como yo.	Although he appears brusque at times, at heart he's as understanding as I am.	MRF: PR
12	Rev. Pendrake	Ain't you done washing that boy yet?	¿Todavía no has lavado al muchacho?	Haven't you washed the boy yet?	MES: LF
13	Mrs Pendrake	I'm giving the boy important religious instruction, Silas.	Le estoy dando importantes enseñanzas sociales, Silas.	I'm giving him important social education, Silas.	MC: PR
14	Rev. Pendrake	I want to eat.	Tengo hambre.	I'm hungry.	=
15		Looks like a pretty well-growed child if you ask me.	Si quieres saberlo, te diré que me parece un chico bien parecido.	If you want to know, I'd say he's a good-looking boy.	MC: LF
16	Mrs Pendrake	All right now, dear. Please stand up and let me dry you off.	Muy bien. Ahora levántate y déjame secarte.	All right. Now stand up and let me dry you.	=
17		I'll avert my eyes, of course.	Apartaré la vista, desde luego.	I'll look away, of course.	=
18		Now step out of the tub.	Ahora sal de la bañera.	Nos get out of the bath.	=
19	Mrs Pendrake	Actually, you are rather well-grown, Jack, You're small, but…nice looking. Did you know that?	Ya lo has oído, eres un muchacho bien parecido, Jack, eres pequeño pero apuesto, ¿no lo sabías?	You heard him, you're a good-looking boy, Jack, you're small but nice-looking. Didn't you know that?	MC: LF
20	Jack Crabb	No, ma'am	No, señora.	No, ma'am	=
21	Mrs Pendrake	Well, you are.	Pues sí, lo eres.	Well, yes, you are	=

22		All the more reason for you to receive complete religious instruction.	*Razón de más para que recibas una completa instrucción social.*	All the more reason for you to receive a complete social education.	MC: PR
23		The girls I am sure, will be after you. And Jack…?	*Las chicas te irán detrás, estoy segura de ello, y Jack.*	The girls will be after you, I am sure of it, and Jack.	=
24	Jack Crabb	Yes, ma'am	*Dígame, señora*	Yes, ma'am	=
25	Mrs Pendrake	That way lies madness.	*Ahí puede estar el pecado.*	That's where sin may lie.	MC: PR
26	Jack Crabb	Ah-h, what way, ma'am?	*¿Qué pecado?, ¿Señora?*	What sin, ma'am?	MC: PR

The first change introduced consists of a commutation of *Reverend Pendrake* for *mi hermano* 'my brother' (TU1), a modification that must have left the audience perplexed as the previous scene had made it clear that the reverend and Mrs Pendrake were husband and wife. This semantic shift is an instance of prophylactic censorship similar to the notorious case in *Mogambo*, where to avoid presenting the adulterous attraction of Grace Kelly towards Clark Gable, Spanish censorship via dubbing converted a married couple into brother and sister, thereby insinuating an incestuous relationship (Gubern 1981: 137; Santoyo 1985: 152).

In *Little Big Man* this first change is one of a series of refocalisations through which references are diverted away from religious themes and centred on the putative "brother" (the righthand column is my backtranslation of the dubbed dialogue):

TU3	"Well, Jesus is your savior"	'Well, he [my brother] will be your protector'
TU6	Are you thinking of Jesus, Jack?	'You're thinking of my brother, aren't you, Jack?'
TU9	Oh, no ma'am. I love … Jesus, and Moses and all of 'em	'Really, I was thinking of your brother, I assure you'

In the original dialogue, mention of religious figures of Jesus and Moses is avoided and replaced by a description of the "brother's" character:

TU10	Well, there is quite a difference, dear.	'He's not so severe as he seems.'
TU11	Moses was a Hebrew, but Jesus was a gentile like you and me	'Although he appears brusque at times, at heart he's as understanding as I am'

This series of refocalisations of religious references is due to the highly erotic content of the scene and its irreverence, for as Mrs Pendrake holds forth on religious themes, the tone of her voice and the rhythmic movements she makes as she washes Jack's leg, together with his facial response, betray the lascivious thoughts behind her words.

The bath scene is interrupted by the sudden appearance of Reverend Pendrake, who impatiently asks: "Ain't you done washing that boy yet?" The reverend's idiolect with its incorrections marks him as unrefined in spite of the social status afforded to a man of his religious stature. However, as occurs with all sociolects and idiolects in Westerns, both in narrative and in films (Camus 2009: 418), this characterisation is lost in translation through the use of standard Spanish, equivalent in this case to 'Haven't you washed the boy yet?'

Mrs Pendrake tries to calm her husband and justifies her tardiness claiming that she is giving Jack important religious instruction. In the dubbed version, in keeping with the previous changes, religious instruction is replaced by 'social education' (TU13).

The reverend, showing signs of gluttony as well as impatience, makes a pointed remark about Jack's maturity: "Looks a pretty well-growed boy, if you ask me" (TU15). This is replaced in the dubbed version by a reference to his physical appearance: 'If you want to know, I'd say he is a good-looking boy'. This commutation is then maintained in identical terms when Mrs Pendrake herself whispers to Jack: "Actually, you are rather well-grown, Jack" (TU19). However, again the characterisation through the contrast in the reverend's "well-growed" and Mrs Pendrake's "well-grown" is neutralised in the dubbed version through the use of standard register.

Similarly, when Mrs Pendrake resumes Jack's education, she repeats the reference to "social instruction" (TU22) as she warns him against the danger that girls will represent for him: "That way lies madness" (TU25). In the dubbed version, "madness" is changed to *pecado* 'sin', a commutation that is maintained in the following unit but between the terms "way" and *pecado*.

In this dialogue, the only addition is a partial addition in TU5, where the translator has added *querido Jack* 'dear Jack' to Mrs Pendrake's speech. The inclusion of this term of endearment is probably intended to convert Mrs Pendrake's lascivious role into a more maternal one and thereby attenuate the erotic tone of the scene.

Similarly, the two suppressions are also partial ones. In TU4 the exclamation "Lordy" was eliminated because of the direct connotation with the religious theme.

Then, as Mrs Pendrake takes up her mission to educate Jack, she says: "You mustn't fib to me, you know". In the dubbed version, this instruction on sincerity is depersonalised to 'You mustn't tell lies, you know', with the elimination of the personal pronoun.

When the semantic shifts were correlated with their pragmatic effects in terms of the censorship criteria used in the study, the most significant effect (11 of 16 changes) was to favour the postulates of the regime. This was assigned to all the modifications eliminating and replacing allusions to religion together with the complementary substitution of the stigma of madness with that of sin. Three changes were considered to limit the form of expression, elevating the reverend's manner of speech to that of Mrs Pendrake. One was directly attributed to reducing the erotic tone and one deemed to have no pragmatic effect with regard to censorship. Although no change was directly attributed to the improvement of the image of one of the protagonists, the neutralisation of the reverend's idiolect and the more maternal attitude introduced into Mrs Pendrake's discourse would indirectly contribute to an enhancement of their moral roles in detriment to the satirical tone of the original version.

In the scene in the Cheyenne camp (Table 8), Old Lodge Skins is saying goodbye to Jack, who is about to leave in search of his wife Olga. The Indian chief tells Jack that he had a dream in which he saw him copulating with his 3 or 4 Cheyenne wives, and was perfectly able to satisfy them all. Jack is surprised by this revelation, especially as the Cheyenne are monogamous. Of the 8 TUs in the dialogue, 6 are conceptually similar in the original and dubbed versions. In TU3 there is a partial addition of *contento y feliz* 'content and happy' and, instead of Jack crawling from one wife to the other, he is depicted as playfully romping (*retozando*) with them. In TU 6, another refocalisation, in which "But it was a great copulation" becomes 'And you coped with them all, my son", avoids the direct allusion to sexual intercourse, shifting the focus to a more macho-like vigorous sex in the Spanish version. The pragmatic effect of both refocalisations is to reduce the erotic content in association with the limitation in the form of expression through euphemism, while the partial addition of contentedness and the paternal vocative add to the attenuation and present Jack in a less cynical light. It is worth mentioning that in *PGH* this verbal description is all that remains of the scene between Jack and his

Indian wives since, as seen in Section 4.2, it was removed completely in the Spanish version.

Table 8. Fragment 2: comparison of original and dubbed dialogues.

TU	1.01,40"	Original Dialogue	Dubbed Dialogue	Backtranslation	Comparison
1	Old Lodge Skins	Don't worry, my son. You'll return to the Human Beings.	No te preocupes, hijo mío. Volverás con los Seres Humanos.	Don't worry, my son. You'll return to the Human Beings.	=
2		I dreamt it last night	Lo soñé la noche pasada.	I dreamt it last night	=
3		I saw you and your wives as you crawled from one to the other in your tepee.	Te vi en tu tienda, contento y feliz, retozando con tus esposas.	I saw you in your tepee, content and happy, romping with your wives.	AP: I MRF: E + LF
4	Jack Crabb	Wives, grandfather?	¿Esposas, abuelo?	Wives, grandfather?	=
5	Old Lodge Skins	Oh, yes. 3 or 4. It was dark and they were hidden under buffalo robes.	Oh, sí. 3 o 4. No había luz y estaban escondidas bajo pellizas de búfalo.	Oh, yes. 3 or 4. There was no light and they were hidden under buffalo robes.	=
6		But it was a great copulation.	Y tú podías con todas, hijo mío.	And you coped with them all, my son.	MRF: E + LF PA: I
7	Jack Crabb	Grandfather, the Human Beings only take one wife. How could I have 3 or 4?	Abuelo, los Seres Humanos sólo toman una esposa. ¿Cómo voy a tener 3 o 4?	Grandfather, the Human Beings only take one wife. How could I have 3 or 4?	=
8	Old Lodge Skins	I don't know. It worries me	No lo sé y eso me preocupa.	I don't know and that worries me.	=

The third dialogue fragment (Table 9) contains six TUs, two of which are semantically identical in the original and dubbed versions. It corresponds to an interchange between an American soldier and Jack just after the former has killed Jack's Indian brother, Shadow, by shooting him in the back. In the original version, the soldier justifies killing the Cheyenne and threatens to have Jack hanged for desertion: "I just took care of him. I'm saving you for the hanging" (TU 1 and 3).

This dialogue is refocalised in the dubbed version and is expanded with the addition of a new unit (TU2): "You can't trust them. You saw it. He wanted to kill you". This refocalisation avoids attributing an unjust killing to a member of the American army by transferring the intent to kill from the soldier to the Indian. The remodelling of this dialogue with two refocalised units and one addition presents an image of the military more in accordance with the postulates of the regime. In the last TU of this fragment, Old Jack Crabb makes a philosophical comment on life: "The world was too ridiculous even to bother to live in". In the dubbed version, this is reduced semantically to the exclamation: 'What a crazy world that was!' (TU6), but no significant censorship-related pragmatic effect was assigned to this reduction in content.

Table 9. Fragment 3: comparison of original and dubbed dialogues.

TU	1.06,48"	Original Dialogue	Dubbed Dialogue	Backtranslation	Comparison
1	Grizzled Sergeant	I just took care of him.	Para que te fíes de ellos.	You can't trust them.	MRF: PR
2			Ya lo has visto.	You saw it.	TA: PR
3		I'm saving you for the hanging.	Quería matarte.	He wanted to kill you.	MRF: PR
4	Old Jack Crabb	There's no describing how I felt.	No puedo describir cómo me sentía.	I can't describe how I felt.	=
5		An enemy had saved my life by the violent murder of one of my best friends.	Un enemigo me había salvado la vida gracias al violento asesinato de uno de mis mejores amigos.	An enemy had saved my life thanks to the violent murder of one of my best friends	=
6		The world was too ridiculous even to bother to live in it.	¡Qué disparatado mundo era aquél!	What a crazy world that was!	MSR: NE

The final modified dialogue (Table 10) takes place when Jack takes his leave of the homosexual Indian Little Horse, who invites him to stay in the camp and offers to be his wife. Of the 5 TUs that make up the dialogue, three are semantically coincidental in the original and dubbed versions, but the other two have undergone shifts in meaning, semantic reduction and refocalisation: "Why don't you live with me and I'll be your wife? (TU3 and 4). In the dubbed version 'Why don't you stay? I can cook for you', the omission of the personal pronoun and the offer to cook eliminates the implication of homosexual co-habitation and converts this offer into a simple invitation to dine together as a marital relationship between males contravened the moral precepts of the regime.

Table 10. Fragment 4: comparison of original and dubbed dialogues.

TU	1.20,00"	Original Dialogue	Dubbed Dialogue	Backtranslation	Comparison
1	Little Horse	You look tired, Little Big Man.	*Pareces cansado, Pequeño Gran Hombre.*	You look tired, Little Big Man.	=
2		Do you want to come into my tepee and rest on soft furs?	*¿Quieres venir a mi tienda y descansar sobre blandas pieles?*	Do you want to come into my tepee and rest on soft furs?	=
3		Why don't you live with me...	*¿Por qué no te quedas?*	Why don't you stay?	MSR: PR
4		and I'll be your wife?	*Yo puedo guisar para ti.*	I can cook for you	MRF: PR
5	Jack Crabb	Thanks for inviting me.	*Gracias por la invitación.*	Thanks for the invitation.	=

5 Discussion

Although González Ballesteros, in his study of legal aspects of film censorship in Spain, attributed the cuts in *LBM/PGH* to "amorous and sexual content" (1981), this study, which used a three-stage analysis, has shown that the grounds for the suppressions and modifications made to the Spanish dubbed version of the film were more varied. The censors showed a concern for the precepts propounded by the regime that went beyond those related only to sexual morality and involved the protection of the images of institutions such as the army and the church, two of the pillars of the regime's ideology.

While the film is situated in the legendary Far West, the satirical caricature of General Custer extends beyond the frontiers of that mythical space, and beyond the borders of the USA, and thus could be seen as a threat to other military figures. Even before the film was presented to the censorship board for authorisation, Filmax, the distribution company, considered it wise to remove the scene in which Custer is seen conversing in a familiar tone with his subordinates and making his pseudo-scientific pronouncements on gargling and the elimination of toxins produced by the gonads, a scene that would be deemed as debasing the standing of the military. Of the other two scenes involving the military, one was suppressed because it portrayed a soldier blatantly disobeying orders to spare women and children and brutally killing Jack's wife and child, and in the second the dialogue was refocalised to make it appear that the Indian Shadow was shot in legitimate defence in battle, thus protecting the army against the accusation of the use of excessive and unjust violence.

Although the censors ordered the suppression of a large part of the bath scene, the analysis has shown that this was retained in its entirety because of the skilful adaptation of the dialogue. In the modifications introduced, the standing of Reverend Pendrake is enhanced and his manner of speech is elevated by translating his idiolect into the standard Spanish register befitting his social status. In addition, Mrs Pendrake's discourse was purged of all the religious allusions, thereby dissociating this theme from the eroticism displayed by her in this scene and thus safeguarding the image of the Church as an institution. The refocalisation of the dialogue also covers up the satire of Mrs Pendrake's evident lack of religious knowledge when in her instruction of Jack she tells him that Jesus was a gentile. However, the adaptation of the scene displays one flagrant flaw when Mrs Pendrake refers to the reverend as her brother, which distorts the coherence of the episode.

Nevertheless, sexual morality was the major preoccupation involved in many of the cuts and modifications introduced by Filmax. The portrayal of Mrs Pendrake was changed not only in the bath scene but also in the scene in the store cellar through the elimination of her most effusive exclamations. This modification is in line with those made to the leading female characters in other films, such as *Duel in the Sun* and *Hud* (Camus 2009), and were clearly aimed at ensuring that the representation of women was in tune with the passive, submissive role propounded by the regime through their *Sección Femenina* ('Women's Section'). Moreover, this holds true not only of the representation of the white women in *LBM* since the suppression of the scene of Jack with his Indian "wives" and the manipulation of the references made by Old Lodge Skins on the sexual mores of Cheyenne and Snake women show that, in this respect, even a civilisation foreign to the target culture was subjected to the same censorship. The removal of all the direct references to sex from the Indian chief's discourse in the dubbed version show a concern for the use of a more decorous register as well as reducing the morbid, erotic content of the script to accommodate this to the regime's moral precepts.

Also of interest is the portrayal of Little Horse, the homosexual Indian. The various scenes where he appears were not cut and the adaptation of the dialogue in which his offer of homosexual cohabitation was replaced with the anodyne invitation to a meal may reflect the more tolerant attitude towards homosexuality prevailing at the time of the release of *LBM*. In 1968, the renowned Spanish psychologist López Ibor had said "Homosexuals should be considered more as sick people than as criminals. But the law should still prevent them proselytising in schools, sports clubs and army barracks" (1968: xxvii). In fact, in 1970, the year *LBM* was released, the 1954 Vagrancy and Delinquency Law, which treated homosexuals as delinquents, was replaced by the Law of Social Danger and Rehabilitation, introducing the concept of rehabilitation rather than punishment.

From a translation studies perspective, the predominant technique that was applied to the dialogues of *LBM* was modification rather than suppressions or additions. The pragmatic effects of adjustment to the regime's postulates, reduction of erotic content and elevation of style with more moderate language were achieved mainly with commutations and refocalisations. These techniques require considerable skill on the part of the translator to maintain the coherence of the script and its relationship with the visual track. The exchange of suitable meanings in commutation and the change of semantic focus in refocalisation allow the translator to meet the constraints of synchronisation with lip movements and, at the same time, to adhere to the dictates of the censorship board, whereas the techniques of addition and suppression would make synchronisation far more difficult.

The analysis of *LBM* has shown that Filmax acceded to some of the censors' demands by removing scenes that violated the censorship norms. However, it is also clear that the company was aware of the censorship constraints and resorted to self-censorship when cutting the Custer scene. In addition, they must have negotiated with the censorship board and introduced modifications in order to retain many of the scenes discussed here. A previous study of film censorship found that negotiation was mostly aimed at lowering the age limit of viewers, thereby achieving a wider audience and greater economic benefit (Camus 2008: 93). However, in the case of *LBM*, which was classed as a film for adults over the age of

18, the negotiation clearly had a different purpose, that of maintaining the integrity of the film as far as possible. Nevertheless, the detailed analysis has revealed that the changes introduced either through self-censorship or in the negotiation process after the initial resolution from the censorship board served to make the film more "acceptable" to the target audience and culture within the moral constraints imposed by Franco's dictatorship.

References

A. Primary sources

Alcázar (1971): "Pequeño gran hombre, de Arthur Penn". 27 de noviembre.
Arriba (1971): "Pequeño gran hombre, de Arthur Penn".
Cine Asesor. (1971): "Hoja archivable de información". *Hoja número 273–71.*
Fotogramas (1971): "Pequeño gran hombre". No. 1199, 8 de octubre.
Braudy, Leo (1971): "The Difficulties of *Little Big Man*". In: *Film Quarterly* 25, 30–33.
French, Philip (1971): "Little Big Man". In: *Sight and Sound* 40, 102–103.
Gow, Gordon (1971): "Gordon Gow sees Arthur Penn mock the western myth". In: *Films and Filming* 17, 73.
Murphy Arthur D. (1970): "Little Big Man". In: *Variety*, 16th December, 17.

B. Secondary sources

Berger, Thomas (1964): *Little Big Man*. New York: Dial Press.
Camus, Carmen (2008): "Translation, censorship and negotiation in Western films". In: O'Sullivan, Carol [ed.] (2008): *Proceedings of the 7th Annual Portsmouth Translation Conference*. Portsmouth: University of Portsmouth. 77–93.
Camus, Carmen (2009): "Traducciones censuradas de novelas y películas del Oeste en la España de Franco". Unpublished PhD Thesis, University of the Basque Country.
—— (2010): "Censorship in the translations and pseudotranslations of the West". In: Gile, Daniel / Hansen, Gyde / Pokorn, Nike K. [eds.] (2010): *Why Translation Studies Matters*. Amsterdam and Philadelphia: John Benjamins. 41–58.
González Ballesteros, Tomás (1981): *Aspectos jurídicos de la censura cinematográfica en España*. Madrid: Editorial de la Universidad Complutense.
Gubern, Román (1981): *La censura: función política y ordenamiento jurídico bajo el franquismo (1936–1975)*. Barcelona: Península.
Gutiérrez Lanza, Camino (2000): *Traducción y censura de textos cinematográficos en la España de Franco: Doblaje y subtitulado inglés-español (1951–1975)*. León: Universidad de León.
López Ibor, Juan J. (1968): *El libro de la vida sexual*. Barcelona: Ediciones Danae.
Merino, Raquel (2005): "From Catalogue to Corpus in DTS: Translations Censored under Franco. The TRACE Project". In: *Revista Canaria de Estudios Ingleses* 51, 85–103.

Rabadán, Rosa (2000): "Modelos importados, modelos adaptados: Pseudotraducciones de narrativa popular inglés-español 1955–1981." In: Rabadán, Rosa [ed.] (2000): *Traducción y censura inglés-español: 1939–1985. Estudio preliminar.* León: Universidad de León. 255–290.

Santoyo, Julio C. (1985): *El delito de traducir.* León: Universidad de León.

Toury, Gideon (1995): *Descriptive Translation Studies and Beyond.* Amsterdam and Philadelphia: John Benjamins.

Postcolonial Hong Kong Drama Translation

Chapman Chen
University of Eastern Finland, Joensuu

Abstract

Mainstream postcolonial (translation) theories focus on the deconstruction of colonialism but seldom consider the case of one colonized subject between two colonizers, postcolonial drama translation per se, and possible benefits of European colonialism to the Third World. The objective is to study the applicability of postcolonial theories to the Western drama in Hong Kong (HK) translation. Mainstream postcolonial theories are juxtaposed with alternative ones, e.g., Fanon's (1967) vs. Ferguson's (2003); Bhabha's (1994) mimicry vs. Rey Chow's (1998) hybrid third space between two aggressors; Tymoczko's (1999) anti-English translation in Irish literature vs. Gilbert Fong's (2007) "strategic alliance" with the UK in HK drama. Two Western plays performed in HK Cantonese since the Sino-British Joint Declaration (1984), R. Chan's (1997) version of Shaw's *Pygmalion* (relocated in HK in the 30s) and H. Tsoi's (2008) version of Bolt's *A Man for All Seasons* (in the form of an entertainment in a modern HK party), are examined in their socio-political context with rereading of the original divided into the translator's, the director's, the critic's and the audience's. It is found that postcolonial HK drama translation reflects nostalgia for British colonial rule and a need to interrogate China as the second colonizer. Mainstream postcolonial theories apply more to HK–Peking than to HK–London relations.

1 Introduction

Mainstream postcolonial theories maintain that Western colonizers always exploit, brainwash and discriminate against their colonies and the task of postcolonial translation is to deconstruct colonialism. The objective of this article is to find out whether mainstream postcolonial theories adequately apply to the case of Hong Kong (=HK), in particular, to Western drama in HK Cantonese translation, or whether they should be balanced or complemented by alternative postcolonial theories. (Cantonese is the mother tongue of most Hong Kong people. Chinese, unspecified as Cantonese or Mandarin, and English are the official languages of Hong Kong; whereas Mandarin, oral as well as written, is the official language of China.) The hypothesis is that postcolonial HK drama translation often manifests nostalgia for, or reluctance to part with, British colonial rule and a need to negotiate with the new colonizer, Peking.[1]

According to Anne McClintock (see Childs and Williams 1997: 227), colonization is the "appropriation and exploitation of another geopolitical territory, together with an organized interference in its rule and culture". Based on this definition, Hong Kong was an overseas colony of Great Britain from 1841 to 1997. Gilbert and Tompkins (1996) think that the term postcolonialism is not a temporal concept but an "engagement with and contestation of colonialism's discourses, power structures, and social hierarchies." This article adopts the temporal concept as well as the ideological definition of postcolonialism. Postcolonial HK translated plays for the purpose of this research are defined as plays rendered since 1982, when Peking first mentioned to London that HK must be returned from the UK to China by 1997. According to Lo Wai-luk (2004) and Lin Kehuan (2007), this event triggered off the identity search of HK citizens and, in my submission, the postcolonial period of HK drama, in which the main target of query is China as its second colonizer. According to Sonny Lo (2007: 222), recolonization is a process in which "a powerful metropole is exerting influence on its colonial enclave politically, economically, socially and culturally", and recolonization takes place in Hong Kong in the form of mainlandization, i.e., policies to render Hong Kong more and more reliant on the Chinese Mainland (Sonny Lo 2007: 179).

In order to familiarize the readers with the background of HK drama translation, a brief history of HK and a literature review will first be given. Then crucial concepts and mainstream and alternative postcolonial (translation) theories will be summarized. Based on their responsiveness to major socio-political events in HK history, such as the handover of HK to Peking (1997), the reinterpretation of the Basic Law (the mini-constitution of HK) by National People's Congress in 2004, and the tenth anniversary of the handover, two plays are selected. They are Rupert Chan's (2003) translation of Bernard Shaw's (1916) *Pygmalion,* and Hardy Tsoi's (2008a) translation of Bolt's (1960) *A Man for All Seasons.* In the light of postcolonial theories, they will be examined and the manipulation of the original will be categorized as the translator's, the director's, critics' and the audience's.

---

[1] According to Lo Wai-luk (2004: 97), in mid- and late 1980s, for HK drama, as "1997" became clearer and clearer, the future "maternal body" – the Chinese mainland – was actually the target to "negotiate with".

HK's attitudes towards its two colonizers will thereby be inferred, for which an explanation will be offered in terms of the socio-political dynamics among HK, the UK and China. Finally, a conclusion will be drawn concerning the applicability of postcolonial theories to the case of HK drama translation.

2 Background

2.1 HK history

HK Island was formally ceded by Qing Dynasty authorities to Britain at the end of the Opium War in 1841. Kowloon, the second part of HK, was ceded to Britain in 1860. The third part, New Territories, was leased to Britain in 1898 for 99 years. In 1967, as a ramification of Cultural Revolution on the Chinese Mainland, a riot broke up in HK, which, however, did not receive much support from the local people, and was soon rooted out. In 1984 Britain and China signed the Sino-British Joint Declaration, by which HK would be returned to China in 1997. Under the principle of "One Country, Two Systems" agreed between the two countries, HK would be governed as a special administrative region, retaining the British Common Law and a high degree of autonomy for at least 50 years after the transfer.

On 28 May 1989, 1.5 million HK citizens, one fourth of HK's population, led by Martin Lee (1938–), Szeto Wah (1931–) and other organization leaders, paraded through HK Island in support of Mainland students on Tiananmen Square demonstrating against governmental corruption and urging for democracy. The crackdown on 4 June severely affected HK's perceptions of the mainland. On 1 July 2003, more than 50 million HK people took to the street, protesting against an anti-subversion bill proposed by the Chief Executive, Tung Chee-hwa (1937–), handpicked by Peking, and his inefficient governance.

Tung abashedly resigned in 2005 and was succeeded by Donald Tsang (1944–). Hong Kong's Gini co-efficient became the highest of all Asian cities in 2008 (UN-Habitat 2008). In 2006 and 2007 respectively, a number of young people born in the 1980s, the so-called post 80s, began their protest careers in the mini-campaigns to try and stop demolition of the unpretentious but much-loved cultural heritages,

Star Ferry Pier and Queen's Pier. In January 2010, thousands of members of the 1980s generation besieged the Legco Building in protest against the proposed Hong Kong section of the Guangzhou–HK Express Rail Link, which was un-eco-friendly and non-cost-effective. In the same month, five lawmakers from two pro-democracy parties resigned and the resignations, which prompted a by-election in May 2010 that the five meant to be a de facto referendum on introducing greater democracy before the next elections in 2012, instead of waiting until 2017 or later, as Peking has demanded. The parties have named their venture a "new democracy" movement that challenges HK citizens to follow the model of the post 80s by taking the initiative on their own when nobody else will.

2.2 Literature review

Drama in the modern sense was not imported into China and HK until late 19th Century. Translated plays occupy an important place in Chinese drama, the beginning of which are marked by Lin Shu's translations (1901; 1898) of *A Postcript to Uncle Tom's Cabin* and *Lady of the Camellias*. According to Jessica Yeung's survey (2008), since 1962, more than 900 Western plays have been translated into HK Chinese (Cantonese) and performed in HK.

Postcolonial studies, however, have seldom paid attention to East Asian drama, even less to HK drama translation. Luk (2007) traces the development of Western drama in HK translation as performed by the HK Repertoire Theatre in the social context of HK. Applying Rey Chow's modified postcolonial theory (see below), Fong (2007) points out that through its postcolonial translated drama and original drama, HK carves its own flexible hybrid identity between its two colonizers. Chen (2006) argues that Anglo-American plays translated and performed between 2002 and 2003 in HK echo the anxieties of HK citizens amidst a postcolonial socio-economic crisis that climaxed in 2003.

Mainstream postcolonial theories almost unconditionally negate Western colonialism, while alternative postcolonial theories note the merits of Western culture and its possible benefits to the colonized. For instance, whereas Fanon (1967) condemns the Western colonizer for its enslaving and brutal exploitation of the colonized, D'Souza (2003) and Ferguson (2003) point out the benefits of British legacy, e.g., rule of law, reason, education, human rights. This is corroborated by Freyrer and Sacerdote (2006). Based on meteorological, historical, and socioeconomic data collected for many islands throughout the Atlantic, Pacific and Indian Oceans, they find that the number of years spent as a European colony and the density of settlement by Europeans is strongly *positively* related to the island's GDP per capita and *negatively* related to infant mortality.

Fanon (1967) also puts forth a 3-stage model for cultural evolvement of the colonized – assimilation, return to cultural nationalism, and revolution. But the third stage has never occurred in HK (cf. Fong 2007: 6). On the contrary, rule of law, human rights, liberty, democracy and professionalism in the European or British sense have become core values of HK (cf. W.K. Chan 2007).

Bhabha (1994: 115) points out that hybridity is a kind of peculiar "replication", which interrogates the colonial culture via mimicry and emerges through opening up 'a third space', where the negotiation of incommensurable differences between global and national cultures occurs. Batchelor (2008: 54) sees this Third Space as "the time-lag between event and enunciation", "through which all acts of speaking/writing about culture pass" and which leads to "the same cultural signs carrying different meanings on different occasions of their enunciation"; whereas, as pointed out by Batchelor (2008: 54), Wolf (2000:135, 138) interprets the Third Space in spatial terms as "a sort of 'in-between space' between existing referential systems and antagonisms" or "the space between two poles or binaries". On the other hand, Rey Chow (1998) shows HK to be carving a third hybrid space between its two aggressors (London and Peking). Similarly, Kwok-kan Tam (2005) argues that the postcoloniality of HK lies in its in-betweenness of cultural anomaly, that HK literature, including drama, tries to construct a HK identity that is neither British nor Mainland Chinese nor Taiwanese.

Bhabha (1994: 85–92) also asserts that the menace of mimicry lies in its double vision, which in disclosing the ambivalence of colonial discourse also disrupts its authority. In contrast, Fong (2007) points out that as a "strategic alliance" existed between colonial HK and the UK, the "mimicry" in Western drama in HK translation is unlikely to be against Britain.

Memmi (1991) thinks that the colonizer brings to the colonized inevitable economic collapse and insidious psychological destruction. In contrast, the HK scholar, Perry Lam (2007: 11, 20) argues that the colonial realities of HK prove that the imperialist is not necessarily just an aggressor; they could also be a benefactor bringing to the colonized law, effective governance, science, civilization and prosperity. As a colonial master, Chris Patten, the last governor of HK, fell in love with his colony; and as colonial subjects, HK people have placed their colonial master in eternal nostalgia (Lam 2007: 10).

Just like most postcolonial theories, most postcolonial drama/translation theories, e.g., Bassnett and Trivedi (1999) and Bandia (2009), focus on how postcolonial plays/translations deconstruct colonialism but seldom consider possible benefits of European colonialism to the colonized subject as may be cherished in postcolonial translations, the hybridity of one colonized subject caught between two colonizers, translations from the Western colonizer's language to the natives', and postcolonial drama translation per se. Moreover, Tymoczko (1999) shows the varied ways that translators articulate resistance to British colonialism and cultural oppression in their translations of Ireland's "national literary heritage". Examining English translations of Indian texts from the eighteenth century to the present, Niranjana (1992) calls for literal English re-translation of colonized people's texts for the purpose of decolonization. Gilbert and Tompkins (1996) develop performative and theoretical frameworks regarding articulation of history, language, body, voice and stage space in postcolonial drama for dismantling imperialism. The frameworks are useful for analyzing how postcolonial HK drama translation interrogates Mainland Chinese imperialism (much more intensely than with British imperialism).

Having gone through relevant postcolonial theories, we are now going to examine Chan's *My Fair Lady* and Tsoi's *A Man for All Seasons* in their light.

3 Will the Cantonese Fair Lady marry the UK professor?

In November 1997, four months after the handover of HK to China, a Cantonese musical entitled *Miutiu Sukneoi* [My Fair Lady] was performed by Spring-Time Group. In our submission, this translated play is a response to the handover, reflecting HK people's reluctance to part with British colonial rule and their gratefulness to it. The play was translated from Bernard Shaw's (1916) English play, *Pygmalion*, by Rupert Chan; the director was Ko Tin-lung and the producer Clifton Chi-Sum Ko.

3.1 The translator's manipulation

The translator relocated Bernard Shaw's *Pygmalion* in HK in the 1930s, with a combination of Chinese cheongsams and Western dresses. Whilst the conversion of a lower-class girl through training in the hands of a phonetics professor into a lady was kept, the English flower girl, Eliza Doolittle, who spoke Cockney English, was rendered into a Chinese flower girl named To Lan-heong speaking Cantonese with a strong Taishan accent. The phonetics professor Higgins became Tam Ying-kit, the only Chinese professor in the elitist University of HK. Probably, To Lan-heong — "heong" referring to the same Chinese character as "Hong" — symbolizes Hong Kong; and Tam Ying-kit, whose first name means English elite, symbolizes British elitism (cf. Li 2007: 456). Tam sets out to coach To primarily pure and high-class Cantonese and secondarily Oxford English, suggesting the predominance of Cantonese and English in HK as a colony. The ordeals at Mrs. Higgin's home in and the embassy ball in Shaw's version became respectively a garden party at the Governor's House and the convocation of the University of HK.

According to Rupert Chan (2000) himself, after discussing with the producer and the director, he added a new meaning to the ending of the play when the flower-selling girl breaks up with the phonetics professor. To says to Tam, "I am grateful to you for teaching me the British style, which has transformed me into an upper-class person", and no corresponding lines can be found in the original. Rupert Chan (2000: 85) confesses,

> This is the kind of feelings that I believe most HK people shared with me when they bid farewell to the colonial days on the 30th June 1997, in sharp contrast with the Mainland Chinese who fervently celebrated the "redressing of the 100-year-old national shame".

3.2 The director's and producer's manipulation

The director's and the producer's manipulation can been seen in the alternative endings of the play, its musical arrangement and use of accent. The HK production offers both the Shavian ending and Alan Jay Lerner's romantic ending. The production with cast A, with the older Chung King-fai, ends with Shaw's separation of the Higgins and Eliza counterparts. The ending with Cast B, with the younger Tse Kwan-ho, ends with the forthcoming marital union of To Lan-heong and Tam Ying-kit. Probably, the Shavian ending represents the reality of HK while the romantic ending represents Hong Kong's wishful fulfilment.

The HK people's reluctance to part with the British is corroborated by results of public opinion polls. According to the 1997 observation of David Bottomley, managing director of Asian Commercial Research Ltd., "We still have 60 per cent of people who ideally would prefer HK not to be a part of China" (see Wood and So 1997). According to Chung Ting-yiu (2007), ten years after the handover, 31 percent of the population of HK still preferred being a colonial citizen before 1997.

According to Gilbert and Tompkins (1996: 194), hybrid song and music often function to protest the domination of the coloniser's linguistic/musical tradition by liberally interspersing it with the words, forms, or musical structures of a less well-recognised and validated system of communication. Songs in Rupert Chan's *My Fair Lady*, however, function to stress the hybridity of the colonized people's linguistic/musical tradition as one dominated by the Cantonese language and supplemented by the two colonizers' languages. For example, the opening and ending presentations feature more than 18 actors/singers/dancers singing a theme song in mainly Cantonese, plus English, Mandarin, Shanghaiese, Taishan, etc. (cf. Li 2007: 456).

Also, according to Gilbert and Tompkins (1996:194), "in addition to its own signification, music [...] enhance[s] a mood, or effect an atmosphere". Further, "if postcolonial theatre provides an occasion for a vocal expression of solidarity, resistance, or even presence, song can intensify the reactions of both the actors and the audience". Its effects can be multiplied by a chorus, reinforcing communal action or interaction. The theme song of *My Fair Lady* has a similar function. For example, the line therein, "The colony has fair ladies, honourable gentlemen, as well as street sleepers – hundreds of kinds of people", especially the first segment, is high-pitched and melodious. They convey a festive mood or atmosphere, which seems to celebrate not the return of HK to China but the diversity or hybridity of HK as a colony.

According to Lefevere (1992: 58), "Dialects and idiolects tend to reveal the translators' ideological stance toward certain groups thought of as 'inferior' or 'ridiculous,' both inside their culture and outside." At the convocation of the University of HK in the translated play, a VIP guest, Hu Shi (1891–1962), a world-renowned Mainland Chinese scholar with a doctoral degree from Columbia University, recited a poem of his in Cantonese with a strong ridiculous Mandarin accent. This seems to reveal HK people's feeling of superiority over the Mainland Chinese.

3.3 Audience's response

This translated play was very popular. It was performed from 30 October 1997 to 23 November 1997, with 41 theatre performances, unusually long for HK drama as most HK plays are only performed for a couple of days. So much the more, Ada To, who played the heroine in the translated play, was awarded the Best Actress Prize by the Hong Kong Drama Awards (1997).

3.4 Critics' reviews

Harry (2007) appreciates the translated play for its alternative endings, its Cantonese localization, Cantonese lyrics and use of dialects. Kay Li (2007: 456), as aforementioned, argues that this translated play "explores how far the traditional ethnic Chinese and the colonial Westernized HK can blend […] a central concern at the end of 1997" or whether globalism and nationalism can co-exist in harmony in HK after the handover.

In a word, by mimicking the classic English play, *Pygmalion*, Rupert Chan's *My Fair Lady*, unlike the original, mainly aims at expressing HK's emotional attachment to the colonial days and the superiority of Cantonese and English over Mandarin and other Chinese dialects rather than at satirizing British pride and prejudice.

4 A HK Man for All Seasons

In December 2008, Hardy Tsoi translated and directed Robert Bolt's *A Man for All Seasons*. It is probably a response to the Tenth Anniversary of the handover of HK to China, in particular, to Communist China's suppression of full democracy in HK.

The plot is based on the true story of Saint Thomas More, the 16th Century Chancellor of England, who, being a devoted Catholic, declined to endorse King Henry VIII's wish to divorce his wife and to break England's connection with the Vatican Church. The play depicts More as a person of principle, envied by rivals such as Thomas Cromwell.

4.1 Possible effects on the audience

The play was performed against such a background of HK that it probably led to certain associations with pro-democracy politicians on the part of the HK audience. Firstly, in April 2004, the Standing Committee of the National People's Congress reinterpreted the Basic Law of HK and ruled out universal suffrage for both the HK Chief Executive election in 2007 and the HK Legislative Council election in 2008. In December 2007, the same committee again ruled out HK general elections in 2012, despite many HK people's repeated demonstrations for universal suffrage and protests made by pro-democracy politicians, e.g., Martin Lee.

Secondly, on 17 October 2007, one year before the performance of the translated play concerned, Martin Lee published an article entitled "China's Olympic Opportunity" in *The Wall Street Journal*, in which he criticized China for not living up to its promise to improve its human rights status during the Chinese Olympic bid, though he also urged the West not to boycott the 2008 Olympic Games. This immediately stirred backlashes from the Peking loyalists in HK, who virtually accused Lee of being an evil traitor to China (see *The Standard* 2007).

Given such a background, Thomas More in the translated play probably represented to the HK audience pro-democracy HK politicians, such as Martin Lee and Szeto Wah, Emily Lau (1956–), Leung Kwok Hung (1956–) and Audrey Eu (1953–). They are major targets of attack by pro-communist media in HK. And they are denied access to the Chinese Mainland. Martin Lee seems to resemble Thomas More most. Both are lawyers in vigorous support of British-style rule of law.[2] Both are devoted Catholics ready to defy the authorities and die for their

---

[2] Thomas More hides himself and his family in "the thickets of the law" (Bolt 1960: 39).

principle.[3] Just as Thomas More was unjustly convicted of treason and beheaded, Martin Lee has been without good reason labelled a traitor to China by pro-communist elements in HK and by Peking.

According to Tsoi himself (2008b), "every man has a price", one of the main themes of the play, applies to the contemporary situation of HK. He also revealed in a personal telephone interview (2009) that since the handover of HK to China in 1997, it has been widely perceived by the HK public that West Point (the location of Liaison Office of the Central People's Government in HK) is leading Central (the location of the Main Wing HK Government Offices), and that quite a few people have steered according to the wind and changed course for convenience. By way of the play, he wanted to explore how a person who persists in his or her principle so unswervingly as to be willing to give up his or her life for it would be viewed in contemporary HK. He said that an example of More-like persons in HK could be Szeto Wah though he was not completely sure whether Szeto has any hidden political agenda.

Moreover, the character of the Common Man who plays, by changing clothes on the stage, various small parts in *A Man for All Seasons* – More's servant, a publican, a boatman, More's jailer, jury foreman and executioner – probably signifies to the HK audience those HK political "chameleons" who have steered according to the wind and changed course for convenience during the postcolonial period.[4] For example, according to David Tang (2005),

> For years, we Chinese were all deferential to the British rule. I remember... As late as 1996, many HK friends of mine, all now fervent Chinese patriots, would jump at the chance of meeting the British Prime Minister of the day...overnight. That deference shifted to the Chinese leadership.... Loyalty and life-long friendships seemed to count for nothing.

Moreover, during the Tiananmen Square Massacre, all HK politicians and wealthy businessmen supported the demonstrating Peking students and condemned the

---

[3] Martin Lee was the target of an assassination during the 2008 elections but he was never frightened because, "as a Catholic, death to me is like pushing the door to another life" (CathNews 2009).

[4] As pointed out by Bareham (1980: 59), the Common Man serves as a Brechtian bridge between historical setting and modern audience. Also, as reminded by Bolt's own preface (1960: viii), "common" has two senses. The first one is certain elements of the character being shared by the audience. The second one is the baseness, the worldliness, and the ethical weakness of the character.

Communist government of China. Since the handover, however, a lot of them have defended the CCP (see *Appledaily* 2009).

4.2 The director's manipulation

A Man for All Seasons was presented by Tsoi as a play within another play from a 21st Century HK perspective, i.e., a form of entertainment performed during a New Year Eve's party held and joined by a group of HK business executives and office ladies. Every actor on the stage, in both the meta theatre and the theatre per se, was dressed in modern costumes, though somewhat glamorous as they are supposed to be participants in a fancy party. Immediately before More was executed, they started counting down loudly. When he was beheaded, they all applauded hilariously. The purpose of this arrangement is probably to wake up the silent majority of the HK people from their indifference to political and social justice.

According to Gilbert and Tompkins (1996: 166–167), "language functions as a basic medium through which meaning is filtered, but it also acts as cultural and political system that has meaning in itself". Altogether five languages were spoken in the performance. Cantonese was spoken by most of the characters most of the time, including More, Cromwell, etc. But More's son-in-law, played by the English actor, Mike Ingham, spoke pure English. More's daughter Margaret spoke in English to her husband and in Cantonese to her father. The Spanish ambassador, played by a Spanish, talked in Spanish. In the middle part of Act 1, Henry VIII and Margaret exchanged a few lines with each other in Latin. In Act 2, the archbishop, Cranmer, helped to interrogate More in Mandarin. This reflects the hybrid, multilingual and cosmopolitan nature of HK, as confirmed by Tsoi (2008c) himself in a radio interview. The archbishop's interrogation of More in Mandarin reminds one of the National People's Congress Standing Committee's ruling out universal suffrage for electing the Chief Executive of HK and the entire HK Legislative Council in 2007/2008 and 2012. It also reminds one of Peking officials' condemnations in Mandarin of pro-democracy HK politicians, e.g., An Min's (Deputy Minister of Ministry of Commerce, China) open, hateful and disdainful denunciation of Martin Lee as a traitor on 7 March 2004 (see *Wenweipo* 2004). The political significance of this use of the Mandarin language is confirmed by the audience's response. No sooner had the archbishop begun to speak in Mandarin than "the audience found themselves between tears and laughter" (Fatlam 2008).

4.3 The translator's manipulation

Although Hardy Tsoi (2009), as the translator, claimed that he was absolutely faithful to every word of the original, one can still find allusions to China in the wording of the translation. For example, the word, "treason" as the accusation against Thomas More is at times translated as *mai-gwok* (selling the country) instead of *bun-gwok* (betrayal of the country). And *mai-gwok* is exactly the term used by many pro-communist elements in HK to attack pro-democracy politicians in HK, in particular, Martin Lee after the publication of his essay, "China's Olympic Opportunity". Another example: "kings" (Bolt 1960: 1) and "the King" as in Wolsey's line, "The King needs a son" (Bolt 1960:11), or in More's line, "the King needs no advice from me on what to do about it" (Bolt 1960: 12), are translated as "the Emperor". And as pointed out by Chip Tsao (2009), an extremely popular HK columnist, "emperor" "crown prince", "eunuch", "lackey", etc. are concepts at the core of Chinese culture. Further, Cromwell's line, "we'll [...] fix these quicksands on the Law's plain chart!" (Bolt 1960: 89) is translated as "we'll give these quicksands a law suppression". Now, *zan-aat* (suppression) in Chinese is frequently used to describe the Chinese Communist Party's armed suppression of demonstrations, e.g., the Tiananamen Square Massacre. So "a law suppression" might remind the HK audience of the National People's Congress' arbitrary reinterpretation of the Basic Law in order to suppress full democracy in HK. In addition, "great native country" (Bolt 1960:93) is translated as *weidai zougwok* (great ancestral country), a term frequently used by the Chinese Communist Party and pro-communist elements in HK when referring to their mother country.

4.4 The critics' reviews

All 6 available critics' reviews confirm and praise the translated play's relevance to the contemporary situation of HK. For instance, Kuk Fei (2008) states that this is a tragedy of the times. In any significant era, those in power mostly classify and look at people in terms of their "value" or "function". Whenever there is a conflict, the more conscience you have, the more miserably you will die, just as Thomas More is often reprimanded by the authorities that his conscience is his personal matter and has nothing to do with the overall situation. Cheung (2008) and Fat Lam (2008) recognize the use of language as politics in the play.

To sum up, by mimicking the story of Saint Thomas More of England, this translated play made in HK aims at challenging not London colonialism but Peking's suppression of HK democracy and interference with its rule of law. It eulogizes at the same time the traditional British hero as well as pro-democracy activists of HK.

5 An account of the inferred phenomenon

Now an account will be given for the emotional attachment to the UK and the need to negotiate with Communist China as manifested in postcolonial HK drama translation.

The relationship between HK and its former colonizer, Great Britain, was not the classic slave-master colonial model but, as aforementioned, a "strategic alliance", as put by Fong (2007: 6). The UK practised an active non-interference policy in relation to HK and never seriously suppressed its local culture or language. At the beginning of the colonial rule, HK was an insignificant fishing port with a GDP approaching zero. At the end of the colonial rule, HK gained[5] not only a reserve of 67 billion euro but also rule of law, freedom, human rights, a non-corrupt governmental system, universal education, a sophisticated financial system, etc. Then HK was handed over to another colonizer rather than became independent. And the second colonizer appears to lag significantly behind both the former colonizer and the colony in terms of press freedom, environmental protection, human wellbeing, human rights, anti-corruption, integrity, etc.

For example, Freedom House (2009) ranked the UK as having the 27th freest media, HK the 75th and China the 181st among the 195 countries assessed. In the

---

[5] DeGolyer (2006) points out that "HK's 156 years of colonial rule left an indelible appreciation for the British legacy of personal rights, rule of law and limited government."

2005 Environmental Sustainability Index prepared by Yale Center for Environmental Law (2003), the UK ranks 65th while China ranks 133rd. Prescott-Allen's (2001) Well-being Index (a combination of Human Well-being and Ecosystem Well-being Indices) surveys 180 countries, ranking the UK 33rd and China 160th. In the Corruption Perceptions Index 2007 prepared by Transparency International, HK ranks 12th, the UK ranks 16th, while China ranks 72nd.

Concerning human rights, reports compiled by Human Rights Watch and International Amnesty regularly confirm that the UK in general respects human rights while China's human rights record remain way below average. Moreover, according to Chang and Halliday (2005), The Communist Party of China, under the leadership of Chairman Mao, was responsible for the deaths of 70 million people and has never apologized to the people. Thus, the UK fulfils international requirements of a civilized country much more than China. This is probably the reason why the citizens of HK prefer the UK to China as its colonizer.

Equally important, according to Cheng (2007), which contains 24 essays written by a team of distinguished HK experts in different domains, HK has declined in political development, economy, social welfare, freedom of press and speech, education, transport, health care, income equality, urban planning, environmental protection, etc., in the first decade after its handover.

6 Conclusion

Mainstream postcolonial theories need to be modified or balanced by alternative postcolonial theories. General mainstream postcolonial theories, e.g., Fanon's (1967) maintain that European colonialism invariably oppresses and exploits the colonized, and that the latter should and will resist and fight against it. But the heroine in Rupert Chan's (1997) translation of Shaw's *Pygmalion*, representing HK, shows loving gratefulness to British colonialism incarnated in the person of the linguistics professor graduated from Oxford, and celebrates the good old colonial days of HK. This confirms Perry Lam's (2007) argument that HK people experience eternal nostalgia for their former colonial master. Similarly, Hardy Tsoi's (2008a) direction and translation of Bolt's (1960) *A Man for All Seasons* depicts allegiance to British-style rule of law on which Thomas More relies to protect himself and his family. And rule of law is one of the merits of British colonial legacy as expounded by Ferguson (2003) and D'Souza (2003).

Homi Bhabha (1994) talks about the subversion of European colonial authority by hybridity, mimicry and the third space. The mixture of Chinese cheongsams and Western dresses and the multilingual songs in the HK version of *Pygmalion* (*My Fair Lady*), and the blending of Cantonese with English, Mandarin, etc. in both *My Fair Lady* and *A Man for All Seasons* highlight the importance of Cantonese in mingling with other languages and dialects in HK. But the main target of challenge seems to be the Chinese Mainland rather than the UK, especially when the audience's response upon hearing the archbishop interrogating Thomas More in Mandarin was "between tears and laughter". By mimicking British classics, postcolonial HK drama interrogates not British colonialism but Communist Chinese imperialism. In both plays concerned, the heroine/hero has to carve a Rey Chovian hybrid third space – in the case of *My Fair Lady*, between the flower-selling girl's Taishan accent and uncouth manners representing her Chinese origin, on the one hand, and the Oxford professor's British elitism, on the other hand; and, in the case of *A Man for All Seasons*, between Vatican representing British imperialism and Henry VIII representing Mainland Chinese authority.

Postcolonial translation theories, like Tymoczko's (1999) and Niranjana's (1992), see translation as a site for resistance against European colonialism. But the translator of *My Fair Lady* puts words of thankfulness to British colonialism in the mouth of the heroine, and the director and producer add an alternative ending in which the heroine actually marries her professor-coacher graduated from Oxford. In addition, the translator's certain choices of diction in referring to Henry VIII and to his lackey's persecution of Thomas More in *A Man for All Seasons*, as well as the timing of performance and the local contemporary setting of the meta theatre, insinuate that Henry VIII and his regime stand for Communist China suppressing democracy and freedom of HK people rather than for Britain.

Therefore, when a postcolonial community is caught between two colonizers, and provided that one is more compliant with international standards of civilization, e.g., Corruption Perception Index, than the other, the colonized people, in its drama translation, may manifest preference or nostalgia for the more compliant colonizer and a need to negotiate with the other one. By mimicking the culture of the more enlightened colonizer, the colonized may resist, not the colonizer being mimicked, but the less enlightened one. In other words, mainstream postcolonial (translation) theories apply more to HK–Peking relations than to HK–London relations. And they need to be modified with the help of alternative postcolonial theories like those of Ferguson (2003), Chow (1998), Fong (2007) and Lam (2007).

References

Bandia, Paul F. (2008): *Translation as Reparation: Writing and Translation in Postcolonial Africa*. Manchester: St Jerome Publishing.
Bassnett, Susan / Trivedi, Harish [eds.] (1999): *Post-colonial Translation (Theory and Practice)*. London and New York: Routledge.
Batchelor, Kathryn (2008): "Third Spaces, Mimicry and Attention to Ambivalence". In: *The Translator* 14:1, 51–70.
Bhabha, Homi (ed.) (1994): *The Location of Culture*. London: Routledge.
Bolt, Robert (1960): *A Man for All Seasons*. London: Heinemann Educational Books.
Bareham, Tony (1980): *Robert Bolt: A Man for All Seasons: Notes*. London: Longman.
CathNews (2009) "Hong Kong's Martin Lee Targeted for Assassination". In: *CathNews* 1 June. Available at http://www.cathnews.com.au/article.aspx?aeid=14134. Visited April 2010.
Chan, Rupert (trans.) (1997): *Miutiu Sukneoi* [My Fair Lady]. Dir. Ko, Tin Lung . Prod. Ko, Clifton. Trans. of *Pygmalion*. By Shaw, Bernard. Perf. Chung, King Fai / Cheung, Dominic. The Spring Time Group Production, HK. 31 Oct. – 30 Nov.
―― (2000): "*Zizukze Pan Jiklok* [The Joy of One who Translates Hard]". In: *Hong Kong Drama Review* 2, 83–90.
Chan, W.K. (2007): "Urban activism for effective governance". Available at http://74.125.77.132/search?q=cache:kCXJkyI-6JkJ:susdevhk.org/resource_download.php%3Fcat_id%3D1%26resource_id%3D18%26download_lang%3Dch+%22hong+kong+core+values+network%E2%80%9D&cd=1&hl=fi&ct=clnk&gl=fi&client=firefox-a. Visited April 2010.
Chang, Jung / Halliday, Jon. (2005): *Mao: The Unknown Story*. London: Jonathan Cape.
Chen, Chapman (2006): "Western Drama in HK Translation". In: *International Journal of the Humanities* 2.2, 973–981.
Cheng, Joseph Y.S. (ed.) (2007): *The Hong Kong Special Administrative Region in its First Decade*. HK: City University of HK Press.
Cheung, Ping Kuen (2008): "*Ngo Syun 2008 Nin Bundei Sapgai Moudoikek* Sauzing Ban [My Choice of the Ten Best Plays in 2008 Revised Edition]". Available at http://www.theatreborderless.com/abchk/a/news.do?method=detail&id=52913c5f1e42b01d011ef397e9060002&mappingName=FORUM. Visited April 2008.
Childs, Peter / Williams, Patrick (1997): *An Introduction to Post-Colonial Theory*. London and New York and Toronto: Prentice Hall.
Chow, Rey (1998): "Between Colonizers: Hong Kong's Postcolonial Self-Writing in the 1990s". In: *Ethics after Idealism: Theory, Culture, Ethnicity, Reading*. Bloomington and Indianapolis: Indiana University Press. 149–167.

Chung, Ting-yiu (2007): "HKU POP Site Findings on Hong Kong and Taiwan People's Views on the 10th Anniversary of Hong Kong's Handover". 27 June. Available at http://hkupop.hku.hk/english/release/release477.html. Visited July 2009.
Cronin, Michael (1996): *Translating Ireland*. Cork: Cork University Press.
D'Souza, Dinesh (2002): "Two Cheers for Colonialism". In: *What is So Great About America*. New York and London: Penguin. 37–68.
DeGolyer, E. Michael (2006): "Hong Kong as a Clue to the Future China". In: *Hong Kong Journal* 1 June. Available at http://www.hkjournal.org/archive/degolyer.html. Visited July 2009.
Fanon, Frantz (1967): *The Wretched of the Earth (Les damnes de la terre)*. Trans. Farrington, Constance. Harmondsworth: Penguin.
Fat Lam (2008): "*Jatjyut Zingzung dik Seigwai Jan* [The Faithful Man for All Seasons]". In: *Takungpao*, HK 23 December. Available at http://dagong.iflove.com/news/08/12/23/MFTX-1008509.htm. Visited 3 July 2009.
Ferguson, Niall (2003): *Empire – How Britain Made the Modern World*. London: Penguin.
Fong, Gilbert (2007): "*Junzi dik Zi-ngo Jingtong – Hoenggong Heikek Faanjikkek dik Buihau* [Suspended self – Behind HK drama translation]". In: *Hong Kong Drama Review* 6, 1–14.
Freedom House (2009): *Freedom of the Press 2009*. 1 May. Available at http://www.freedomhouse.org/uploads/FreedomofthePress2009.pdf. Visited July 2009.
Freyrer, James / Sacerdote, Bruce (2006): "Colonialism and Modern Income – Islands as Natural Experiments". National Bureau of Economic Research Working Paper No. 12546. September. Available at http://www.nber.org/papers/w12546. Visited 6 April 2010.
Gilbert, Helen / Tompkins, Joanne. (1996): *Postcolonial Drama*. London and New York: Routledge.
Kuk Fei (2008): "*Seikwai leongsam* [A Conscience for All Seasons]". 13 December. Available at http://101arts.net/101artscontent/101_column_Pen/08Dec/A_man_for_all_season_KF.htm. Visited Jan. 2010.
Lam, Perry (2007): *Heonggong Nei Wan Singha Dosiu* [Hong Kong, how much of you is still left]. HK: Sub-culture.
Lefevere, Andre (1992): *Translation, Rewriting, and the Manipulation of Literary Fame*. London and New York: Routledge.
Li, Kay (2007): "Performing the Globalized City: Contemporary Hong Kong Theatre and Global Connectivity". In *Asian Theatre Journal* 24:2 (Fall), 440–469.
Lin, Kehuan (2007): *Heikek Hoenggong, Hoenggong Heikek* [Dramatic Hong Kong, Hong Kong drama]. HK: OUP.
Lo, Sonny (2007): "The Mainlandization and Recolonization of HK: A Triumph of Convergence over Divergence with Mainland China". In: Cheng, Joseph (ed.): *The HK Special Administrative Region in its First Decade*. HK: City University of HK Press. 179–223.
Lo, Wai-luk (2004): *Hoenggong Moutoi* [HK on Stage]. HK: International Association of Theatre Critics (HK).
Luk, Y.T. Thomas (2007): *Translation and Adaptation of Western Drama in Hong Kong: From Script to Stage (in Chinese)*. HK: Chinese University Press.
Memmi, Albert (1991): *The Colonizer and the Colonized*. New York: Orion.
Niranjana, Tejaswini (1992): *Siting Translation*. Berkeley: University of California Press.
Prescott-Allen, Robert (2001): *The Wellbeing of Nations*. Washington D.C.: Island Press.
Shaw, Bernard (1916): *Pygmalion*. New York: Brentano.
Tam, Kwok-kan (2005): "Voices of Missing Identity: A Study of Contemporary Hong Kong Literary Writings". In: Shi, X. / Kienpointner, M. / Servas, J. [eds.]: *Read the Cultural Others*.

Forms of Otherness in the Discourses of Hong Kong's Decolonization. Berlin: Mouton de Gruyter. 165–176.

Tang, David (2005): "It's too Early to Tell". In: *Appledaily* 9 October.

The Standard (2007): "Lee Fires Bullet at Beijing, Asks Bush to Meddle". In *The Standard* 26 October.

Transparency International (2007): *Corruption Perceptions Index 2007.* Available at http://en.wikipedia.org/wiki/Corruption_Perceptions_Index. Visited July 2009.

Tsoi, Hardy (trans.) (2008a): *Seigwaijan* [A Man for All Seasons]. Dir. Tsoi, Hardy. Trans. of *A Man for All Seasons*. By Bolt, Robert. Perf. Tu, Mac. TNT Theatre, HK. 5–7 December.

—— (2008b): "Category 2.5 Theatre of *A Man for All Seasons*". In: *Chinese Drama Society Bulletin* 14 (December). Available at http://com2.tw/chta-news/2008-12/chta-0812-001.htm. Visited July 2009.

—— (2008c): Interview. "*Seigwaijan* [A Man for All Seasons]". New Cultural Campaign. Radio 5, RTHK, HK. 21 November. Available at http://gbcode.rthk.org.hk/TuniS/www.rthk.org.hk/rthk/radio5/newculturalcampaign/20081121.html. Visited July 2009.

—— (2009): Personal telephone interview. June 1.

Tsao, Chip (2009): "Jyuman Gaiduk [Detoxification of Language]". In: *Appledaily* 4 June.

Tymoczko, Maria (1999): *Translation in a Postcolonial Context. Early Irish Literature in English Translation.* Manchester: St Jerome Publishing.

UN-Habitat (2008): *State of the World's Cities 2008/2009 – Harmonious Cities.* New York: UN-Habitat.

Wenweipo (2004): "On Man: Meimaa Leifu Maigwok [An Min: Did not Accuse Lee's Father of Treason]". In: *Wenweipo* 8 March.

Wolf, Michaela (2000): "The Third Space in Postcolonial Representation". In: Simon, Sherry / St-Pierre, Paul [eds.]: *Changing the Terms: Translating in the Postcolonial Era.* Ottawa: University of Ottawa Press. 127–145.

Wood, Chris / So, Lillian (1997): "Hong Kong Prepares for Chinese Rule". In: *The Canadian Enclopedia* 3 February. Available at http://www.thecanadianencyclopedia.com/index.cfm?PgNm=TCE&Params=M1ARTM0011069. Visited April 2010.

Yale Center for Environmental Law, Yale University / Policy and Center for International Earth Science Information Network, Columbia University (2006): *2005 Environmental Sustainability Index.* Available at http://sedac.ciesin.columbia.edu/es/esi/ESI2005_policysummary.pdf. Visited July 2009.

Translating Slogans: Advertising Campaigns Across Languages

Katarína Nemčoková
Tomas Bata University in Zlín, Czech Republic

Abstract

As market became global, migrating products were accompanied by migrating advertising campaigns, which created new challenges for translators worldwide. A substantial number of trends and problems in the translation of advertising language have already been dealt with extensively. This paper offers an observation of the global advertising campaigns entering the small markets of the Czech and Slovak Republics since the markets opened to western products 20 years ago and it maps the major stages of the development of advertising slogan translation of that period. The first stage of using untranslated slogans for the local market was followed by a stage of rather poor translations, which now again seems to have been replaced by a wave of untranslated advertising texts. This paper tries to find reasons behind this development, pinpointing the specific problems during each stage. It charts the development as it was experienced by small-market translators and consumers and offers examples and case studies that help clarify the motives of the advertisers for their choice of translating strategy. Finally, it evaluates the choices and suggests the continued use or abandonment of some strategies.

1 Introduction

Advertising slogans, together with the products to which they are related, travel across national markets, speech communities and cultures. During such a process, they may be translated into the languages of the new audiences, adapted to new cultural settings, or designed anew to fit local needs. The aim of this paper is to observe the trends within the process of advertising slogan transplantation from the perspective of small markets and "small languages", specifically slogans of advertising campaigns used to sell various products in the Slovak and Czech markets. With such a narrow focus, larger trends in ad translation may remain veiled. However, such a micro-study can contribute to the general picture by helping to determine to what extent ad translation is a monolithic experience. Small markets and small languages often receive only a marginal notice, as being small is often associated with being unimportant. Nevertheless, a translator must do his/her work regardless of how big the language is and how many recipients absorb the translation. The year 2009 marked the 20th anniversary since the Western markets expanded eastward into the former Soviet sphere, a sufficient time span to observe relevant development, comment on it and learn from it. It is a considerably extended time to observe major trends, yet a short enough period to remember the details.

This paper presents a long-term observation rather than a statistically supported corpus research. The trends in advertising slogan translation were observed personally during the whole transformation period, first through the eyes of a student of languages and later as a professional in linguistics and translation. For the purposes of this paper, approximately 50 issues of various mainstream Slovak and Czech magazines dating from 1993 to 2009 were studied for the product ads appearing in them. The trends in translation practices observed in the print ads seem to confirm personal observations.

The translation problems of slogans as they seem to have developed from the early 1990s until the present are presented here. Both Slovak and Czech-language ads are used to exemplify the relevant points, since the two languages are very similar in structure and are mutually understandable without much effort. This fact has been used by the advertisers themselves, when the global campaigns entering Czech and Slovak markets were frequently localized only once (usually for the Czech market); the second version was a mild grammar or vocabulary adaptation of the localized one.

2 Theoretical framework

Recent studies by translation researchers in the former Eastern Bloc suggest that the role of translation prior to the 1989 Velvet Revolution and the one following it have a common denominator: in both eras, translation has served ideological purposes. While before 1989 it was political propaganda and the dictate of political power, after 1989, it was consumerism and impositions of marketing force. Debeljak (2007) proposes that translation is inevitably political, because what is foreign, becomes understandable through translation. Keníž (2006), Kusá (2005) and Djovčoš and Pliešovská (2010) discuss various aspects of this view and claim that intercultural dialogue, so often remarked by translation researchers, is rather a dictating monologue of the dominant culture and dominant language. Kusá (2005) states that in the case of Slovakia (and the Czech Republic), the social and cultural scope has always been heavily determined by surrounding cultural contexts: first Russian and later mainly Anglo-Saxon. During the period of the communist regime, the connections with foreign cultures were characterized by the relative absence of contacts with the Anglo-Saxon culture. There were historically-conditioned contacts with the Russian, German, Hungarian and French cultures, however, direct connections with the Anglo-Saxon culture were almost non-existent. Now, the situation has changed – Czechs and Slovaks are primarily dominated by the European Union and the United States.

In the Czech and Slovak markets since 1989, the "dictate" of political influence in translation has changed into the "dictate" of global product brands and their global advertising campaigns. The Czech Republic and Slovakia have reared a typical subordinate small-market consumer ingesting what is being served. For such a target audience, very rarely are the advertising campaigns translated with appropriate care and attention. Foreignization has been a major trend in both receptor cultures. Keníž (2006: 29) views translation in the two societies as commercial commodities and recognizes this phenomenon as a tool of propaganda of the dominant (consumerist) ideology. He states:

> Sixteen years after the Velvet Revolution that changed us, determined warriors against American and western imperialism, into its fiery promoters, in the times when the globalization wave took the essence of our economy and some level of self-sufficiency, we come to see that it is also robbing us of the last thing that we had – national culture and national identity. (Keníž 2006: 29)

We often witness such development when translation (or more specifically "non-translation") of migrating advertising campaigns is considered. However, the development in this particular area has its unique features and does not stay immune to reactions of the ad recipients. These, subsequently, promote changes in the translation routine.

3 Advertising slogans and their translation

The observations of translating advertising campaigns cover the translation of one part of translation messages: the slogans. Slogans are usually very short, but the means by which they represent the advertised product make them prominent textual parts of the majority of advertising campaigns. They tend to build the strongest trace in the consumers' memory. Angela Goddard (2002: 127) defines slogan as a "phrase designed to be memorable". Křížek and Crha (2003: 98) state that the two major functions of slogans are reminding the consumer of the product or the company and giving the consumer "the reason-why" by frequent repetition. If consumers remember the words by which a product is advertised, they usually remember the slogan. Slogans do not sell the product directly; their information content is low. Their value is in creating a symbolic image of the product in consumers' minds. That is why slogans should be handled with extreme care when the product they represent moves to new markets. Symbols in one culture may have differing meaning elsewhere, and achieving the same symbolic meaning may not be possible with the target language means, especially if the source and target languages are not genetically related.

Generally, three strategies can be identified when considering globetrotting slogans: a source language slogan (most frequently English, German or French) is used in the target market; a translation (with or without respect to the target culture) is made; and a completely new slogan is crafted in the target language for the target audience. Each category will be looked at, commented on and illustrated with specific examples taken from the Slovak and Czech markets.

4 The stages of slogan translation

Central and Eastern Europe opened up as a new market for goods sold in the West in a revolutionary way. There was no time to prepare. Almost overnight, the Easterners became members of a consumer capitalist community. At the same time, being only vaguely aware of what had been hidden behind the Iron Curtain, Westerners could not fully grasp the cultural differences and the market specifications of the newly added territories. The spontaneity and speed of this process was significantly reflected in the translation (or *attempted* translation) of product-related texts such as content information, instructions and warnings on packaging, manuals, advertising copies and product-promoting slogans. As a result of speed and a lack of education in the field, good quality translations of non-literary texts from that era are not easy to find.

4.1 Stage I: Source-language slogans in the target market

The usage of source language slogans changes over time and so does their effect. By observing the Czech and Slovak markets for almost two decades, a trend related to using translated as opposed to untranslated slogans seems to be detectable: untranslated, source language slogans used in the early period of open markets in Eastern Europe were later replaced by translated ones (in varying quality), many of which are currently being replaced by a new wave of source language slogans.

In her recent study on English in advertising, An H. Kuppens (2009: 115–117) outlines several possible reasons for the use of source-language text with a target-language audience: first, the advertisers may choose it to build a global, consistent marketing strategy. Another reason appears to be the availability of expressions in the source language and possibilities of linguistic creativity, which may both be lacking in the target language. The third reason is connected with intended transferring of the source culture characteristics, for which the source language may serve as a vehicle. The final reason is the power and influence of the "big languages", the use of which simply feels natural to the foreign advertisers in "small language" markets.

In the Slovak and Czech context of the early 1990s, source language slogans seem to have been used for two major reasons: first, the power of big source languages combined with a lack of quality translation services to create a wave of source-language (usually English) slogans. Second, foreign languages spoken in the West symbolized everything the new market consumers had not had during the old era but longed to get through the new arriving culture: high quality and reliable products and trendsetting 'western' status. One of many examples is Coca Cola, which had its first massive advertising campaign in Slovakia in 1993 headed by the English slogan *Always Coca Cola*. Problems arising from the consumers' not knowing the source language soon became obvious. A slogan should work as a symbol. However, the empty contents of the expression resulted in a missing link in the minds of consumers. They were unable to identify the slogan as a symbol for the product. Since it was only the sound representation that reminded them of the soft drink, it operated at a surface level, as an icon, and thus lost some of its image-building potential. A different category of problems appeared as well: the consumers remembered the sound of *always* (not knowing its meaning) and associated it with the product in unintended ways. Such was the case of an overheard conversation in the mid-1990s during which the English *Coca Cola* slogan was mixed-up with a product bearing the brand name *Always* (feminine hygiene product), leading to the saying *Always Coca Cola with wings*.

The "wow" factor of the western market products on new markets was rather short-lived. The source language slogans taking advantage of it soon faced criticism from new consumers regaining their self-confidence and becoming fed up with the force-fed ideas they did not understand. Norman Fairclough in his book *Language and Power* describes it in terms of the "powerless" (the consumers in this case) resisting the "power holders" (the producers of the discourse, the advertisers). He claims that "The effectiveness of resistance and the realization of change depend on people developing a critical consciousness of domination and its modalities" (1989: 4). He further argues that advertising discourse positions the "powerless" into the roles of consumers and even attributes that position with the qualities of desirability. Within the frame of this paper, this fact can be seen in how often advertising language becomes a part of consumers' language in the form of catchphrases, funny bon-mots, popular jokes, etc. (see Kovácsová 2008). Of course, this is a dream fulfilled for any advertiser, since they all want their products to be talked about and become an indivisible part of our lives. However, this transfer only happens if the consumers understand the language used for advertising. While Slovak and Czech slogans were often becoming catchphrases and richly circulated as a part of popular culture in the underworld of everyday communication, the foreign words never entered that world. The ties between the product and the slogan were not as strong as the advertisers could make by using a target language.

The advertisers learned more about the new consumers as quickly as the consumers learned about themselves. As Kuppens (2009: 119) pointed out, "Savvy, media-literate viewers [...] present advertisers with a challenge". The non-understood source language appearing in the ads seemed to be a sign of arrogance of power of the advertisers (similar in effect to direct commands or overtly pushy selling tactics in case of an understood language use). Fairclough (1989: 33) argues that the power can be exercised directly, through "coercing others to go along" or, indirectly, through "winning others' consent". The second strategy is generally much more effective, less risky and less costly when reaching objectives. Imposing a foreign-language ad on the consumer who does not speak the language may easily feel as exercising power over them, and may in turn invoke rather strong resistance. Fairclough (1989: 72) further claims: "One dimension of power in discourse is arguably the capacity to determine to what extent that power will be overtly expressed". This may be one of the decisive reasons why many advertisers switched to translated slogans as the criticism and resistance from the consumers became more obvious.

4.2 Stage II: Translated slogans

At the beginning of the 21st century, many advertisers had already switched to translated slogans in both the Czech Republic and Slovakia. A plentitude of translatological studies has been published describing the crucial problems in the translation of advertising slogans (see e.g. Jettmarová 2008, 2004; Pym, Shlesinger and Jettmarová 2007; Guidere 2007; Barancic 2005; de Mooji 2004; Adab 2000). Many slogans of this period simply did not work because the translators could not handle the transfer of stylistic devices such as puns, rhymes, metaphors, fixed phrases or cultural references. While the low-quality translations of manuals and instructions of this era originated in the poor language skills of the translators, the low quality of translated slogans was often caused by the insistence of the advertisers on following their global advertising strategy. In many cases the advertisers felt they had a great slogan so they insisted on its precise (near word-for-word) translation. This can be illustrated with a case of the mobile-phone operator Orange and their slogan translation from English to Slovak in 2000. At that time, the company was about to undergo a re-branding process, and the marketing department was collecting ideas about the future slogan. It was supposed to be translated from the original, English one, which was a linguistic play on words making use of a homonymy and partial synonymy connected with one of the meanings. It read: *"The future is bright, the future is Orange."* Slovak as a synthetic language operates with 6 declinations, 3 grammatical genders, numerous patterns of conjugations in both singular and plural, all marked by dozens of inflectional suffixes. The directly translated slogan missed the point, because the word *bright*, when translated, was obviously marked an adjective, while the word *Orange* was only identifiable as a proper noun, even keeping its source-language pronunciation and spelling. The possible semantic and collocational connection of *bright* and *orange* was completely lost. What is more, the monosyllabic (and thus phonetically highly effective) word *bright* has two possibilities of translation. One meaning, *žiarivý*, fits perfectly for its higher expressivity, which the advertiser most probably wanted to reach (the proof of that being the bright orange color against the pitch black background of the ads). However, it does not collocate with the Slovak word for *future (budúcnosť)*. On the other hand, *jasný* is rather mild in its meaning and tones down the message, yet it collocates with *future*. However, in the collocation with *future* it gains additional meaning of *clear*. Since all these linguistic problems were obvious, it would seem logical to have a completely new slogan designed for the rebranding. Nevertheless, the instructions were to follow the general advertising strategy of the company. The final translation eventually used was the word-for-word one, using the milder word *jasný*. The slogan showed no meaning connection of *bright* and *Orange*, it shifted the meaning of *bright future* into the *clear future* so instead of saying "Orange is the light of the future, the torch of hope, the optimism to come" it said "we know what is going to happen, it is clear". The customers, instead of seeing the hope, understood the company to be a power player because they knew already what was to happen (not necessarily in the best possible sense). Even though the company earned a sizeable profit for many years to follow, it seems that this profit was closely tied to the specific market situation with limited competition and not because of the slogan. This claim can be supported by the fact that once the market became saturated, profits declined and the fight for the consumer was really happening through advertising campaigns, the slogan was abandoned altogether, and Orange started to advertise with its bright orange logo against a black background rather than with a slogan.

Similar problems can be observed in the slogans of *Maybelline* (*Maybe she was born like that, maybe it is Maybelline*) where the wonderful chime of *maybe-Maybelline* is lost in translation. This slogan is still used, though, possibly because at least its alliterative power of M-m was preserved (*Možno sa už taká narodila, možno je to Maybelline*). The *KitKat* candy bar slogan reads *Have a break, have a Kitkat* which, translated, did not keep its homonymous play on the word *break* – a piece of bar broken off and a pause for relaxation while enjoying the bar. However, the translated slogan (*Daj si pauzu, daj si KitKat*) is pleasant to the ear, is highly rhythmical and thus very catchy and easily remembered. This is not a frequent case, because English, unlike Czech or Slovak, has a high tendency to monosyllabicity. The rhythm and fast pace of English advertising texts is hard to reach in translation due to this phenomenon. This can be further illustrated by the Nivea for Men slogan *What Men Want* translated as *Muži vědí, co chtějí*, which lost its pace because of the two-syllable words [*Mu-ži vě-dí, co chtě-jí*] replacing the appealing monosyllabic rhythm in translation. Other features lost here are the alliteration and the graphic similarity between W and M, which all cooperate in creating an image of the product. Compared to the English one, the Czech translation only preserves the word and sentence meaning. Hellmann's mayonnaise slogan translator came with a substitute strategy. The original monosyllabic and rhythmical *Bring out the best* was replaced by one with a slightly shifted meaning (literally *Simply the Best*) yet preserving the rhythm and pace by having two multi-syllabic words in an ear-pleasing chant of *Jednoducho to najlepšie* [*Jed-no-du-cho to-naj-lep-šie*]. The exact meaning transfer was sacrificed for a pleasing form and that seems to be a better strategy when slogans are adapted for a target audience.

Alliteration is another powerful device frequently appearing in slogans, but easily lost in translation. Attempts should be made to preserve it since it is a useful over-coding device having a profound influence on the senses and memory of the consumer. An example where this capacity has been lost appears in the Microsoft slogan *Your potential. Our passion*, translated word-for-word as *Vaše možnosti. Naša inšpirácia*. Here, not only is the alliteration lost but the rhythm is gone together with the syllabic pace. The original two-times four syllables is replaced by five plus seven which ruins the possibly well-working effect of over-coding. The message is approximately the same in word meaning, yet the translated slogan sounds uninspiring, boring, and difficult to remember. For consumers, this slogan may cease to exist as soon as their eyes rest upon some other text, which is not the best investment for Microsoft.

If low-quality work is done in the translation of a slogan at the beginning, it can return as a boomerang even years later. Tesco Stores in the Czech Republic and Slovakia are now facing such an effect. The English Tesco slogan *Every Little Helps* is an inviting, playful, creative text with a high impact factor. For an unknown reason it was translated as *S nami ušetríte*, which is a completely ordinary, boring and uninspiring sentence meaning 'you'll save with us'. Not only is there a complete absence of any language figure, sense-pleasing use of words and inventiveness, there is a very poor meaning transfer as well. The English slogan covers a much larger spectrum of Tesco's advantages: a little savings help, but also little things such as good and quick customer service, etc. The translated slogan can only be applied to two items we can save: money and time. The store image becomes shallow in not caring about anything else but the very materialistic essence of consumerism, which bears rather negative connotations. What is more, during the 2009 Christmas season, Tesco added a seasonal Slovak-language slogan in Slovakia. Loosely, it says: *Little things make Christmas,* which seems to be nicely in line with the original English slogan *Every Little Helps*. However, it has no connection with the translated general slogan ('you'll save with us'). There is no consistency, no "story of the little things" to be said. If the English slogan had been translated with more skill and closer observance of what it was meant to say, the 2009 Christmas slogan would make much more sense in that general picture.

If the translated slogan is to function as effectively as the one in the language of the global advertising campaign, it should be in line with the global advertising policy and the general message the producer wants to spread about the product. However, with regard to the functions of a slogan, experience shows that the literal translation is lower in importance than the device used to make an impact on the consumer's senses and memory. Slogans do not exist to give information but to associate the product with a certain idea, causing the product to be remembered and recollected even when consumers are not reading or watching commercials. Syllable-based rhythm, alliteration, puns based on homonymy, creative exploration of word combinations and other similar sense-inspiring devices all serve these purposes. If the translation does not allow the usage of such figures in the target text, a deviation from the word and sentence meaning in order to "make space" for such a device is highly justifiable. A copywriter rather than a translator should always be the one in charge when the advertising campaigns move globally. A translator is ideally a language and culture expert. It should be his/her responsibility to inform the advertiser which effects are lost and how the translated slogan may (or may not) work with the target consumers.

4.3 Stage III: Return to the source-language slogans

With all the gradually gained experience in the difficulties of slogan translation, many advertisers have nowadays returned to a single, global source-language slogan for all markets. However, there are more reasons behind this shift than just the difficulties in translation. In a broad perspective, globalization has reached deep and far and has produced a more experienced consumer. In a narrower, local perspective, new markets have matured as have new consumers. These consumers have improved in foreign languages and have learned more about other (usually western) cultures. They associate more characteristics with the product when it is advertised with a slogan *Das Auto* (by Volkswagen) since they have quite an extensive idea of the German-speaking world. The same applies to Citroën that launched its global advertising campaign with the untranslated French slogan *Créative Technologie* (as compared to the previous, translated one, *Fantasy in Motion*, *Fantázia v pohybe*). In regards to cars, perfumes and some other commodities, this may be the case, as Helen Kelly-Holmes (2000: 67–82) has argued, of a source language as a fetish. She claims the symbolic value of language used in certain types of advertising has become prevalent over its communicative function. However, some producers seem to opt for global world-wide slogans because their functionality would get lost in most translations and because the new global customer understands the untranslated slogans much better than 20 years ago. Such is the case of McDonald's that switched from its translated Slovak/Czech slogan (*McDonald's je skrátka fajn*) into an English – and a global – one: *I'm Loving It*. As the market matures, the consumers do not feel foreign language slogans as direct imposition of power by the advertisers, since now the majority of them understands the message. The slogans for some advertised products are simply so good they cannot be translated or reproduced in a comparable quality: *LG Life's Good*, *You Can Canon*, *Play Station 2 Fun, anyone?*, *Today Tomorrow Toyota*, etc., will never compare in effect and impact factor if they are translated.

Where the possibilities allow it or even ask for it, my suggestion is to make the translation into small languages, such as Czech or Slovak. The cases of English-language slogans used in Slovak and Czech markets seem unjustified with Honda (*The power of dreams*), JVC (*The perfect experience*) or Kenvelo (*Anywhere*). In these examples the potential of the slogan as a strong marketing tool seems to be wasted since the target languages offer good possibilities for their translation.

The question remains why some Slovak or Czech producers insist on using English slogans in the local market. Kuppens (2009: 117) argues: "Advertisers often [...] use English to market locally produced products to local customers, in hope that they will think they are produced abroad." This does not seem to be the case of the auto manufacturer Škoda, a rich source of Czech national pride. Their slogan reads *Simply Clever* (and for the purposes of this article it may stay omitted that this English slogan does not work well in English, as argued by Bendl (2008)). The explanation of using English in this case may lay in its unquestionable market position in the Czech Republic, regardless of its slogan. It is secure at home, and by using an English slogan it tries to address the foreign markets. Another example is Matador, a Slovak tire producer, using an English slogan *Leading the Way*. It sells most of its production abroad, which justifies the existence of the English slogan, but instead of using a Slovak slogan in the Slovak market and thus helping to strengthen its own position locally, it gives an impression of a pretender.

4.4 Original target-language slogans as a special category

The last category of products and their slogans traveling globally is the one when the product is launched on the market and its slogan is created completely anew with no connection to the existing advertising campaign abroad. The American car producer Chevrolet realized how harmful the *American* label might be abroad nowadays. Unlike Volkswagen and Citroën, that strengthened the ties with their German/French origin by using German/French for the global slogan, Chevrolet deleted any connection to the USA by crafting a completely new slogan for the Slovak and Czech markets. It reads *Veľké plus*, translated as *The big plus*, which has several praiseworthy features: first, it is short and clear; second, it is a frequently used fixed expression with the meaning of 'a great advantage'; and third, its literal meaning is in direct connection with the logo of Chevrolet – a big golden cross, or a plus. Slogans seem to work more effectively if more devices operate at the same time. Chevrolet managed this with seemingly little effort.

The financial company Aegon opted for the strategy of a new slogan when it entered Czech and Slovak markets back in 2003. Its widespread English slogan reads *Local knowledge. Global power*, and that is how Aegon really seems to operate, since they came to Slovakia and the Czech Republic with a skillful local slogan:

Myslite aegonomicky (the back-translated version would be 'think aegonomically'). It is unconnected in meaning with the English slogan but speaks to the local clientele: unusual in its play on word-formation (Slovak is not very creative in this sense due to the difficulties imposed by inflections), it shows it can handle difficult situations with wit and grace, it can relate to what already exists (*aegonomically* strongly reminds *economically*); its message of addressing clients with economic issues is presented clearly and unmistakably.

More excellent cases of advertising campaigns led locally can be found in the car ads for Kia and Peugeot (both companies started their production plants in Slovakia recently). Kia sells with a wonderful slogan crafted for the region where its cars are born: *SlovaKIA* and *CzeKIA*. Peugeot came with a similar idea and sells its 206cc model, produced north of the capital Bratislava, by the slogan *Rodený Slovák*, translated as *Slovak by birth*.

5 Conclusion

Observing the slogans of world advertising campaigns crossing the borders of the Czech Republic and Slovakia confirmed the belief that knowing the consumer, or the client, is the essence of marketing success. This applies to the translators of ad campaigns as much as to the advertisers. The translators are the experts to point out weaknesses of their translations and possibly even persuade the advertiser to go for the untranslated slogan if circumstances require. Translation, in my opinion, should be applied where the body text of the ads are transferred. The best strategy for the slogans seems to be crafting them completely anew, from scratch, which ensures that the local cultural touch and the local language means work together in reaching the best results.

References

Adab, Beverly (2000): "Towards a More Systematic Aproach to the Translation of Advertising Texts." In: *Inverstigating Translation.* Amsterdam and Philadelphia: John Benjamins, 223–234.
Barancic, Maximiljana (2005): "The Language of Advertisements in Translation from English into Croatian." In: *Folia Translatologica,* Vol. 9, 9–23.
Bendl, Thomas (2008): "Simply Good or Not? Analýza sloganů mezinárodních výrobců aut." Transl. Tereza Pavlíčková. In: *Strategie,* March 3, 2008. www.strategie.cz/ scripts/detail.php?id=347377. Visited December 2009.
Carter, Ronald / Goddard, Angela / Reah, Danuta / Sanger, Keith / Swift, Nikki (2008): *Working with Texs: A Core Introduction to Language Analysis.* London and New York: Routledge.
Cook, Guy (2001): *The Discourse of Advertising.* London and New York: Routledge.
Debeljak, Erica Johnson (2007): "Gained in Translation." In: *Kritika a kontext* 33 (10th Anniversary Issue). Bratislava: Samuel Abraham.
De Mooij, Marieke (2004): "Translating Advertising." In: *The Translator* 2, 179–198.
Djovčoš, Martin / Pliešovská, Ľubica (2010): "Questionable Identity in Intercutural Monologue." Paper presented at the conference *Identity in Intercultural Communication: 3rd Triennal Conference in English and American Studies.* Budmerice 21–22 October 2010.
Fairclough, Norman (1989): *Language and Power.* Harlow: Pearson.
Goddard, Angela (2002): *The Language of Advertising: Written Texts.* London and New York: Routledge.
Guidere, Mathieu (2007): "The Translation of Advertisements: from Adaptation to Localization." www.translationdirectory.com/article60.htm . Visited November 2009.
Jettmarová, Zuzana (2004): "Norms and other factors in advertisement translation." In: *Und Sie bewegt sich doch... Translation Wissenschaft in Ost und West.* Frankfurt am Main: Peter Lang, 163–175.
────── (2008): "Překladovost ve vývoji reklamního žánru." In: *Translatológie a jej súvislosti* 2, 197–214.
Kelly-Holmes, Helen (2000): "Bier, parfum, kaas: language fetish in European advertising." In: *European Journal of Cultural Studies;* Vol. 3, No. 1, 67–82.
Keníž, Alojz (2006): "Preklad ako odraz spoločensko-kultúrnej situácie." In: *Preklad a tlmočenie* 7, 29–34.
Kovácsová, Katarína (2008): "Reklamné slogany v hovorovej reči: Postupová práca." http://www.katkakovacsova.estranky.cz/clanky/etnologia/zenska-muzska-rola_dve-generacie-v-bratislave---postupova-pracak. Visited November 2009.
Křížek, Zdeněk / Crha, Ivan (2003): *Jak psát reklamní text.* Praha: Grada.
Kuppens, An H. (2009): "English in Advertising: Generic Intertextuality in a Globalizing Media Environment." In: *Applied Linguistics* 31(1), 115–135.
Kusá, Mária (2005): *Preklad ako súčasť dejín kultúrneho priestoru.* Bratislava: Ústav svetovej literatúry SAV.
Pym, Anthony / Shlesinger, Miriam / Jettmarová, Zuzana (2007): *Sociocultural Aspects of Translating and Interpreting.* Amsterdam and Philadelphia: John Benjamins.

Target Readers' Expectations and Reality: Conformity or Conflict?

Minna Ruokonen
University of Turku, Finland

Abstract

This case study explores to what extent translations meet target readers' expectations and what causes underlie possible conformity and conflict. After discussing the relationship between expectations and norms and also possible causes for deviating from expectations, I analyse the Finnish translations of Dorothy L. Sayers' (1893–1957) detective novels, translated in the 1940s and the 1980s. Analysis of contemporary documents indicates that target readers' expectations about translations were fairly similar in both periods. However, the 1940s' TTs include mistranslations, omissions and modifications that were likely to conflict with contemporary expectations. This conflict is probably linked to translators' working conditions, SL skills and target readers' expectations concerning detective fiction. The 1980s' TTs meet contemporary expectations to a greater extent, probably due to increased professionalisation, more stable working conditions and the improved status of crime/detective fiction, although there were some differences between individual translations. The findings raise the question of whether the concept of norms is relevant when a large part of translation practice manifests deviant behaviour and suggest that future research is needed on conflicts between expectations and reality, as well as on translations brought out by different publishers.

1 Introduction

Readers' expectations play a major role in interpreting texts. Being able to anticipate the characteristics of a text helps the reader to process the text and construct a coherent interpretation more efficiently. If the text defies the reader's expectations in some manner, this sometimes enriches the interpretation; however, such deviance may also disturb the reader, particularly if it is felt to break a norm, or to avoid what would have been a more acceptable choice.

In this case study, I examine to what extent and why the translations of Dorothy L. Sayers' detective novels published in Finnish in the 1940s and the 1980s were likely to correspond to contemporary expectations concerning translations. As target readers' expectations are closely related to translation norms, I first consider the relationship between expectations and norms, the methods for studying them, and possible reasons for why the textual characteristics of translations may conform to or conflict with contemporary expectations. After a brief characterisation of the source texts studied, I outline target readers' expectations concerning literary translations in the Finland of the 1940s and the 1980s. Then, I analyse the translations from the two periods, considering to what extent they were likely to meet target readers' expectations and discussing causes behind possible conformity and deviance. Apart from throwing new light on the history of literary translation and detective fiction in Finland, the case study suggests valid topics for further research and raises the question of whether translation norms are a valid concept in a situation where there is an evident conflict between expectations and reality.

This paper is an offshoot of my dissertation (Ruokonen 2010), which examines the translated allusions in the same material. However, the present paper covers broader aspects of style, characterisation and themes in the translations and focuses on the relationship between target readers' expectations and the socio-cultural contexts.

2 Expectations, norms and underlying causes

Target readers' expectations about translations are closely related to *translation norms*, the ways of behaviour that a community finds correct or acceptable in a particular translational situation (Toury 1995: 55; Chesterman 1997: 54). Readers' expectations may exert a normative influence on translators' solutions (see *expectancy norms*, Chesterman 1997: 64–67, 81–84), and, conversely, norms give rise to various expectations concerning translations.

Readers' expectations are also usually investigated by methods common in studying norms, by analysing statements made by critics, translators and editors (Toury 1995: 65; Pym 1998: 111–112; Brownlie 2003: 125–126). The main difference is that, with regard to norms, this must be accompanied by an analysis of actual translations. In other words, while expectations may only express what is desirable, norms must also reflect a common practice.

The present case study investigates target readers' expectations concerning translations, the extent to which the translations studied were likely to correspond to those expectations, and the reasons for possible correspondence or lack of it. My focus is on expectations concerning textual characteristics, including which strategies are considered appropriate for dealing with the structure and style of the source text, for translating shorter segments and for formulating the TL wording; these are closely connected to Toury's *operational norms* (Toury 1995: 58–59) and Chesterman's *expectancy norms* (Chesterman 1997: 64).

The scope of the case study is not sufficient for proving the existence of any norms. However, the findings may provide evidence suggesting a possible norm or, perhaps even more interestingly, draw attention to conflicts between expectations and reality.

There are several possible causes for why a translation may fail to meet readers' expectations. Studies on norms point out that a community may have alternative or competing norms of varying prevalence (Toury 1995: 59, 62–64; Toury 1999: 27–28). Translations may also conform to a norm to a varying degree (Chesterman 1997: 64–65), for reasons ranging from translators' individual preferences to larger literary and socio-cultural issues.

Below, I outline those factors that seem likely to have exerted a major influence on the extent to which the translations studied correspond to contemporary readers' expectations. For the sake of clarity, the factors are divided into *cognitive, textual* and *socio-cultural* categories. The division is based on Chesterman (2000: 20) and Williams and Chesterman (2002: 54), with some modifications to reflect the nature of the study.[1]

Cognitive factors are related to the translator's thought-processes during translation, and they are also affected by the translator's personal history and experiences (Williams and Chesterman 2002: 54). In a historical study, the translators' decision-

---

[1] In Chesterman's original classification (2000: 20), textual factors are one of the causes related to the *translation event*. Other similar factors include, for example, an individual translator's working environment (computers) and conditions (deadline, pay). In a historical context, such details about an individual translation assignment can rarely be determined. As the translators' working conditions have to be examined on a more general level, they are more closely linked to Chesterman's *socio-cultural causes* (history, norms, ideologies, etc.).

making can no longer be 'tapped', but their professional backgrounds are reconstructed on the basis of biographical documents, publication histories and interviews. Factors affecting motivation are also suggested.

Of possible *textual factors,* the source text is of particular interest here. ST properties, such as stylistic variation or the perceived function of a passage, act as stimuli for formulating the translation, with a varying degree of influence on the form of the final product (cf. Pym's *material* or *initial cause* [1998: 149]). Particularly translators with little experience may find it difficult to 'let go' of the SL form, as argued by an experienced instructor of literary translation (Pennanen 1979: 257–258). Low-level SL skills may also encourage word-for-word renderings, as the translator needs to puzzle out the meanings of individual words or expressions instead of being able to process larger wholes (cf. Kujamäki 2007: 412).

Both translators' backgrounds and their treatment of ST properties are affected by the *socio-cultural context* of the translations. Context has been analysed in terms of polysystems, norms, ideologies, poetics and, recently, of social networks. However, although emphases vary, the basic approach remains similar: the researcher familiarises him- or herself with certain aspects of the socio-cultural context and the translations and looks for connections between them.

The socio-cultural aspects relevant for the present study include the historical and material circumstances in which the translators worked, the development of literary translation as a profession, and the status of detective fiction in Finland. To some extent, these could be outlined on the basis of previous research, such as Kukkola (1980), Ratinen (1992) and Eskola (2004), but contemporary documents also needed to be consulted. I also interviewed those Sayers translators that I was able to reach (Pekkanen 2005; Rikman 2005; Eräpuro 2009).

As the material includes two retranslations (of *Whose Body?* and *The Nine Tailors*), a few observations on the so-called *retranslation hypothesis* are also in order. The hypothesis argues that later translations represent a 'return to the source text', remaining closer to it than first translations (Gambier 1994: 414). Recent research has drawn attention to the fact that the characteristics of retranslations also depend on socio-cultural factors, which indicates that the hypothesis is hardly universally valid (see, for example, Paloposki and Koskinen 2004). Nevertheless, the hypothesis needs to be borne in mind as a possible explanation for differences between the translations.

The expectations that the Sayers translations were likely to face in the target context are commented on in some previous studies, including Heinämäki (1993), Sorvali (1996), Leppihalme (1997: 85–90) and Kujamäki (2007). These observations were complemented by a more detailed analysis of contemporary statements made by translators, critics and other actors. As contemporary newspaper reviews rarely comment on the quality of translations (Heinämäki 1993: 23; Kujamäki 2007: 406, 411), I focused on translation reviews published in various journals with explicit comments on translation quality.

With regard to the 1940s, I follow the example of Kujamäki (2007), analysing texts published in:

- The cultural journal *Valvoja-Aika* (title shortened to *Valvoja* in 1944): 2 articles, 27 reviews;
- The cultural journal *Suomalainen Suomi*: 19 reviews;
- The journal for Finnish Studies, *Virittäjä*: 6 reviews of individual translations; 39 articles with short examples from several unidentified translations.

With regard to the 1980s, I focus on material more closely related to translated detective fiction:

- *Ruumiin kulttuuri*, the journal of the Finnish Whodunit Society, est. 1984: 64 reviews;
- *Kääntäjä*, the journal of the Finnish Association of Translators and Interpreters: comments on the criteria of the annual Mikael Agricola Award for an outstanding literary translation.

The material is likely to reflect the expectations of the cultural elite and of professionals in the fields of language, literature and translation. There is hardly any relevant data on average Finnish readers' expectations concerning translations or detective fiction. On the other hand, the expectations of the literati are probably the most relevant to the Sayers translations, as the following discussion of the material shows.

3 Why Sayers? Introducing the source and target texts

My material consists of five novels written by Dorothy L. Sayers (1893–1957) and of their Finnish translations. The source texts are set in the England of the 1920s and the 1930s, and they were written between 1923 and 1934, during the Golden

Age of traditional detective fiction. The translations were published in the 1940s and the 1980s.

In some respects, Sayers' novels resemble traditional whodunits. They feature an aristocratic amateur detective, Lord Peter Wimsey, and they are structured as complex but logical puzzles that readers can at least partly solve if they pay attention to the clues (on this principle of 'fair play', see Haycraft 1941: 226, 247, 251–252). Some novels even include lists of motives or suspects that make it easier for readers to keep track of clues (Sayers 1930: 47–51; Sayers 1931: 27–28).

However, what makes Sayers' works an interesting object of study is the fact that they go beyond the pure whodunit. Traditional detective fiction was to be an intellectual but popular genre (Pyrhönen 1994: 15), clearly distinguished from quality fiction with its supposedly more distinct, individual style and profound commentary on life (Shaw 1972: 223; Strinati 2004: 11–13). To maintain the division, elaborate development of style, complex themes and realistic milieus or characterisation were considered unnecessary and even undesirable in whodunits, as such features distracted readers from the intellectual workout (Haycraft 1941: 242–248; Symons 1992: 117–119). Sayers' works, in contrast, address serious themes, criticise social ills and incorporate stylistic variation and rich characterisation, often expressed by means of allusions, or intertextual references conveying implicit meaning. Such a mixture of popular and quality fiction may be particularly likely to be translated differently in different contexts.[2]

Sayers was also an "intellectualising" author (Knight 1980: 124), who did not want to write down to her readers (Brabazon 1981: 191–193) and expected them to cope with stylistic variation, Latin and French quotations and often complex allusions. Sayers' ideal reader would thus be a literature enthusiast receptive to nuances and deeper meanings rather than someone looking for a moment's diversion – although Sayers' novels are humorous and witty enough to entertain the latter kind of reader as well.

---

[2] In reality, the status of a literary work is not determined by its intrinsic properties but by the actions of various agents in a socio-cultural context (Storey 2003: 92–94, 104–105; for applications in Translation Studies, see notably Lefevere 1992). However, the traditional distinction between popular and quality fiction described above is relevant for this study because it was valid both in Sayers' days and in the Finnish target contexts.

Sayers' novels have been translated into Finnish over a long period of time, from the 1930s to the 1990s. I analyse the novels translated in the 1940s and the 1980s, as this provides me with seven target texts by seven translators working in two very different target contexts (see Table 1 below). Two source texts (*Whose Body?* and *The Nine Tailors*) were even translated in both periods. Full bibliographical data are given in the references.

Table 1. The source texts and translations studied

Source text	1940s' translation	1980s' translation
Whose Body? (1923)	*Kuka ja mistä?*, 'Who and where from?' (1944) By Niilo Lavio	*Kuka ja mistä?*, 'Who and where from?' (1986) By Kristiina Rikman
Clouds of Witness (1926)	*Kuolema keskiyöllä*, 'Death at midnight' (1948) By Oiva Talvitie	–
Strong Poison (1930)	–	*Myrkkyä*, 'Poison' (1984) By Paavo Lehtonen
The Five Red Herrings (1931)	–	*Yksi kuudesta*, 'One of the six' (1985) By Hilkka Pekkanen
The Nine Tailors (1934)	*Kolmesti kuollut*, 'Three times dead' (1948) By V. Vankkoja	*Kuolema kirkkomaalla*, 'Death in the churchyard' (1989) By Annika Eräpuro

The following section considers what kinds of expectations these translations were likely to meet in their target contexts.

4 Expectations concerning translations in the 1940s and the 1980s

Historically speaking, the 1940s and the 1980s were very different periods in Finland. In the 1940s, the Second World War and the subsequent war reparations made hardship and shortages a part of daily life. In contrast, the 1980s were an era of abundance, with a booming economy and extensive social security.

In spite of these differences, target readers' expectations of translations were described in similar terms in both periods. The expectations can be divided into those characterising the quality of the target language and those commenting on the relationship between the source text and the translation.

Broadly speaking, translations were expected to be written in natural and fluent Finnish (Heinämäki 1993: 75–77; Kujamäki 2007: 411–412). Word-for-word translations and source-language interference met with harsh criticism (Saarimaa 1941: 261; Saario 1988; Raitio 1989). The translation was also to sound lucid and make sense (Saarimaa 1943: 352; Rantanen 1987; Leppihalme 1997: 87), to be a coherent text in its own right. In the words of the traditional praise, a good translation makes "one forget that one is reading a translation" (Koskenniemi 1943: 241, my translation; see also Mannila 1983: 95 and Sorvali 1996: 152).

There were also similarities in the expectations concerning the ST–TT relationship. On the macro-level, source texts were to be translated in their entirety without omissions or abridgements (Saarimaa 1943: 352; Hollo 1943: 1; Leppihalme 1997: 88–89). Conveying the style of the source text was considered important, particularly in quality fiction (Hollo 1943: 9–12; Agricola 1983; Agricola 1987). On the micro-level, mistranslated words and phrases drew criticism in both periods (Saarimaa 1943; Heinämäki 1993: 67).

In both periods, reviewers' comments on translation quality are often accompanied by examples from actual translations. These examples indicate that the similar expectations are not a mere illusion produced by similarities in the discourse of talking about translation.

On the other hand, the similarities are fairly general in nature, and in practice the characteristics expected of translations did differ to some extent. For example, the criteria of 'natural and fluent Finnish' had obviously changed between the 1940s and the 1980s, simply because the Finnish language had changed. Splitting sentences may also have been more acceptable in the 1940s than in the 1980s (Nopsanen 1948: 92; Ruokonen 2010: 178). Further differences are covered in my dissertation (Ruokonen 2010: 177–179, 190–192), but they do not affect the broad tendencies described above.

The following sections show that the Sayers translations of the 1940s and the 1980s met the contemporary expectations to varying degrees. The reasons for this can probably be found in the different target contexts.

5 The Sayers translations of the 1940s: conflict between expectations and reality

Below, I first describe the backgrounds of the individual translators and consider to what extent the three Sayers translations of the 1940s were likely to correspond to target readers' expectations (Section 5.1). I then discuss possible causes for the conflict evident between the expectations and the actual characteristics of the translations.

5.1 The Sayers translators and translations of the 1940s

All three Sayers translators received their assignments from Tammi, an at that time recently-founded publisher with the ambitious agenda of bringing out modern world literature and popular fiction with some literary merit (Utrio 1968: 24; Helminen 1999: 44). Contrary to many new wartime publishers, Tammi was not simply looking for profit but operated professionally and soon became a pioneer in having modern American fiction translated into Finnish (Helminen 1999: 40–42; Rekola 2007: 436–437).

At least two of the Sayers translators worked part-time. The most productive of them was Oiva Talvitie: in the 1940s, he brought out up to eight translated novels per year while working as a newspaper editor (Poijärvi et al. [eds.] 1949).[3] Before the Sayers translation, Talvitie had translated 15 novels; since 1945, he had also been a member of the Finnish Literature Society's committee of the Finnish language, the highest authority on correct Finnish (Poijärvi et al. [eds.] 1949).

Another translator, who worked under the pseudonym Niilo Lavio, has been identified as Unto Varjonen (Hellemann 1968: 67; Rekola 2007: 436). Lavio/Varjonen worked as editor-in-chief at a news agency and was even elected party secretary of the Finnish Social Democratic Party in the same year as his Sayers translation was published (Poijärvi et al. [eds.] 1949). Like Talvitie, Lavio/Varjonen had a background in journalism; however, the Sayers novel was his

---

3   Data on the translators' publications have been retrieved from Fennica, The National Bibliography of Finland, at https://fennica.linneanet.fi/.

first published literary translation, and he only translated three novels in all under the pseudonym Lavio.

The third translator, "V. Vankkoja" is more of an unknown quantity, as s/he probably used a pseudonym. The translator's name also appears in the forms "V.V. Vankkoja" and "Vankka Vankkoja", and such combinations are very unlikely. According to the records of the Finnish Population Register Centre, which go back to the 19th century, only four Finns have ever had the surname Vankkoja and less than 40 Finns the first name Vankka (http://www.vaestorekisterikeskus.fi – Name Service). At any rate, "Vankkoja" is very likely to have worked part-time as well: barring the use of other pseudonyms, s/he translated only two to three titles per year.

Considering that the translators worked part-time and in wartime or post-war conditions, it is perhaps not surprising that the three Sayers translations of the 1940s probably failed to meet contemporary expectations, at least with regard to the ST–TT relationship. None of the translations were reviewed in the journals studied, but all three translations contain numerous examples of semantic shifts that seem to be more closely linked to the translators' SL skills than to a conscious decision to modify the source text. Such mistranslations appear on virtually every page and sometimes involve even basic vocabulary and structures, as illustrated by the following examples. Their frequency suggests that the translators would have benefited from more time to decipher the ST meanings with the help of dictionaries.

(1) **ST** he selected a dark-green tie to match his socks (Sayers 1923: 5)
  TT hän valitsi tummanvihreän nauhan sitoakseen sukkansa kiinni (Lavio 1944: 9)
  'he chose a dark-green lace to fasten his socks'

(2) **ST** what's the bit you haven't solved (Sayers 1934: 230)
  TT minkä kohdan te olette saanut selväksi (Vankkoja 1948: 189)
  'what's the part you have solved'

On the other hand, most TL passages with semantic shifts still sound fluent and coherent in their text-context. The mistranslations are mainly unnoticeable unless one compares the source and target texts. By and large, the translations function well as independent texts, and probably largely met TT readers' expectations of TL quality in this respect.

This impression of fluency is partly connected to the fact that ST sentences have often been split into shorter ones in all three translations. This makes the texts easier to read, and it was perhaps an easier solution for the translators as well; it may even have been an acceptable solution (Nopsanen 1948: 92; Ruokonen 2010: 178). Nevertheless, the split sentences do change the stylistic effect. Consider the following description of a village plagued by crop failure and its translation:

(3)   **ST**[I]n that summer the water lay on the land all through August and September, and the corn sprouted in the stocks, and the sodden ricks took fire and stank horribly, and the Rector of Fenchurch St Paul, conducting the Harvest Festival, had to modify his favourite sermon upon Thankfulness, for there was scarcely sound wheat enough to lay upon the altar and no great sheaves for the aisle windows or for binding about the stoves, as was customary. (Sayers 1934: 279)

TT [T]uona kesänä olivat maat koko elokuun ja syyskuun veden vallassa. Vehnänjyvät itivät kuhilaissa, ja kaatuneet aumat mätänivät hirveästi löyhkäten. Fenchurch St. Paulin pastorinkin oli elonkorjuujuhlaa johtaessaan lievennettävä kiitollisuutta koskevaa mielisaarnaansa, sillä kunnollista vehnää riitti tuskin alttarille. [End of ST sentence omitted.] (Vankkoja 1948: 231)

Back translation: 'That summer the land was submerged for the whole of August and September. Wheat seeds sprouted in stacks of sheaves, and fallen ricks rotted, stinking horribly. Even the Rector of Fenchurch St. Paul, when leading the harvest festival, had to tone down his favourite sermon on thankfulness, for there was hardly enough sound wheat to put on the altar.' [End of ST sentence omitted.]

In the ST, the initial repetition of co-ordinated clauses makes a solemn, even Biblical impression, connecting the passage to the religious themes of the novel. The failed harvest is a metaphor for how an unsolved murder is poisoning the village community; it may even symbolise divine wrath. The translated description does feature some evocative expressions (*veden vallassa*) and lyrical use of marked syntax (*olivat maat, riitti tuskin*), but it is considerably less detailed, and the split sentences make the statements more matter-of-fact.

The translated description above also contains an omission. Omissions occur in all three translations of the 1940s, targeting individual words, allusions, sentences and even entire paragraphs. Two of the translations (Talvitie 1948 and Vankkoja 1948) have been heavily abridged. Talvitie, for example, cuts down a discussion on an aged, undrinkable wine. One of the deleted lines compares the wine to *the taste of a passion that has passed its noon and turned to weariness* (Sayers 1926: 199; Talvitie 1948: 138). This allusion to John Donne's (1572–1631) poem, "A Lecture Upon A

Shadow", emphasises the futility of passion, which is one of the ST themes. Leaving out the allusion weakens the thematic impact.

On the whole, although the translations mainly read fluently, the modifications and omissions were likely to conflict with contemporary expectations of ST–TT relationship, as they dilute or even omit aspects of style, characterisation and themes. The following section shows that this deviation is probably connected to the socio-cultural contexts in which the translations were produced.

5.2 Possible causes for deviating from expectations in the 1940s

Translators' working conditions in the Finland of the 1940s were far from ideal. It was already observed above that the three Sayers translators worked part-time, and this reflects a general trend in the profession at the time: assignments were often taken on by writers, teachers or journalists to supplement a meagre living (Cronvall 2007: 363). There was also no formal training for literary or non-fiction translators.

In addition, particularly schedules for popular-fiction translations had been hurried even before the war (Cronvall 2007: 364). The situation was unlikely to have improved during the 1940s, when the publishing process was beset with many wartime obstacles, including the rationing of paper, which continued until 1949 (Utrio 1968: 27; Turunen 2003: 192). The rationing of paper may be at least partly responsible for the omissions and abbreviations manifested in two of the Sayers translations: Talvitie's and Vankkoja's efforts may have been cut down to bring them to approximately the same length as Lavio's (cf. Turunen 2000: 65–66).

The semantic shifts in the Sayers translations suggested that the translators were hampered by insufficient SL skills, and this seems even more likely on the basis of previous research and contemporary documents. Since the 1920s, English had been the most common source language for Finnish literary translations (Jalonen 1985: 64; Kovala 1992: 35–41), but it was mainly taught as an optional language in secondary school and learned by fewer than 10% of each generation (Paasivirta 1991: 182; Sipilä and Anttonen 2008: 50). As a result, English texts were sometimes translated from a pivot translation rather than the original (Cronvall 2007: 363). With regard to the Sayers translations studied, comparisons with the source texts and with possible pivot translations show that the translators had most likely relied on the English originals alone (Ruokonen 2010: Appendix 4). However, insufficient

SL skills were still likely to cause difficulties in understanding the source texts and, together with the probable time pressure, may have encouraged the Sayers translators to opt for strategies contrary to TT readers' expectations.

The low status of detective fiction may well have been another contributing factor. In the 1940s, translated fiction and popular fiction in general were suspect categories for major cultural actors (Utrio 1968: 14–16; Cronvall 2007: 364–365). Detective fiction met with particular disapproval because it transformed crime into light entertainment that could ruin readers' taste for quality fiction and even promote lawlessness (Jokela 1989: 57; Eskola 2004: 87). As a rule, detective novels were not recommended for public libraries (Jokela 1989: 34–46; Eskola 2004: 85–86, 214). All in all, translated detective fiction was hardly a merit for either the publisher or the translator. The publisher of the Sayers translations was thus unlikely to encourage spending much time and effort on a whodunit, and the low status of detective fiction may even have affected the translators' motivation.

Perhaps the translators were also aware of target readers' more specific expectations concerning detective fiction. In spite of the cultural authorities' negative attitudes, traditional whodunits were popular: frequently-translated authors before and in the 1940s included Agatha Christie, John Dickson Carr and Edgar Wallace (Kukkola 1980: 73). As in the English-speaking world, whodunits were expected to be believable and captivating puzzles (Sara 1940; Kukkola 1980: 117; Jokela 1989: 43; Eskola 2004: 85). Descriptions and conversations were to be brief and to the point (ibid.).

In this context, Sayers was probably perceived as an author of whodunits, which suggests her serious themes and complex characterisation were not quite in line with TT readers' expectations. This may partly explain the omissions in the translations. The passages omitted from the Sayers translations can often be characterised as 'literary digressions': passages like *the taste of a passion that has passed its noon* that affect style, characterisation or even themes but do not contribute to solving the murder-puzzle. The omissions certainly bring the translations closer to the traditional whodunit (cf. Turunen 2000). The streamlined target texts perhaps even corresponded to TT readers' expectations concerning whodunits better than more 'faithful' translations would have done; on the other hand, deviating from faithfulness probably impaired correspondence with expectations concerning translations.

As a matter of fact, similar conflicts between target readers' expectations about translation quality and actual translations seem to have been fairly common in the 1940s in general. Translation reviews in *Virittäjä* often include long lists of misunderstood SL meanings, found even in the work of experienced translators (Saarimaa 1943: 350, 352–353; Kujamäki 2007: 412). There are also comments to the effect that translators should not leave out "difficult passages", which suggests omissions may actually have been frequent (Saarimaa 1943: 352, my translation; see also Hollo 1943: 1).

Reviews in *Virittäjä* may partly offer too pessimistic a view of the state of literary translation. The examples were sometimes taken from manuscripts handed in for revision rather than from published translations, and the translations, when identified, do not usually represent quality fiction. Translated classics, which were mainly reviewed in *Suomalainen Suomi* and *Valvoja-Aika*, seem to have corresponded to reviewers' expectations to a greater extent.

On the other hand, omissions and abridgements could apparently occur even in quality-fiction translations completed by experienced translators for well-established publishers. For example, the Finnish translation of Henry Fielding's classic *Tom Jones* (1749, transl. 1950) was criticised for having been "arbitrarily abridged" (Anhava 1950: 503; my translation). The translator, Olli Nuorto, argues in his preface that the omissions were deliberate and intended to cut down philosophical, political and literary discussions that would have required too extensive explanations and been of little interest for Finnish readers (Nuorto 1950: 8; see also Leppihalme 2007: 159, 161). Whichever view is the more accurate, the omissions are there, and in principle they are in conflict with contemporary expectations.

On the whole, the reviews studied appear to reflect a persisting conflict between readers' expectations and the actual characteristics of translations. In spite of the criticism, translations with similar problems continued to be published. Further research comparing translations of popular and quality fiction would be needed to establish how frequent mistranslations, modifications and omissions were in the 1940s. If conflicts between expectations and actual characteristics of translations are revealed to have been common, this raises questions about the validity of translation norms in the period. However, before going further into these implications, I turn to the Sayers translations of the 1980s and the extent to which they corresponded to contemporary expectations.

6 The Sayers translations of the 1980s: reality meets expectations, with some exceptions

As in the previous section, I first cover the backgrounds of the Sayers translators and consider to what extent the translations were likely to meet target readers' expectations (Section 6.1). All four translations corresponded to contemporary expectations to a greater extent than the 1940s' translations, although one translation manifested more deviance; possible causes are considered in Section 6.2.

6.1 The Sayers translators and translations of the 1980s

All four Sayers translators of the 1980s had studied relevant subjects at university level, including English, Finnish and literature. Three of the translators, Paavo Lehtonen, Hilkka Pekkanen and Kristiina Rikman, worked for the established publishing house WSOY; they had also accumulated considerable experience as literary translators (34 to 39 translated titles each). They were also able to make a living as full-time translators: Rikman focused on literary translation, Pekkanen also translated some non-fiction and Lehtonen was a productive subtitler (Rikman 2005; Pekkanen 2005; Helasvuo 2005).

In contrast, Annika Eräpuro was only starting her career (Eräpuro 2008). She worked for a small publisher, a one-man enterprise called Viihdeviikarit. The firm was known for its ambitious agenda to bring out previously untranslated classics of detective fiction, but also for its self-acknowledged lack of resources and varied translation quality (Rantanen 1987; Raitio 1989).

All four translations received positive reviews in *Ruumiin kulttuuri*. Lehtonen's and Rikman's efforts were praised (Lindström 1985; Huhtala 1986), and Eräpuro's translation also made a favourable overall impression (Huhtala 1989). The reviewer of Pekkanen's work did not explicitly comment on the translation but was pleased, for example, with the rich characterisation (Gustafsson 1985).

A closer examination of the translations indicates that these four Sayers translations indeed seem to have met contemporary expectations more closely than the 1940s' target texts. There are no extensive abridgements, unlike in the translations of the 1940s, and there are hardly any drastic mistranslations or shortened sentences. The following TT passage contains some changes in the sequence of clauses, perhaps for the sake of TL fluency, but conveys the meaning, rhythm and structural complexity, as well as the humorous tone.

(4) ST [...] Inspector Sugg had no words for the interferingness of Lord Peter. He could not, however, when directly questioned, deny that there was to be an inquest that afternoon, nor could he prevent Mr Parker from enjoying the inalienable right of any interested British citizen to be present. (Sayers 1923: 47)

TT [...] komisario Sugg [ei] löytänyt tarpeeksi kuvaavaa sanaa lordi Peterin sietämättömyydelle. Mutta eihän hän voinut kieltääkään, että kuolemansyyntutkimus pidettäisiin iltapäivällä, kun sitä suoraan kysyttiin, eikä voinut evätä Parkerilta läsnäolo-oikeutta, joka kiistämättä kuului jokaiselle asiasta kiinnostuneelle Britannian kansalaiselle (Rikman 1986: 110)

Back translation: '[...] Inspector Sugg could [not] find a sufficiently descriptive word for Lord Peter's intolerability. But he could not deny, could he, that the inquest was to be held in the afternoon, when this was directly asked, nor could he refuse Parker the right to be present, which undeniably belonged to any British citizen interested in the matter.'

Semantic shifts can be spotted here and there in the 1980s' translations, but these are considerably rarer than in the 1940s' target texts, and they do not interrupt the flow of the text.

Another contrast to the 1940s' target texts is the way in which the 1980s' translators have retained even literary digressions. *Strong Poison*, for example, contains a lengthy discussion on the character of Philip Boyes, the murdered lover of Harriet Vane. Boyes first insisted on Vane's living with him against her moral principles and then, after a few months' 'probation', condescended to offering marriage. Vane refused, realising that Boyes would never treat her as an equal. In the discussion, Boyes' Victorian ideas of woman being subservient to man are criticised by means of allusions to Tennyson's and Milton's poems (Sayers 1930: 41–42). The discussion is not relevant to solving the murder, but it is significant as a characterisation of Boyes and as an expression of two major themes: the importance of mutual respect in a relationship and critique of lingering Victorian attitudes. In the Finnish translation, the discussion is retained in full (Lehtonen 1984: 52–53). TT readers were unlikely to recognise the allusions, but their characterising and thematic functions can largely be deduced from the TT context.

Similar examples of retained literary digressions can be found in all the translations of the 1980s, and quite often they convey at least part of the stylistic impact and of the functions of the ST passage.

The differences in the individual translators' circumstances show particularly in the relatively high number of omitted allusions in Eräpuro's translation. None of the 1980s' translations has been abridged as were two of the 1940s' target texts, but Eräpuro has omitted many epigraphs and even a few in-text allusions. The three other translations contain only one or two omitted allusions. The larger number of omissions in Eräpuro's translation is probably connected to the fact that a fair number of omitted epigraphs include puns relying on bell-ringing terminology with no Finnish equivalents. It also seems clear that the publisher did not have the time or staff resources to support the translator in finding solutions more 'faithful' to the source text.

On the other hand, Eräpuro's translation of *The Nine Tailors* still remains considerably closer to the source text than Vankkoja's. The same also applies to Rikman's translation of *Whose Body?* in comparison with Lavio's, which means that these translations conform to the retranslation hypothesis. However, the other two translations of the 1980s, Lehtonen's and Pekkanen's, also manifest a closer ST–TT relationship than the third translation of the 1940s (Talvitie 1948), and they do not involve retranslation. This indicates that other, socio-cultural factors are the more likely explanation for the differences between Lavio vs. Rikman and Vankkoja vs. Eräpuro as well.

By and large, all four translations of the 1980s thus both read fluently and convey the major aspects of ST style, characterisation and themes. The reasons for this correspondence to contemporary expectations are considered below.

6.2 Possible reasons for meeting the expectations

As a rule, translators' working conditions had improved considerably by the 1980s. The publishing industry operated on a more stable and professional basis than in the 1940s, although growth and profits remained modest in spite of the general economic boom (Brunila and Uusitalo 1989: 61–62). The field was dominated by three large, well-established publishing houses (Brunila and Uusitalo 1989: 64–66), including WSOY, the publisher of three Sayers translations.

Literary translation had also become more professionalised. According to a survey conducted in 1991, over seventy respondents had made their living as full-time literary translators at least since 1985 (Ratinen 1992: 2). Schedules were also more reasonable than in the 1940s. Although grants were a welcome supplement to translation fees, a full-time translator could make a living on three to four translated novels per year (Jänicke 1989; Jänicke 1990; Ratinen 1992: 3).

There was still no full-length training for literary translators (unlike for non-fiction translators), but almost four out of five Finnish literary translators held a university degree (Ratinen 1992: 10), typically in foreign languages, Finnish or literature (Mannila 1985a: 42). Shorter courses and seminars on literary translation had been offered on a regular basis since the late 1960s (Halme 2007: 341). English remained the most common source language (*Joukkoviestintätilasto* 1991: 107–108), and, since the 1960s, it had also been the most commonly taught foreign language (Kovala 2007: 143). With regard to English, translators' SL skills were thus likely to have improved considerably since the 1940s, and this probably shows the scarcity of semantic shifts in the Sayers translations.

The general quality of literary translations may also have become more even by the 1980s (Riikonen 2007: 438), which is perhaps reflected in the examples discussed in *Virittäjä*. In the 1940s, the examples of incorrect Finnish were largely attributed to translations. In the 1980s, the unsatisfactory examples often came from newspapers or from Finnish papers written for the final exam of upper secondary school (*ylioppilastutkinto*): the errors had been made by students and hurried journalists rather than professional translators (e.g., Pulkkinen 1983; Kuusi 1986; Metsä-Heikkilä 1988).[4]

The improved status of crime/detective fiction may also have influenced the publishers' attitudes and the translators' motivation. The genre had been welcomed into Finnish public libraries in the 1970s (Jokela 1989: 53–55, 60–61), and the first history of detective fiction in Finland had been published in 1980 (Kukkola 1980).

---

[4] The change in the sources of examples may also partly depend on what kind of material was the most readily available to the reviewers. In the 1940s, at least two frequent contributors, E.A. Saarimaa and Matti Sadeniemi, proof-read manuscripts for publishers (Kujamäki 2007: 412; Sadeniemi 1949: 345); a similar opportunity was perhaps not available in the 1980s.

Another milestone, in 1984, was the founding of The Finnish Whodunit Society (*Suomen Dekkariseura*).

Expectations concerning crime/detective fiction had also undergone some changes since the 1940s. Traditional detective novels or whodunits had become a sub-genre of crime fiction, accompanied by categories such as the American hard-boiled detective fiction and the spy novel. Whodunits were still popular in Finland: Agatha Christie remained a best-selling author (Jokinen 1987: 56–59). The critics of *Ruumiin kulttuuri* were also able to appreciate a well-executed, traditional murder puzzle (e.g., Raitio 1985a). However, the novels to receive the most acclaim were expected to feature psychologically believable characters in realistic milieus and to address issues relevant to contemporary society (e.g., Ekholm 1985). Sayers' novels thus probably stood a better chance than in the 1940s of being appreciated for their characterisation and themes, at least by critics and translators, which may have influenced the translators' treatment of the source texts.

On the other hand, detective fiction was still surrounded by some ambiguity. Translation fees in general were lower for popular fiction than for quality fiction (e.g. Mannila 1985b; Jänicke 1989; Jänicke 1990). Crime/detective novels may have been more likely to be assigned to novice translators (Rikman 1988: 44), perhaps being considered less valuable or easier to translate. Some experienced translators even had the impression that publishers did not want to waste time or effort on "disposable" crime/detective fiction (Rantanen 1987: 51; my translation; see also Nyytäjä 1988: 66–66).

As illustrated by the example of Viihdeviikarit, the publisher that Eräpuro worked for, translated crime/detective fiction was also sometimes published by small firms with insufficient resources. At least in the case of the publisher Viihdeviikarit, this could result in careless editing (Raitio 1988), frequent translation errors (Rantanen 1987; Raitio 1989) and even abridgements (Lindström 1984; Raitio 1985b), although some translations, such as Eräpuro's Sayers translation, evoked favourable responses.

On the whole, translators' working conditions and the status of crime/detective fiction made the socio-cultural context of the 1980s considerably more favourable for producing translations that corresponded to target readers' expectations. On the other hand, the characteristics of Eräpuro's Sayers translation and reviewers' comments on other translations brought out by the publisher Viihdeviikarit show that conflicts with contemporary expectations were still possible, although now they were perhaps more closely connected to a publisher's lack of resources and/or a translator's lack of experience. This has implications for further research, which are considered in more detail in the next section.

7 Discussion and proposals for further research

This case study has illustrated that the Sayers translations of the 1980s probably met contemporary readers' expectations to a greater extent than the Sayers translations of the 1940s. The 1980s' target texts convey ST style and meanings more faithfully and, like their source texts, can be read for their style, characterisation and themes, not simply as whodunits. This is also in line with what critics expected of a good crime novel in the 1980s. On the other hand, the omissions and modifications made by the 1940s' translators probably brought the target texts closer to the traditional whodunit, and in this respect the translations perhaps corresponded to TT readers' expectations better than more 'faithful' translations would have done. Nevertheless, in terms of the ST–TT relationship, the 1940s' translations were unlikely to meet contemporary expectations to as great an extent as the 1980s' translations.

The discussion of the causes for theses cases of conformity and conflict offers a glimpse into the history of literary translation and detective fiction in Finland. Possible causes range from something as concrete as shortage of paper to the wider issues of translation as a profession and the status and typical features of detective fiction. The analysis of the socio-cultural contexts suggests that improved working conditions and increased professionalisation of literary translation, together with changes in the status of detective fiction, made the conditions in the 1980s more favourable for translating Sayers' novels in such a way that they met contemporary expectations about translated fiction to a greater extent than the 1940s' translations. The 1980s' translations also convey the ST mixture of popular and quality fiction better than the 1940s' target texts.

The case study has also drawn attention to broader issues calling for further research. Firstly, there are indications that there was a rather wide gap between readers' expectations and translation practice in the Finland of the 1940s. Particularly translations of non-canonised fiction could manifest problems in TL fluency and ST–TT relationship. As the flow of criticism continued throughout the 1940s, new translations were apparently published with similar flaws. Perhaps, with the wartime and post-war conditions and the generally low level of English skills, at least some publishers contented themselves with less-than-perfect translation quality. If this was the case, popular genres like detective fiction may well have been among the most severely affected. Further investigation of both popular and quality fiction translations brought out by various publishers would be of interest to throw more light on the matter.

If there was a widespread conflict between expectations and translation practice in the 1940s, this may have interesting implications for the study of translation norms. Of course, a conflict could simply mean that the translations were produced in unfavourable conditions and therefore did not adhere to contemporary norms to as great an extent as they could have; after all, not all translations follow a norm to the same degree (Chesterman 1997: 64–65). Another possibility could be an alternative or conflicting norm that sanctioned a cavalier approach to the source text in the translations of popular genres, such as detective fiction (cf. Toury 1995: 62; Chesterman 1997: 66; Pym 1998: 112). However, at least the material studied included no comments defending, for example, semantic shifts; this makes it more likely that mistranslations, modifications and omissions were overlooked by tacit agreement or negligence rather than embraced as an alternative form of desirable behaviour.

Perhaps it is even worth considering whether the concept of norm is relevant at all in a situation where a large part of translation practice persists in deviant behaviour. Of course we can still collect normative statements from reviews and other documents, but what if actual translations provide little corroborating evidence for such postulated norms? After all, a norm is hardly a norm if it fails to describe 'normal' or common behaviour (Chesterman 1997: 56). On the other hand, a conflict between readers' expectations and reality should actually be a more fascinating object of study than a more 'normal' situation (cf. Pym 1998: 112): a conflict can illustrate the dynamics of how some agents try to establish or uphold a norm and others ignore or undermine it.

Secondly, the analysis of Eräpuro's translation of the 1980s and of the reviews in *Ruumiin kulttuuri* draws attention to a conflict between TT readers' expectations and the characteristics of some crime/detective fiction translations. At least in the case of the small publisher called Viihdeviikarit, the conflict seems to have been closely linked to the publisher's lack of resources: the publisher was apparently able to offer little support to the translator, which made translation quality more vulnerable and dependent on an individual translator's skills and experience. In the Sayers translation by Eräpuro, this shows mainly as omissions, although the translation still mostly corresponded to contemporary expectations.

Further research could delve more deeply into issues of popular vs. quality fiction and large vs. small publishers. This case has shown that crime fiction translations by a small publisher could manifest variable translation quality; but is the quality systematically higher in translations brought out by well-established publishing houses? The three Sayers translations brought out by WSOY would suggest so, but they were produced by experienced translators, which means we should also investigate translations completed for WSOY by novice translators. Furthermore, if the quality of translated crime/detective fiction should be revealed to be at least partly dependant on the publisher's resources, does this also apply to other popular genres?

Studying translations published by large and small publishers could yield other interesting results, too. At least in Finland, the 1980s would be one relevant period to examine as the distinction between popular and quality fiction was still well-established, and small publishers of fiction often focused on popular genres such as crime and romance fiction. The results could then be compared with the situation today. In the 21st century, small Finnish publishers have begun to bring out translations of quality fiction that often make just as professional an impression as translations published by large companies. If differences in translation quality between large and small publishers have faded, it would be of interest to discover what has caused this.

The present paper has shed light on a thought-provoking case in the history of literary translation in Finland that draws attention to valid issues to be studied further. I hope I have been able to present something new and unexpected for the readers to consider: after all, in research, as in detection, it is often the anomalous and the unpredictable that inspires the researcher or detective to investigate and leads to new discoveries.

References

A. Source texts and Finnish translations studied

Eräpuro, Annika (1989/1997): *Kuolema kirkkomaalla.* ['Death in the churchyard'. The second Finnish translation of *The Nine Tailors.*] Hyvinkää: Viihdeviikarit.
Lavio, Niilo (1944): *Kuka ja mistä?* ['Who and where from?' The first Finnish translation of *Whose Body?*] Helsinki: Tammi.
Lehtonen, Paavo (1984): *Myrkkyä.* ['Poison'. The Finnish translation of *Strong Poison.*] Porvoo, Helsinki and Juva: WSOY.
Pekkanen, Hilkka (1985): *Yksi kuudesta.* ['One of the six'. The Finnish translation of *The Five Red Herrings.*] Porvoo, Helsinki and Juva: WSOY.
Rikman, Kristiina (1986): *Kuka ja mistä?* ['Who and where from?' The second Finnish translation of *Whose Body?*] Porvoo, Helsinki and Juva: WSOY.
Sayers, Dorothy L. (1923): *Whose Body?* In: *Four Complete Lord Peter Wimsey Novels: Whose Body? Clouds of Witness. Murder Must Advertise. Gaudy Night,* 1–106. New York: Avenel Books (1982).
—— (1926): *Clouds of Witness.* In: *Four Complete Lord Peter Wimsey Novels: Whose Body? Clouds of Witness. Murder Must Advertise. Gaudy Night,* 107–260. New York: Avenel Books (1982).
—— (1930/1998): *Strong Poison.* New York: HarperCollins.
—— (1931/1995): *The Five Red Herrings.* New York: HarperCollins.
—— (1934/1981): *The Nine Tailors: Changes Rung on an Old Theme in Two Short Touches and Two Full Peals.* Boston: G.K. Hall.
Talvitie, Oiva (1948): *Kuolema keskiyöllä.* ['Death at midnight'. The Finnish translation of *Clouds of Witness.*] Helsinki: Tammi.
Vankkoja, V. (1948): *Kolmesti kuollut.* ['Three times dead'. The first Finnish translation of *The Nine Tailors.*] Helsinki: Tammi.

B. Other primary sources cited

Agricola 1983 = "Mikael Agricola -palkinto Arto Häilälle." ['Mikael Agricola Award to Arto Häilä.'] In: *Kääntäjä* 38 (May 1983), 1.
Agricola 1987 = "Mikael Agricola -palkinto Pentti Saaritsalle." ['Mikael Agricola Award to Pentti Saaritsa.'] In: *Kääntäjä* 4/1987, 2.
Anhava, Tuomas (1950): "Mestariteos ja mestarin teos." ['A masterpiece and a piece by a master.' A review of the Finnish translations of Henry Fielding's *Tom Jones* and Somerset Maugham's *The Narrow Corner.*] In: *Suomalainen Suomi* 18, 502–504.
Ekholm, Kai (1985): "Mainiota, Harjunpää." ['Excellent, Harjunpää.' A review of Matti Yrjänä Joensuu's *Harjunpää ja rakkauden lait.*] In: *Ruumiin kulttuuri* 3/1985, 47.
Eräpuro, Annika (2008): Interview. 30th May 2008 and 9th June 2008.

Gustafsson, Dorrit (1985): "Taiteilijat murhasilla." ['Artists playing murder.' A review of the Finnish translation of *The Five Red Herrings*.] In: *Ruumiin kulttuuri* 4/1985, 46.

Hollo, J.A. (1943): "Kaksi 'Seitsemän veljeksen' käännöstä." ['Two translations of *The Seven Brothers*.'] In: *Virittäjä* 47, 1–15.

Huhtala, Liisi (1986): "Lajinsa ansarista." ['A representative of its genre.' A review of the second Finnish translation of *Whose Body?*] In: *Ruumiin kulttuuri* 3/1986, 44.

—— (1989): "Kuolinkellot." ['Death bells.' A review of the Finnish translation of *The Nine Tailors*.] In: *Ruumiin kulttuuri* 3/1989, 45–46.

Koskenniemi, V.A. (1943): "Sten Stolpe: Armoton maailma." [A review of the Finnish translation of Sten Stolpe's *Världen utan nåd*.] In: *Valvoja–Aika* 63, 241.

Kuusi, Matti (1986): "Kirjasuomen julkinen runtelu." ['Mutilating written Finnish in public.'] In: *Virittäjä* 90, 251–254.

Lindström, Juha (1984): "Kolme mestaria eli lukitusta huoneesta paperilappusen kitaan." ['Three masters, or from a locked room into the maw of a piece of paper.'] In: *Ruumiin kulttuuri* 2/1984, 36–41.

—— (1985): "Tunteita pääkallossa." ['Emotions in a skull.' A review of the Finnish translation of *Strong Poison*.] In: *Ruumiin kulttuuri* 2/1985, 17–21.

Metsä-Heikkilä, Kaija (1988): "Vajaasta ilmaisusta." ['On elliptical expressions.'] In: *Virittäjä* 92, 446–450.

Nopsanen, Aulis (1948): "Käännöstyön pulmakysymyksiä." ['Problems of translation.'] In: *Valvoja* 68, 91–93.

Nuorto, Olli (1950/1959): *Tom Jones*. [A Finnish translation of Henry Fielding's *Tom Jones*.] Porvoo and Helsinki: WSOY.

Nyytäjä, Kalevi (1988): "Dekkarikirjailijat Raymond Chandler, Ed McBain ja Donald Westlake kääntäjän kiikarissa." ['The whodunit authors Raymond Chandler, Ed McBain and Donald Westlake in the translator's sights.'] In: Rantanen, Aulis [ed.] (1988): *Suomentajan pyhää ja arkea*. Helsinki: Helsingin yliopisto. 55–69.

Pekkanen, Hilkka (2005): Interview. 4th and 12th May, 2005.

Pennanen, Eila (1979): "Suomentamisen ja sen opettajan vaikeuksia." ['Difficulties of literary translation and its instructor.'] In: *Virittäjä* 83, 255–260.

Pulkkinen, Paavo (1983): "*Tuoda mukanaan* turhissa paikoissa." ['Unnecessary use of *tuoda mukanaan*.'] In: *Virittäjä* 87, 572–573.

Raitio, Risto (1985a): "Vuosikerta-Agatha." ['A vintage Agatha.' A review of the Finnish translation of Agatha Christie's *Murder on the Links*.] In: *Ruumiin kulttuuri* 2/1985, 43–44.

—— (1985b): "Keitossa ei edes kärpäsiä." ['Not even flies in the soup.' A review of the Finnish translation of John Dickson Carr's *Patrick Butler for the Defence*.] In: *Ruumiin kulttuuri* 3/1985, 44–45.

—— (1988): "Kun ei kulje." ['When it just won't work.' A review of the Finnish translation of Rex Stout's *The Final Deduction*.] In: *Ruumiin kulttuuri* 3/1988, 61–62.

—— (1989): "Liian iso keikka." ['Too big a job.' A review of the Finnish translation of Lawrence Sanders' *Caper*.] In: *Ruumiin kulttuuri* 1/1989, 52, 54.

Rantanen, Aulis (1987): "Kääntämisen ihanuus ja kurjuus." ['The joy and misery of translating.'] In: *Ruumiin kulttuuri* 3/1987, 50–54.

Rikman, Kristiina (1988): "Viihdekirjallisuus kääntäjän kannalta." ['Popular fiction from the translator's point of view.'] In: Rantanen, Aulis [ed.] (1988): *Suomentajan pyhää ja arkea*. Helsinki: Helsingin yliopisto. 44–54.

—— (2005): Interview. 7th October 2005 and 9th November 2005.

Saarimaa, E.A. (1941): "Epäsuomalaisia attribuutteja." ['Un-Finnish attributes'.] In: *Virittäjä* 45, 261–266.

—— (1943): "Suomentajain kompastuksia." ['Translators' blunders.'] In: *Virittäjä* 47, 350–354.

Saario, Tapio (1988): "Herrasmiesetsivä." ['A gentleman detective.' A review of the Finnish translation of Leo Bruce's *Crack of Doom*.] In: *Ruumiin kulttuuri* 2/1988, 46.

Sadeniemi, Matti (1949): "Hyvää vapaata suomea." ['Good free Finnish.'] In: *Virittäjä* 53, 340–345.

Sara, Rauno (1940): "Suomalaisia salapoliisiromaaneja." ['Some Finnish detective novels.'] In: *Suomalainen Suomi* 8, 34–37.

C. Secondary sources

Brabazon, James (1981/ 1988): *Dorothy L. Sayers: A Biography*. London Victor Gollanz.

Brownlie, Siobhan (2003): "Investigation Explanations of Translational Phenomena: A Case for Multiple Causality." In: *Target* 15(1), 111–152.

Brunila, Anne and Uusitalo, Liisa (1989): *Kirjatuotannon rakenne ja strategiat*. ['The structure and strategies of book production'.] Jyväskylä: Jyväskylän yliopisto, Nykykulttuurin tutkimusyksikkö.

Chesterman, Andrew (1997): *Memes of Translation: The Spread of Ideas in Translation Theory*. Amsterdam and Philadelphia: John Benjamins.

—— (2000): "A Causal Model for Translation Studies". In: Olohan, Maeve [ed.] (2000): *Intercultural Faultlines: Research Models in Translation Studies I: Textual and Cognitive Aspects*. Manchester: St. Jerome. 15–27.

Cronvall, Emilia (2007): "Käännetty naistenromaani uuden ja vanhan risteyksessä." ['The translated women's novel in between the new and the old.'] In: Riikonen, H.K. / Kovala, Urpo / Kujamäki, Pekka / Paloposki, Outi [eds.] (2007): *Suomennoskirjallisuuden historia I*. Helsinki: SKS. 357–368.

Eskola, Eija (2004): *Suositellut, valitut ja luetut: kirjallisuus kirjastoissa 1918–1939*. ['The recommended, the selected and the read: library books from 1918 to 1939.'] Tampere: Tampere University Press.

Gambier, Yves (1994): "La retraduction, retour et detour." In: *Meta* 39(3), 413–417.

Halme, Helkky (2007): "Suomen kääntäjien ja tulkkien liitto: alan ammattilaisten järjestö." ['The Finnish Association of Translators and Interpreters: an organisation for professionals.'] In: Riikonen, H.K. / Kovala, Urpo / Kujamäki, Pekka / Paloposki, Outi [eds.] (2007): *Suomennoskirjallisuuden historia II*. Helsinki: SKS. 337–341.

Haycraft, Howard (1941/1974): *Murder for Pleasure: the Life and Times of the Detective Story*. New York: Biblo and Tannen.

Heinämäki, Margit (1993): "Kirjallisuusarvostelujen rooli ja mahdollisuudet käännöskritiikin esittämisessä." ['The role and possibilities of literature reviews in translation criticism.' Unpublished master's thesis.] Tampere: University of Tampere.

Hellemann, Jarl (1968): "Kirjallinen katsaus." ['Literary review.'] In: *Tammen neljännesvuosisata*. Helsinki: Tammi. 55–82.

Helminen, Soili (1999): "Kahden tulen välissä – Kustannusosakeyhtiö Tammen tasapainottelu vuosien 1941–1948 poliittisissa suhdanteissa." ['Between the rock and a hard place – the publisher Tammi's balancing act in political trends from 1941 to 1948.'] Unpublished master's thesis. Turku: University of Turku.

Jalonen, Olli (1985): *Kansa kulttuurien virroissa: tuontikulttuurin suuntia ja sisältöjä Suomessa itsenäisyyden aikana*. ['A nation in the currents of cultures: trends and contents of imported culture in independent Finland.'] Helsinki: Otava.

Jänicke, Raija (1989): "Kirjallisuuden käännöspalkkiot vuonna 1988." ['Literary translation fees in 1988'.] In: *Kääntäjä* 3/1989, 5.

—— (1990): "Kirjallisuuden käännöspalkkiot vuonna 1989." ['Literary translation fees in 1989'.] In: *Kääntäjä* 2/1990, 5.

Jokela, Pirjo (1989): "Ruumis kirjastossa: Kirjastolehden ja Arvostelevan kirjaluettelon suhtautuminen salapoliisiromaaneihin vuosina 1908–1970". ['A body in the library: the views of the Library Journal and the Critical Book Review on detective novels from 1908 to 1970'. Unpublished master's thesis.] Tampere: University of Tampere.

Jokinen, Kimmo (1987): *Ostajat, lukijat, arvioijat, tukijat: lukijoiden ja kriitikoiden kirjallisuus suuren muuton jälkeisessä Suomessa*. ['Buyers, readers, reviewers, promoters: the literature of readers and critics in Finland since the late 1970s.'] Jyväskylä: Jyväskylän yliopisto.

Joukkoviestintätilasto. ['Mass communication in statistics.'] (1991) Helsinki: Tilastokeskus.

Knight, Stephen (1980): *Form and Ideology in Crime Fiction*. London and Basingstoke: Macmillan.

Kovala, Urpo (1992): *Väliin lankeaa varjo: angloamerikkalaisen kaunokirjallisuuden välittyminen Suomeen 1890–1939*. ['A shadow falls in between: mediation of Anglo-American fiction into Finland from 1890 to 1939'.] Jyväskylä: Jyväskylän yliopisto.

—— (2007): "Kieltenopetus ja kielitaito kääntämisen edellytyksinä autonomian ajan Suomessa." ['Language teaching and language skills as preconditions for translation in autonomous Finland.'] In: Riikonen, H.K. / Kovala, Urpo / Kujamäki, Pekka / Paloposki, Outi [eds.] (2007): *Suomennoskirjallisuuden historia I*. Helsinki: SKS. 140–146.

Kujamäki, Pekka (2007): "Kääntämisen normit sotien välisenä aikana." ['Translation norms between the wars.'] In: Riikonen, H.K. / Kovala, Urpo / Kujamäki, Pekka / Paloposki, Outi [eds.] (2007): *Suomennoskirjallisuuden historia I*. Helsinki: SKS. 401–413.

Kukkola, Timo (1980): *Hornanlinnan perilliset: 70 vuotta suomalaista salapoliisikirjallisuutta*.['The heirs of Hornanlinna: 70 years of Finnish detective fiction.'] Porvoo, Helsinki and Juva: WSOY.

Lefevere, André (1992): *Translation, Rewriting and the Manipulation of Literary Fame*. London and New York: Routledge.

Leppihalme, Ritva (1997): *Culture Bumps: an Empirical Approach to the Translation of Allusions*. Clevedon: Multilingual Matters.

—— (2007): "Britteinsaarten kertomakirjallisuus." ['Narrative fiction from the British Isles'.] In: Riikonen, H.K. / Kovala, Urpo / Kujamäki, Pekka / Paloposki, Outi [eds.] (2007): *Suomennoskirjallisuuden historia II*. Helsinki: SKS. 152–166.

Mannila, Markku (1983): "Kaunokirjallisuuden kääntämisestä – asemasta, olemuksesta, koulutuksesta ja tutkimuksesta." ['On literary translation – status, nature, training and research'.] In: Roinila, Paavo / Orfanos, Ritva / Tirkkonen-Condit, Sonja [eds.] (1983): *Näkökohtia kääntämisen tutkimuksesta*. Joensuu: Joensuun korkeakoulu, kielten osasto. 93–100.

—— (1985a): "Kurssin kautta suomentajaksi." ['Becoming a literary translator by means of a course'.] In: *Kääntäjä* 9/1985, 42–46.

—— (1985b): "Mitä meille maksettiin: palkkiokyselyn tulokset vuodelta 1984." ['What we were paid: results of literary translators' fee inquiry in 1984.'] In: *Kääntäjä* 2/1985, 2.

Paasivirta, Juhani (1991): "Suomi jäsentyy kansakuntana Eurooppaan: kulttuurisuhteet 1800- ja 1900-luvuilla." ['Finland's place as a nation in Europe: cultural relations in the 19th and 20th centuries.'] In: Jokipii, Mauno [ed.] (1991): *Suomi Euroopassa: talous- ja kulttuurisuhteiden historiaa*. Jyväskylä: Atena. 171–192.

Paloposki, Outi and Koskinen, Kaisa (2004): "A Thousand and One Translations: Revisiting Retranslation." In: Hansen, Gyde [ed.] (2004): *Claims, Changes and Challenges in Translation Studies: Selected Contributions from the EST Congress, Copenhagen 2001.* Philadelphia: John Benjamins. 27–38.

Poijärvi, L. Arvi P. / Havu, I. / Jääskeläinen, Mauno [eds.] (1949): *Kuka kukin on 1950: Henkilötietoja nykypolven suomalaisista.* ['Who's Who 1950: personal data on contemporary Finns.'] Helsinki: Otava.

Pym, Anthony (1998): *Method in Translation History.* Manchester: St. Jerome.

Pyrhönen, Heta (1994): *Murder from an Academic Angle: An Introduction to the Study of the Detective Narrative.* Drawes and Columbia: Camden House.

Ratinen, Sirpa (1992): "Kirjallisuudenkääntäjät Suomessa – Ammattikuvatutkimus." ['Literary translators in Finland – A study of the profession.'] In: *Kääntäjä* 6/1992, 1–3 and *Kääntäjä* 7/1992, 10–11.

Rekola, Simo (2007): "Kääntäminen toisen maailmansodan aikana ja heti sen jälkeen." ['Translation during the Second World War and immediately afterwards.'] In: Riikonen, H.K. / Kovala, Urpo / Kujamäki, Pekka / Paloposki, Outi [eds.] (2007): *Suomennoskirjallisuuden historia I.* Helsinki: SKS. 426–442.

Riikonen, H.K. (2007): "Suomennoskritiikin vaiheita 1850-luvulta lähtien." ['Phases of translation criticism since the 1850s.'] In: Riikonen, H.K. / Kovala, Urpo / Kujamäki, Pekka / Paloposki, Outi [eds.] (2007): *Suomennoskirjallisuuden historia II.* Helsinki: SKS. 425–442.

Ruokonen, Minna (2010): *Cultural and Textual Properties in the Translation and Interpretation of Allusions: An Analysis of Allusions in Dorothy L. Sayers' Detective Novels Translated into Finnish in the 1940s and the 1980s.* Turku: Painosalama. Also available electronically at http://julkaisut.utu.fi.

Shaw, Harry (1972): *Dictionary of Literary Terms.* New York: McGraw-Hill.

Sipilä, Jorma and Anttonen, Anneli (2008): "Miten hyvinvointivaltio muutti elämäämme?" ['How did the welfare society change our lives?'] In: Häggman, Kai et al. [eds.] (2008): *Suomalaisen arjen historia 4: Hyvinvoinnin Suomi.* Helsinki: Weilin + Göös. 44–69.

Sorvali, Irmeli (1996): *Unohdettu kääntäjä.* 'The forgotten translator.' Oulu: Pohjoinen.

Storey, John (2003): *Inventing Popular Culture: From Folklore to Globalization.* Malden, Mass.: Blackwell.

Strinati, Dominic (2004): *An Introduction to Theories of Popular Culture.* [2nd edition.] London and New York: Routledge.

Symons, Julian (1992/1994): *Bloody Murder: From the Detective Novel to the Crime Novel: A History.* London and Basingstoke: Pan Books.

Toury, Gideon (1995): *Descriptive Translation Studies and Beyond.* Amsterdam and Philadelphia: John Benjamins.

―――― (1999): "A Handful of Paragraphs on 'Translation' and 'Norms'." In: Schäffner, Christina [ed.] (1999): *Translation and Norms.* Clevedon: Multilingual Matters. 9–31.

Turunen, Risto (2003): *Uhon ja armon aika: suomalainen kirjallisuusjärjestelmä, sen yhteiskuntasuhteet ja rakenteistuminen vuosina 1944–1952.* ['The age of bravado and mercy: the Finnish literary system, its social relations and structuralisation from 1944 to 1952.'] Joensuu: Joensuun yliopisto.

Turunen, Tuula (2000): "Vaatturit kirkontornissa vuonna 1930; kronotooppisuutta ja uudelleenkirjoitusta." ['Tailors in a steeple in 1930; chronotopicality and rewriting.' Unpublished master's thesis.] Tampere: University of Tampere.

Utrio, Untamo (1968): "25 vuotta kustannustoimintaa." ['25 years of publishing.'] In: *Tammen neljännesvuosisata.* Helsinki: Tammi. 7–51.

Williams, Jenny / Chesterman, Andrew (2002): *The Map: A Beginner's Guide to Doing Research in Translation Studies*. Manchester, UK and Northampton MA: St. Jerome.

Translation and Linguistic Innovation: The Rise and Fall of Russian Loanwords in Literary Translation into Dutch

Piet Van Poucke
University College Ghent and Ghent University, Belgium

Abstract

This paper examines the use of Russian loanwords in Dutch translations of Russian literary texts from the period 1970–2009. In an increasingly globalized world, as more information is exchanged across cultural borders worldwide, one might expect a growth in the number and use of loanwords, even between cultures that are relatively distant from each other such as Dutch and Russian. In the case study conducted, which was based on a representative corpus of 20 Dutch translations of Russian novels, we found that while there was a relative growth in the number of loanwords used in the 1970's and 1980's, the trend since the 1990's has been downwards. In the earlier period the public's interest in dissident Russian literature and in the cultural developments of the *Glasnost* period was intense, which in turn stimulated literary translators to use foreignizing translation strategies, bringing the (Russian) source text closer to the (Dutch) target public. With the rise of new genres (postmodernism and crime novels) in Russian literature and the changes in publishing policies this tendency diminished and the number of loanwords in translation decreased, which indicates a rise of domesticating translation strategies in Dutch culture in recent decades.

1 Translation and globalization

This paper examines (literary) translations from a loanword perspective. More specifically it focuses on the influence of current processes (globalization) on the behaviour of Dutch literary translators, i.e. on their decisions to use either a domesticating or foreignizing translation strategy when translating Russian literature into Dutch.

There is a considerable amount of recent research on the complex relationship between globalization and translation (e.g. Cronin 2003; Pym 2006; Ho 2008; Shiyab 2010). However much of this concentrates on translation in general, which means that literary translation is only partially dealt with. It is my opinion that the latter deserves greater attention because literary translators adapt as well to the processes of globalization as general translators, which can be illustrated by an analysis of the use of loanwords as a parameter of foreignizing translation behaviour.

In reference to this issue Venuti (1995: 1–5) stressed more than a decade ago now how domesticating translation had become normative in Anglo-American culture and how reviewers of literary translations responded to this norm by demanding fluent translations and 'invisible' translators. According to the norm the use of foreign elements (stylistic and syntactic features from the source text, but also lexical elements such as loanwords and other borrowings) should be avoided as much as possible in order to accommodate the preferences of Anglo-American readers who supposedly do not like deviations from fluent and transparent English discourse.

As cultures all over the world increasingly feel the impact of globalization and the dominance of the current lingua franca (English), translators working within non-Anglo-American cultures seem, in recent years, to have adapted to the same requirement of fluency and transparency mentioned above. This is especially the case when a minority language at the periphery receives information that is produced at the core, i.e. in English.

The increasing number of political, economic and cultural contacts, indeed, leads to ever greater quantities of information crossing linguistic and cultural borders, mostly in an asymmetrical way, from the bigger languages at the core to minority languages at the periphery (cf. Bielsa 2005: 9), and therefore translation activities are not undiminished.

In this paper we want to investigate whether and the extent to which the changed global linguistic interrelations may have an influence on the activities and individual decisions of literary translators. More specifically this article examines how the translation of Russian literature by Dutch speaking translators has been affected by globalization and the dominance of Anglo-American translation norms. It looks at the extent to which translators consider foreign elements acceptable for readers and therefore use more or less of those elements than the translators of earlier generations.

2 Borrowings and loanwords

According to the *Dictionary of Translation Studies* we speak about a borrowing when "elements of ST are replaced by *parallel* TL elements" (Shuttleworth & Cowie 1997: 17). This means a borrowing is "the simplest type of translation, since it merely involves the transfer of an SL word into TT without it being modified in any way" (Shuttleworth & Cowie 1997: 17).

In articles on translation the terms borrowing and loanword are sometimes used to indicate a similar concept, but the words are by no means synonymous. The former has a double meaning: not only does the word borrowing indicate "a translation procedure where the translator carries over a word or an expression from the source text into the target text", but also "any product of this translation procedure" (Delisle, Lee-Jahnke & Cormier 1999: 122). The latter term loanword is only used in the sense of a product of borrowing, and therefore we prefer the term "loanword" in this paper to refer to particular words that are brought into the target culture by means of translation.

Borrowing is indicated by Vinay and Darbelnet (1958/1995: 85–91) as one of the seven major translation procedures, along with calque, literal translation, transposition, modulation, equivalence and adaptation. Vinay and Darbelnet describe two possible reasons for the use of borrowing: (1) to "overcome a lacuna" in the target language, usually to refer to a "new technical process" or an "unknown concept", and (2) to "create a stylistic effect" or "introduce the flavour of the source language" (Vinay & Darbelnet 1958/1995: 85). Breiter (1997: 90) adds a third reason for borrowing to this list: "the establishment of some positive (or negative) connotations which the equivalent in the target language does not possess". This positive connotation is especially topical in a situation where translation is involved from a dominating language (English) into a minority language.

However, we would like to stress here that the majority of loanwords in literary translations are used for stylistic effect, rather than to overcome a lacuna. This means that only in very particular cases does the translator have no other choice than to borrow the foreign word, for example to refer to very specific culture-related concepts such as monetary units (*rouble, dollar*) or some food names (*vodka, tequila*). In most other cases a borrowing is used by the translator as a result of "a deliberate choice, not the unconscious influence of undesired interference" (Chesterman 1997: 94). Some of the examples of Russian borrowings given by Vinay and Darbelnet are, indeed, used to create a specific stylistic effect, for example words such as *datchas* and *aparatchik* could easily be replaced by "seasonal home" and "(communist) functionary" (or a similar equivalent) in translation where the translator decides to choose a domesticating translation strategy.

Therefore a (literary) translator should always specify the prevalent norms of translation in the target culture with regard to the use of foreign elements before deciding whether or not to use a loanword (cf. also Listrova-Pravda 2001: 120). As the use of loanwords is a relatively provocative way to confront the reader with the foreignness or otherness of a text, translators should always decide on the level of acquaintance with foreign elements they can expect from their audience and on the level of openness of the target culture. Indeed, as Baker indicates, some cultures, "Arabic and French, for instance, are much less tolerant of loan words than Japanese" and others (Baker 1992: 36). In this paper we will concentrate on borrowings from Russian into Dutch, a relatively small culture located in between the larger English, French and German cultures, that is therefore, in Baker's terms, relatively tolerant towards loanwords.

3 Types of loanwords and semantic fields

Vinay and Darbelnet correctly stress the dynamic nature of loanwords by commenting how "[s]ome well-established, mainly older borrowings are so widely used that they are no longer considered as such and have become a part of the respective target language lexicon" (Vinay & Darbelnet 1958/1995: 85). In her dictionary of loanwords in Dutch van der Sijs (2005: 35–36) investigates the dynamic issues of borrowing and she comes to the conclusion that loanwords can be divided into four subsequent levels of development.

In the first instance only a small elite of scientists or specialists use a certain loanword in a certain context with a very specific meaning. In the second instance increasing numbers of people become aware of the meaning of the word and begin to use it, although it clearly remains foreign and mostly does not fit the norms of the target culture. In a third phase the loanword is accepted by the majority of people in the target culture and the word is sometimes assimilated. Finally, a loanword can be totally assimilated and from then on is no longer recognised as such. In this paper we are only interested in the first three phases of the process. Once a word is no longer seen as a foreign element in the target culture, it loses its otherness and can no longer be used to add a particular flavour to a translation.

Whether or not a loanword becomes accepted in another language, depends on a number of factors. As suggested by several authors (Yang 2009: 103; Breiter 1997: 86–88 and also Newmark 1988: 147), some semantic areas or fields are more open to loanwords than others. Small cultures tend to borrow more from the larger ones than vice versa, and the semantic fields involved usually depend on the way(s) in which the two cultures are connected to each other. In a globalized world with changing economic, political and cultural relationships between people and countries, those semantic fields seem to be very dynamic and flexible.

Yang (2009: 104–105) stresses, for instance, how Chinese (Cantonese, Amoy and Mandarin) borrowings in English have tended to be in the first place food items and concepts of high culture (philosophy, religion, history, politics, art and literature), but he foresees new loanwords occurring in various semantic fields as the contact between the two cultures continues to grow.

Borrowings from English in Russian belong to other semantic fields. Breiter (1997: 97) analysed recent English borrowings in Russian and came to the conclusion that those borrowings could be located in several semantic fields, in diminishing order: (1) social and political life, (2) finance, economy and trade, (3) science and technology, (4) travel and tourism, (5) meals and drinks, (6) clothes and fashion, (7) sports, (8) pop music and entertainment, (9) culture and arts and finally (10) standard forms of communication and interjections (Breiter 1997: 87).

In this paper we will investigate whether comparable correspondences exist in the translation process from Russian into Dutch and how this process evolves over time.

4 The use of Russian loanwords in Dutch (literary) translation

At any given moment in the continuous flux of change and exchange between cultures a (literary) translator has to make an individual decision on whether or not to use a loanword. There is a broad range of different factors that he/she will to some degree consider before making that decision.

(1) The nature of the source text is a first factor to deal with. A historical novel evidently contains a different kind of lexicon (more archaic words for example) compared to works on contemporary themes, and therefore a literary translator has greater freedom to use a foreignizing translating strategy, for instance by using assimilated loanwords and sometimes even introducing new loanwords (neologisms) in the translation. For the same reason a crime novel can require a quite different translation strategy to used, for instance, in treating a philosophical treatise.

(2) The source culture and the prestige this culture has in the target culture has also to be taken into account when translating literature. Any pair of source and target cultures have indeed different historical, ideological, political or economic relationships and these cultural differences may considerably diminish the number of choices a literary translator can make. As a rule, loanwords or neologisms are more likely to be accepted quickly when the prestige of the source culture (not only at a cultural, but also at a political and economic level) is high.

(3) A literary translator should also reckon with the traditions, norms and nature of the target culture and the expectations of the audience. As was indicated above, some cultures are more or less open to new foreign elements. French culture, for instance, is known to be more resistant to foreign influences than many others and this kind of situation will have consequences on the work of the translator, whether or not he is providing a literary translation.

(4) Another important agent on the target side of the translation process is the publisher who understandably wants a work to reach the largest possible audience and is therefore looking for products that please rather than irritate the possible readers. In Dutch-speaking countries, for instance, the majority

of publishers impose a ban on the use of footnotes to explain foreign words because the presence of footnotes is considered to be a typical attribute of scientific texts, and by extension not acceptable in literary texts.

(5) However, the final decision on whether or not to use a loanword in translation remains the personal responsibility of the translator him-/herself. As we indicated earlier in this paper, we are convinced that most of the loanwords in literary translations could be avoided fairly easily by using translating methods other than borrowing, although a part of the particular meaning of a culture-specific element can be lost for the reader. It is the translator with his/her openness to foreign elements and willingness to add some local colour to a literary translation who decides on the introduction of new loanwords and other borrowings. However, at times translators wish to avoid the responsibility of taking this decision, and instead make use of Google as a handy internet tool to check the level of assimilation of particular words in the target culture.

5 Case study

As was indicated earlier in this paper we aim to investigate the use of Russian loanwords in Dutch literary translation from a diachronic point of view. In order to study the changes in behaviour of literary translators with regard to Russian loanwords we compiled a limited but representative corpus of 20 translations of Russian 20th and 21st century literary works. The texts were selected from literary translations from the period 1970–2009, and give a good impression of tendencies in both the source and target cultures. However, to make the study as representative as possible within the scope of a limited corpus, the translations are chosen according to the following conditions:

(1) No Russian author is represented twice in the corpus, in order to avoid a situation in which one specific narrative style exerts too much influence on the research data;

(2) Each translation has been produced by a different Dutch translator, in order to avoid, again, the personal style of one person influencing the whole of the data;

(3) The translations are taken from the four decades between 1970 and 2009. Each of the decades is represented in the corpus by 5 translations, which allows us to look at translations from a diachronic perspective;

(4) The source texts cover different periods in Russian cultural history of the 20th and 21st centuries. (Re)translations of classical (19th century or earlier) Russian novels are not included in the corpus in order to avoid an excess of outdated lexicon;

(5) The works represent the different literary prose genres that reflect the trends in literary production of the particular period. The corpus includes prose works and memoires, but pure historical novels were not taken into account, as they usually contain a relatively high proportion of references to culture-specific elements that are no longer known to the public, sometimes even in the source culture.

Within this Dutch language corpus of 20 translations a manual search for the presence of Russian loanwords was conducted.[1] Only Russian loanwords "proper" have been taken into account in the investigation. This means in the first place that all derivates have been brought together under one lemma: e.g. the different translations for the Russian *car', carica, carevič, carskij...* count only as one loanword, namely *car'* ('tsar').[2] The same goes for *sovet* ('soviet') which covers also *sovetskij*, and *ikona* ('icon') which covers *ikonostas* as well.

Several groups of lexicon have been excluded from the study: calques and loanblends for instance, and also toponyms and proper names (including the names of brands), even when they are used in an attributive position (as in Lenin Street for example). For obvious reasons these words are very rarely translated and therefore the use of a Russian toponym or proper name cannot really be considered as a foreignizing element in translation.

Also excluded from the study are loanwords that have been entirely assimilated into Dutch and are no longer recognised as loanwords by the audience, words that are

---

[1] We would like to thank MA students Nele Derde and Elien Decommer who conducted part of the research in preparation of their MA thesis.
[2] Unless otherwise indicated in the text the loanwords are referred to in transcription from the Russian words, using the scientific ISO R/9 system. When a word appears in the text for the first time, the English translation (loanword and/or explanation) is added between parentheses.

included in the translation as part of a pun or a play on words or sounds and the loanwords that are introduced in the text when the foreign origin of this word has to be stressed, for instance when the direct speech of one of the characters is provided, usually followed by an additional phrase, indicating he/she was saying something in Russian. Finally, loanwords that are clearly of non-Russian origin and used as such in the source text are also excluded.

However, as indicated by Podhajecka (2006: 125) this kind of etymology has a certain margin of error and therefore we have to try to understand how such a loanword is perceived by the public. Whenever a word, even from non-Russian origin, might be perceived by the readers as "Russian", that possibly is taken into account in this study. This is the reason why the following Russian words in the Dutch translations have been included in the list of loanwords, although they are not really Russian: *tajga* ('taiga'), *šašlyk* ('shashlik'), *ikona*, *kumys* ('kumis, an alcoholic beverage made from fermented mare's milk'), *mitropolit* ('metropolitan bishop'), *pioner* ('pioneer') and *tundra*. The words *ikona* and *mitropolit* are religious terms, connected with the Orthodox religion and of Greek origin, but equally associated with Russia. *Tajga* and *tundra* are not Russian either, but again many readers do not know the (Turkish and Finnish) origin of the words and associate the terms geographically with Russia. *Kumis* and *šašlyk* belong to the semantic fields of "food and drink". The former word is of Kalmyk origin and the latter is generally associated with the typical Russian barbecue, and therefore included in the list. Finally, *pioner* is added to the list because it reflects an aspect of daily life in the Soviet Union, associated with the Young Pioneer organisation.

The study makes no distinction between isolated loanwords, loanwords with an explanation in the text and loanwords with an explanation in foot- or endnote.

When we applied the described parameters to the corpus of 20 literary translations, we counted a total of 132 different Russian loanwords, with 85 loanwords occurring only once in the corpus and 14 only twice. This means 33 loanwords are used on a more or less regular basis in Dutch and seem to reflect the local colour the translator wants to add. Among these words are the financial *rubl'* ('rouble') and *kopejka* ('kopek'), the food related *kvas* ('kvass, an alcoholic drink of low strength made from cereals and bread'), *samovar*, *šašlyk*, *vodka*, the geographical *step'* ('steppe'), *tajga*, *tundra*, the religious *ikona*, *pop* ('parish priest'), the measures *pud* ('pood, a unit of weight equal to 16.4 kilograms'), *versta* ('verst, a unit of length equal to 1.067 kilometres') and the *trojka* ('troika') as a means of transportation. By far the most productive lexical field for Russian loanwords is that of "social and political life", including among others *banja* ('banya, a Russian sauna'), *dača* ('dacha'), *kazak* ('Cossack'), *car'* (+ derivates), *sovet*, *kolhoz* ('kolkhoz'), *sovhoz* ('sovkhoz') and *bol'ševik* ('Bolshevik').

When we look at the distribution of the loanwords in translation from a diachronic perspective, we notice a clear, decreasing tendency (Figure 1). 5 out of the 7 translations with 20 or more different loanwords belong to the period 1970–1990, while 3 out of the 4 with 10 or less loanwords are situated in the period 1990–2010.

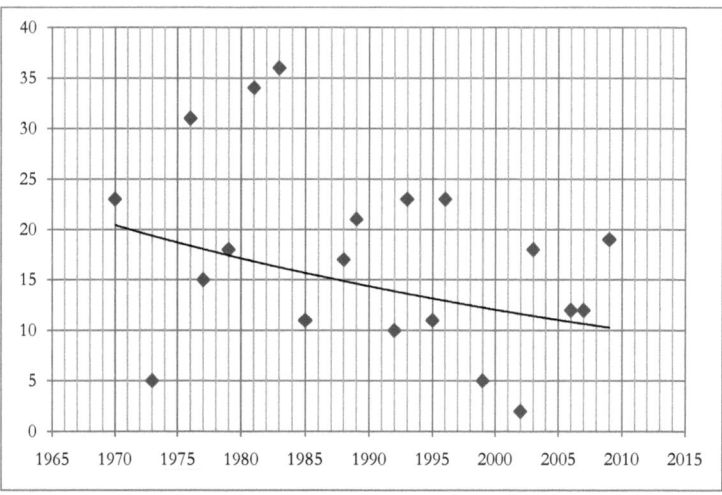

Figure 1. Number of different loanwords in the corpus.

While the average number of used loanwords is still increasing in the 1980's (23.8 Russian loanwords on average per translation) in comparison with the 1970's (18.4), this figure decreases very quickly in the last two decades. The translations in the corpus from the 1990's contain an average of 14.4 different loanwords, compared to 12.6 for the years 2000. This negative trend becomes even more apparent when we take into account the length of the translated text (Figure 2 gives the number of different loanwords per 100 pages of translated text), but the general observations remain unchanged.

We could usefully ask whether changes in both the source and target cultures might help to explain the contradictory decrease in the use of foreign words despite globalization, with its increasing number of political, economic and intercultural exchanges.

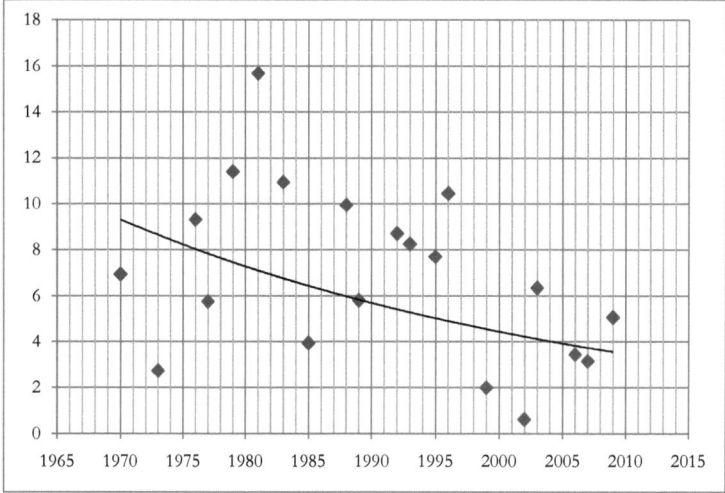

Figure 2. Average number of different loanwords in the corpus per 100 pages of translated text.

6 Literary translators as innovators

The average number of Russian loanwords in the Dutch literary translations of the corpus is higher in the 1980's than in the 1970's although the chosen corpus contains literary works of approximately equal character and genre for both decades: 4 "soviet novels" and 1 autobiographical work in each group of 5 translations (cf. the list of used translations at the end of the paper).

This increase in the use of Russian loanwords in literary translations is most probably influenced by changes both in the source and target cultures. If we look at the total number of published translations of Russian 20th century literature in Dutch, we see a steady increase from 18 books in 1970 to 30 in 1989 (cf. Waegemans & Willemsen 1991; TSL 1987–1991). This means that interest in Russian literature did not diminish in the Dutch-speaking countries, despite the existence of the Cold War which cast Russian literature as part of a culture from "the other side".

This can partly be explained by the prestige that Russian literature enjoyed at that time and has in fact held since the end of the 19th century (cf. Meylaerts 2009: 36; Heilbron 2008: 193). The Russian classics (e.g. Dostoyevsky, Tolstoy, Chekhov) continued to be translated without significant interruption, but the 1970's and moreover the 1980's also marked the public's interest for the growing market of dissident Russian literature. Most notably the works of Nobel Prize winner Aleksandr Solzhenitsyn, but also those of Georgy Vladimov, Aleksandr Zinovyev, Andrey Sinyavsky, Vladimir Voinovich, Lidiya Chukovskaya, Vladimir Maksimov and Varlam Shalamov (works of the last 4 writers are present in our corpus) depict a non-official view of soviet reality, and during this period their books were read with eagerness in the West. Moreover, the 1980's saw the emergence of *Perestroika* and *Glasnost*, which created intense interest in how Russian culture would develop given fewer censorship constraints.

One could expect that the growing interest of the audience in Russian literature and culture would stimulate literary translators to use foreignizing translation strategies, bringing the source text closer to the target public and not vice-versa. This could indeed explain why 4 out of the 5 translations in the corpus of the 1980's contain an above average number of loanwords. It seems, indeed, as if translators used the curiosity of the Western reader regarding the relatively unknown and closed soviet culture to introduce substantial amounts of realia of that culture by means of loanwords, especially in the semantic field of "social and political life". Our corpus of the 1970's and 1980's contains several loanwords that reflect soviet reality: *bol'ševik, kolhoz, komintern* ('Comintern'), *komsomolec* ('member of Komsomol'), *men'ševik* ('Menshevik'), *partorg* ('"party organizer" appointed by the CPSU Central Committee'), *pioner, rabfak* ('workers' faculty'), *revkom* ('revolutionary committee'), *revtribunal* ('revolutionary tribunal'), *sovhoz, sovet, trudovik* ('trudovik, a member of a small workers party in early 20th century Russia') and *čekist* ('member of the Cheka').

Does this observation fit in with general observations on lexical innovation? If we look at the data in the *Chronological dictionary* (CD) written by the Dutch scholar van der Sijs (2001: 286–288) we see that the 1970's and especially the 1980's were indeed relatively productive for the introduction of new Russian words into the Dutch language. No less than 9 out of a total of 55 Russian loanwords became, according to the CD, assimilated in Dutch in the 1970's and 1980's, mostly words connected with the political situation in the Soviet Union as for instance *agitprop* ('agitation and propaganda'), *apparatčik*, *gulag* ('Gulag, or Chief Administration of Corrective Labour Camps'), *glasnost'* ('Glasnost') and *perestrojka* ('Perestroika'). Two of these borrowings are situated in the 1970's, seven in the 1980's.

This is an interesting statement in the discussion on the role of literary translators on linguistic innovation. Newmark (1988: 81–82) and Fawcett (1997: 34–35), for instance, both stress how journalists usually play the role of innovators:

> Like borrowings, calques often make their first appearance not in translations but as an element in a newspaper article or in some other form of original literature, since journalists and creative writers tend more often than translators to see themselves as word creators (Fawcett 1997: 35).

On the other hand

> it seems highly likely that translators will resort more readily to borrowing than to calque, since the guidelines for using the latter are far less obvious than for the former (Fawcett 1997: 35).

Others disagree with Newmark and Fawcett. According to Vinay and Darbelnet (literary) translators indeed take up an innovative position. They stress how "many borrowings enter a language through translation, just like semantic borrowings or faux amis, whose pitfalls translators must carefully avoid" (Vinay & Darbelnet 1958/1995: 85) and Breiter echoes this point of view in her believe "that translation provides the most important impetus for borrowing. Borrowing takes place each time translation is hampered by inner-linguistic (systemic) or extra-linguistic (societal) reason" (Breiter 1997: 95).

In this paper journalistic texts are not involved and therefore the question about who is more innovative – the journalist or the literary translator – will not be addressed, but the paper does give an indication as to the importance of literary translations in terms of the development of language. Although the *Chronological dictionary* (CD) contains the relatively small number of 55 Russian words, our (limited) corpus counts up to 132 different loanwords. Among the words in the corpus we find *duma* and *čekist* with 4 hits and *banja* and *dekabrist* ('Decembrist') with 3, but those words are still not represented in the CD. On the other hand, the loanword *dača* is present in the CD, but with the year 1996 given as its "year of birth" in Dutch, although the word is seen 10 times in the corpus with no less than 5 hits (1988, 1989, 1992, 1993 and 1995) before that year.

The future will tell whether these translators are either pioneers of Russian loanwords or naive idealists who try (in vain) to pass to their public culturally bound information. In fact, the process of borrowing is a never ending continuum and *Chronological dictionaries* will have to be adapted on a continual basis.

7 Paradoxical effects of globalization

In his paper on *Globalization and its Impact on Translation* Shiyab (2010: 8) looks at the enriching possibilities of globalization for the target culture:

> Globalization has always been a significant aspect of translation, simply because translation brings cultures closer. [...] [P]eople as well as translators need to come to terms with the fact that words adopted from the target language can be enlightening to the reader as they genuinely mirror other cultures and their traditions.

This is a very optimistic view on the effects of globalization and the research conducted on our corpus instead shows some paradoxical effects.

On the one hand, cultures have indeed come closer to each other and we know more about the world outside than ever before. On the other hand, the data from the case study (see Figures 1 and 2) indicate a strong decrease in the use of Russian loanwords in literary translation into Dutch in the last two decades. How could this paradox be explained?

One of the possible explanations is to be found in the source culture, namely in the developments in Russian literary production. Since the initial rise of a new geopolitical and economic order from the ruins of the Soviet Union in 1991 much has changed. In terms of literature we can see some of the effects of this change by looking at the new generation of young writers in Russia, who turned en masse to new genres: first postmodernism (Pelevin, Sorokin, Yerofeyev) and later crime novels (Akunin, Marinina, Dashkova, Dontsova, Ustinova, Platova). The conditions of a market economy forced publishers to look for bestsellers, which meant that the pure soviet themes of the *Glasnost* period have increasingly been replaced by softer genres that appeal to a larger audience. The translations in the corpus of this paper are representative of this track, for Pelevin (1995), Marinina (1999), Skorobogatov (2002), Sorokin (2003) Platova (2006) and Akunin (2007) all belong to either postmodernist or crime literature.

One of the effects of globalization here can be found in the fact that modern writers in Russia use a more "Western" style no longer referring to Russian realia, but instead turning to Western loanwords themselves. A good example of this development can be found in the Marinina (1999) detective novel in the corpus where the heroes drink cognac rather than the formerly omnipresent vodka.

In connection with this it should also be stressed how the gradual disappearance of communist vocabulary from the source culture is paralleled by an evident decrease of the use of this vocabulary in translation. This pattern can also be illustrated by using the corpus of this paper. In the last 10 translations some generally assimilated (according to the *Chronological dictionary*) Russian loanwords have become rare occurrences, although they used to appear in almost every soviet novel before: *bol'ševik* (3), *kolhoz* (3), *sovhoz* (1). Other communist vocabulary has totally disappeared, as for instance *kulak* ('a wealthy independent farmer'), *komintern*, *men'ševik*, *revkom*.

However, the decrease in the use of Russian loanwords in Dutch translation in the last two decades has not only to do with changes in the source culture. Publishers and readers in the Dutch-speaking countries have also changed and translators have to adopt to the preferences of the new audience, as was indicated already by Vinay and Darbelnet: the "decision to borrow a source language word or expression for introducing an element of local colour is a matter of style and consequently of the message" (Vinay & Darbelnet 1958/1995: 85).

This idea about the importance of the message corresponds to the fundamental ideas of the Skopos theory. According to Vermeer's Skopos theory "the aim of any translational action, and the mode in which it is to be realized, are negotiated with the client who commissions the action" (Vermeer 1989: 221). In the case of literary translation the real "client" is the reader, and in comparison with the reader of soviet dissident literature the average reader of crime stories seems to be more interested in the story plot than the culture-specific references behind the story.

The translated crime novels in the corpus of this paper confirm this assumption. The contemporary crime stories written by Marinina (1999), Skorobogatov (2002) and Platova (2006) contain in translation 5, 2 and 12 Russian loanwords respectively, which is far below the average of the whole corpus – 17.3.

Apparently, translators of Russian literature in the 1970's and 1980's experienced more stimuli to use borrowings than their contemporary colleagues, who are now more likely to employ a domesticating translation strategy rather than a foreignizing one. On the one hand this is connected to the position of the publishers who follow the laws of the market and are influenced by the huge economic force of the internet. Confronted with an Anglo-American model that demands "invisible" translators, publishers follow a rather conservative policy with respect to translation. Elements in translation that could deter the reader are avoided as much as possible, and therefore the use of footnotes and neologisms (loanwords or other borrowings) in Dutch translations is reduced to the absolute minimum.

On the other hand literary translators themselves also adapt to the laws of the market. They too, apparently, conduct a less foreignizing strategy than their colleagues in previous decades and it now seems that Google has taken over the role of normative word-list provider for the current generation of literary translators.

An experienced translator of Russian literature, Helen Saelman, when asked about her translating strategy, indicated that she prefers to use originally Dutch words as often as possible, even in those cases where the Dutch word is not really a semantic equivalent of the Russian culture-specific element in the source text. She prefers, for instance, the Dutch word *zomerhuis* ('summer house') instead of the loanword *datsja* ('dacha'), even if the local colour of the typical Russian wooden house with wood carvings might be lost to the reader. Her judgement is partly based on the data from the Google database.

The same applies to Russian loanwords such as *versta* and *valenki* ('felt boots'). The former, according to the *Chronological dictionary* (CD), has been an assimilated element of Dutch since 1714 and has been used by most of the translators of earlier literary works. In the translation of Platova's detective novel (2006), however, the translator replaced that word (that was indeed used in the contemporary source text!) by the Dutch domesticating *kilometer*, thus reducing the foreign element to a minimum. The latter is not assimilated in Dutch according to the CD, but it has been used in literary translations before, for instance in the memoires of Paustovsky (1970) in the corpus. Again the word is not retained as a loanword in recent translations, e.g. Shalamov (1996), Platova (2006) and Rzhevskaya (2009), but replaced by the Dutch translation *viltlaarzen* ('felt boots'), although few Dutch readers who have not lived in Russia would have an idea about the culture-specific reference of this word.

The trend to avoid Russian loanwords marks a major change in translation policies. The new lingua franca in the world, English, provides most of the borrowings in Dutch, thanks to the prestige the Anglo-American world has. The borrowings from other languages tend to be controlled by the (purely quantitative) judgement of Google's data. If this tendency was to become normative, then the process of borrowing and the creation of neologisms would be taken out of the hands of literary translators and be moved to the virtual (and barely controllable) world of the internet.

8 Conclusion

If we consider the use of loanwords in a literary translation as one of the parameters for recognizing domesticating and foreignizing tendencies, then we can make some interesting conclusions on literary translation from Russian into Dutch, based on a limited corpus of 20 translations.

At the end of the 20th century, especially in the 1970's and 1980's, literary translators took up their role as cultural intermediaries and introduced several neologisms in Dutch translation, with or without complementary explanation in the text or in foot- or endnote, depending on the level of acquaintance the translator expected from the target public. The number of different Russian loanwords in a translation rose from an average of 18.4 in the 1970's to 23.8 in the 1980's, which might well be explained by the Western public's interest in the dissident tendencies in soviet literature. Because of this general interest, translators were tempted to use Russian loanwords to bring the source culture closer to the reader who could not easily visit the Soviet Union to see the culture-specific elements in the text with his/her own eyes.

Since the fall of the Soviet Union in 1991, the opening up of its old borders and the broad process of globalization, translation strategies have, apparently, altered. Even in those cases where literary translators would have used a Russian loanword in the past to present a culture-specific item to the reader, albeit with an explanation, the translator nowadays tends to use more domesticating translation strategies.

This can be explained, on the one hand, by the huge changes in Russian society and culture since 1991. Globalization has deeply "westernized" most of the literary scene in Russia, which has led to a decrease in the number of Russian culture-specific references in a literary work. On the other hand, the target culture has changed as well, and it seems as if literary translators have to adapt firmly to the demands of the market. Crime novels (the dominant genre in contemporary Russian literature) are clearly translated in a different (more domesticating) way than, for instance, the dissident novels of the Soviet period.

A more detailed research project on a larger corpus, with representatives of different decades and genres, should make clear whether these hypotheses can be confirmed or not.

References

A. Translations used in the corpus

Akunin (2007) = Akoenin, Boris: *De witte buldog: een provinciale roman*. Translated by Arie van der Ent. Breda: De Geus. Original title: *Pelagija i belyj bul'dog* (2001).
Astafyev (1988) = Astafjev, Viktor: *De droevige detective*. Translated by Lourens Reedijk. Amsterdam: Meulenhoff. Original title: *Pečal'nyj detektiv* (1986).
Babel (1979) = Babel, Isaak: *Rode Ruiterij*. Translated by Charles Timmer. Amsterdam: Meulenhoff. Original title: *Konarmija* (1926).
Bitov (1992) = Bitov, Andrej: *Leven in weer en wind*. Translated by Gerard Rasch. Amsterdam: Bert Bakker. Original title: *Žizn' v vetrenuju pogodu* (1989).
Chukovskaya (1973) = Tsjoekovskaja, Lidia: *Duik in de diepte*. Translated by Hans Leerinck. Amsterdam: van Oorschot. Original title: *Spusk pod vodu* (1972).
Gorky (1983) = Gorki, Maksim: *Onder de mensen*. Translated by Maarten Tengbergen. Utrecht/Antwerpen: Spectrum. Original title: *V ljudjah* (1916).
Ilf and Petrov (1993) = Ilf, Ilja & Petrov, Jevgeni: *De twaalf stoelen*. Translated by Frans Stapert. Amsterdam: M Bondi/Pegasus. Original title: *Dvenadcat' stul'ev* (1928).
Maksimov (1976) = Maximow, Wladimir: *Afscheid van het niets*. Translated by Arthur Langeveld, Hans Koens and Anneliet Schönfeld-Vorstman. Amsterdam: Amsterdam Boek. Original title: *Proščanie iz niotkuda* (1974).
Marinina (1999) = Marinina, Alexandra: *De hand van een moordenaar*. Translated by Theo Veenhof. Amsterdam: Luitingh-Sijthoff. Original title: *Stečenie obstojatel'stv* (1993).
Paustovsky (1970) = Paustovskij, Konstantin: *Verre jaren. Herinneringen uit het tsaristisch Rusland*. Translated by Wim Hartog. Amsterdam: Arbeiderspers. Original title: *Dalëkie gody* (1963).
Pelevin (1995) = Pelevin, Viktor: *Omon en de race naar de maan*. Translated by Aai Prins. Amsterdam: Wereldbibliotheek. Original title: *Omon Ra* (1992).

Platova (2006) = Platova, Victoria: *Vaarwel Ladybird*. Translated by Olga Groenewoud. Utrecht: Signature. Original title: *Bitvy bož'ih korovok* (2001).
Rasputin (1985) = Raspoetin, Valentin: *Afscheid van Matjora*. Translated by Anne Pries. Amsterdam: Arbeiderspers. Original title: *Proščanie s Matëroj* (1976).
Rybakov (1989) = Rybakov, Anatoli: *Het zware zand*. Translated by Roel Pieters. Amsterdam: Bert Bakker. Original title: *Tjažëlyj pesok* (1980).
Rzhevskaya (2009) = Rzjevskaja, Jelena: *Tolk in oorlogstijd*. Translated by Monse Weijers. Amsterdam: Mouria. Original title: *Zapiski voennogo perevodčika* (2009).
Shalamov (1996) = Sjalamov, Varlam: *Verhalen uit Kolyma*. Translated by Marja Wiebes and Yolanda Bloemen. Amsterdam: Bert Bakker. Original title: *Kolymskie rasskazy* (1982).
Skorobogatov (2002) = Skorobogatov, Aleksandr: *Aarde zonder water: roman*. Translated by Rosemie Vermeulen. Antwerpen: House of Books. Original title: *Zemlja bezvodnaja* (2002).
Sorokin (2003) = Sorokin, Vladimir: *IJs*. Translated by Helen Saelman. Amsterdam: Ambo. Original title: *Lëd* (2002).
Trifonov (1981) = Trifonov, Joeri: *De oude man*. Translated by Jan Robert Braat. Amsterdam: Arbeiderspers/Meulenhoff. Original title: *Starik* (1978).
Voinovich (1977) = Wojnowitsj, Wladimir: *De merkwaardige lotgevallen van soldaat Iwan Tsjonkin. Een anekdotische roman*. Translated by Gerard Kruisman. Amsterdam: Meulenhoff. Original title: *Žizn' i neobyčajnye priključenija soldata Ivana Čonkina* (1975).

B. Secondary sources

Baker, Mona (1992): *In other words. A coursebook on translation*. London and New York: Routledge.
Bielsa, Esperanca (2005): "Globalisation as Translation: An Approximation to the Key but Invisible Role of Translation in Globalisation." CSGR Working Paper No 163/05. http://wrap.warwick.ac.uk/1956/1/WRAP_Bielsa_wp16305.pdf. Visited November 2010.
Breiter, Maria (1997): "What is the difference between *shashlyk* and *barbecue*?" In: *Perspectives: Studies in Translatology* 5 (1), 85–100.
Chesterman, Andrew (1997): *Memes of translation. The spread of ideas in translation theory*. Amsterdam and Philadelphia: John Benjamins.
Cronin, Michael (2003): *Translation and Globalization*. London and New York: Routledge.
Delisle, Jean / Lee-Jahnke, Hannelore / Cormier, Monique (1999): *Terminologie de la Traduction*. Amsterdam and Philadelphia: John Benjamins.
Fawcett, Peter (1997): *Translation and language. Linguistic Theories Explained*. Manchester: St. Jerome.
Heilbron, Johan (2008): "Responding to globalization: The development of book translations in France and the Netherlands." In: Pym, Anthony / Shlesinger, Miriam / Simeoni, Daniel [eds.] (2008): *Beyond Descriptive Translation Studies. Investigations in homage to Gideon Toury*. Amsterdam and Philadelphia: John Benjamins. 187–197.
Ho, George (2008): *Globalization and Translation. Towards a Paradigm Shift in Translation Studies*. Saarbrücken: VDM Verlag Dr. Müller.
Listrova-Pravda, Ju.T. (2001): "Inojazyčnye vkraplenija-bibleizmy v russkoj literaturnoj reči XIX-XX vv." In: *Vestnik VGU. Serija 1, Gumanitarnye nauki* 1, 119–139.
Meylaerts, Reine (2009): "*Kleine* literaturen in vertaling: buitenkans of gemiste kans?" In: Hinderdael, Michaël / Jooken, Lieve / Verstraete, Heili [eds.] (2009): *De aarde heeft kamers genoeg. Hoe vertalers omgaan met culturele identiteit in het werk van Erwin Mortier*. Antwerpen-Apeldoorn: Garant. 33–49.
Newmark, Peter (1988): *A Textbook of Translation*. New York etc.: Prentice Hall.

Podhajecka, Mirosława (2006): "Russian Borrowings in English: Similarities and Differences in Lexicographic Desription." In: McConchie, R.W. et al. [eds.] (2006): *Selected Proceedings of the 2005 Symposium on New Approaches in English Historical Lexis (HEL-LEX)*. Somerville, MA: Cascadilla Proceedings Project. 123–134.

Pym, Anthony (2006): "Globalization and the Politics of Translation Studies." In: *Meta* LI (4), 744–757.

Shiyab, Said M. (2010): "Globalization and Its Impact on Translation". In: Shiyab, Said M. et al. [eds.] (2010): *Globalization and Aspects of Translation*. Newcastle upon Tyne: Cambridge Scholars Publishing. 1–10.

Shuttleworth, Mark / Cowie, Moira (1997): *Dictionary of Translation Studies*. Manchester and Kinderhook, NY: St. Jerome.

Sijs, Nicoline van der (2005): *Groot Leenwoordenboek*. Utrecht and Antwerpen: Van Dale Lexicografie.

Sijs, Nicoline van der (2001): *Chronologisch woordenboek. De ouderdom en herkomst van onze woorden en betekenissen*. Amsterdam and Antwerpen: Veen.

TSL 1987–1991 = *Tijdschrift voor Slavische Literatuur* 1 (1987), 92–94; 4 (1989), 83–85; 9 (1991), 73–77; 11 (1991), 72–78.

Vermeer, Hans (1989): "Skopos and commission in translational action." In: Venuti, Lawrence [ed.] (2000): *The Translation Studies Reader*. London and New York: Routledge. 221–232.

Venuti, Lawrence (1995): *The Translator's Invisibility. A history of translation*. London and New York: Routledge.

Vinay, Jean-Paul / Darbelnet, Jean (1958/1995): "A methodology for translation". In: Venuti, Lawrence [ed.] (2000): *The Translation Studies Reader*. London and New York: Routledge. 84–93.

Waegemans, Emmanuel / Willemsen, Cees (1991): *Bibliografie van Russische literatuur in Nederlandse vertaling*. Leuven: Universitaire Pers.

Yang, Jian (2009): "Chinese borrowings in English." In: *World Englishes* 28 (1), 90–106.

Intertextuality and Historiography: The New World Popularized, or the Encyclopaedic Language of Historical Discourse

Marieke Delahaye
HUBrussel, Brussels and CETRA/KULeuven, Belgium

Abstract

This article examines the tracks left by translation – and by the intertextual web that has been woven through the last 500 years – in the popularised discourse on the "discovery" and "conquest" of the "New World" by the Spaniards, as they appear in several current European encyclopaedias: the (English) *Encyclopaedia Britannica*, the (French) *Universalis* and the (Dutch) *Winkler Prins*. A limited corpus of encyclopaedia articles on the topic will be examined by means of descriptive analysis (Toury 1980, Lambert & Van Gorp 1985), in order to discover (i) the hybrid character of historiographical discourse on this particular topic in encyclopaedia texts in each of the languages mentioned, (ii) the world views conveyed by the encyclopaedia articles in question and their eventual allegiance to a sort of nationalistic selection and/or presentation of the topic, and (iii) the role played by language and translation in this process, or the techniques used to reduce multilingual and multicultural materials into a quasi monolingual environment. This paper is part of a larger, doctoral project on the role of language/languages and translation in the (West-)European tradition of Spanish-American historiography.

1 Introduction

While scientific research in our modern global communities is carried out increasingly in a "monolingualized", or even, in an "anglicized" way, particular disciplines such as historiography happen to depend up to a large extent on language/languages as the main raw material for their research; for this reason, they try to work with a very precise system of references to a "heterolingual" corpus of historical and historiographical texts. This discourse, or continuous "re-writing" of the (historical and historiographical) texts must necessarily take into account source texts or "intertexts" (Venuti 2009: 157) from several cultures and different languages, and the apparently monolingual nature of many historiographical texts will not surprisingly contain both overt and hidden reminiscences to translated discourse.

Contrary to what we might think, cut and paste techniques are not the privilege of electronic word processing. The procedure is as old as language itself, since language can only develop in dialogue, through reproduction and imitation of fragments of utterances, either in the same form or in new contexts. The analysis of this phenomenon, reflected in the concept of intertextuality, originates in the polyphonic literary theory of Mikhail Bakhtin (1981; 1986) who highlighted the heterogloss nature of literary texts as complex networks of different voices resulting of an ongoing dialogue between own ideas and (past and present) utterances of others. He also points to the presence of polyglossia in literature, or the interaction of several languages in one text. The concept was developed by Kristeva (1966; 1984) who subsequently coined the concept with the term *intertextuality*. Perhaps the most apparent manifestation of intertextuality is the quotation – literal or not – which refers directly to another text, author or "voice", just like translation can be when it is open, not hidden. The notion has further been developed through different approaches; see for instance Compagnon (1979: 27) who considers the quote not as a product but as the key concept or paradigm of writing, meaning by this a creative and constructive concept that he labels "travail productif" or productive work. Genette (1982) uses the metaphor of the palimpsest, or the superposition of a hypertext to a hypotext in one and the same manuscript by which both texts permeate mutually and end up as one plurivocal text. According to Meylaerts (2006: 86) "heteroglossia or literary language plurality is the presence in the text of foreign idioms or social, regional, historical...varieties". Venuti (2009: 162) comments on the relation between intertextuality and translation, especially stressing the idea that "translation is radically transformative. The foreign text is not only decontextualized, but *re*contextualized insofar as translating rewrites it in terms that are intelligible and interesting to receptors, situating it in different patterns of language use, in different culture values, in different literary traditions, in different social institutions, and often in a different historical moment". Tymoczko (1999: 41–42) states that "Every writing is a rewriting" and that "an exploration of the working of retellings or rewritings, of the characteristics and properties of retellings and rewritings, offers potential insight for all levels of literary inquiry". But there is no need of limiting the study of translation to the classical one-to-one comparative analysis, nor to the canonized literary translations. According to Lambert (2006: 88), "We are totally wrong in reducing translations to complete and well identified texts, produced by individual writers and individual translators. Their impact is often much deeper and stronger in the case of text fragments, isolated words and colloquial expressions which penetrate our discourse and replace the so-called normal and original discourse". In this perspective, we propose the study of some (intertextual) tracks left by translation in current encyclopaedic discourse on the "discovery" and "conquest" of the "New World" by Spain, as they appear in several current European encyclopaedias: the (English) *Encyclopaedia Britannica*, the (French) *Universalis* and the (Dutch) *Winkler Prins*.

Encyclopaedias aim at surveying the existing knowledge at a given moment in time and produce meaning on the basis of both external factors such as their social position and prestige, their audience and possible influence, and internal factors like the organization of the discourse, the presence or absence of certain concepts, the reference system, the relationship to the authors and sources, particular didactic intentions, etc. Each encyclopaedia – and usually any of its revised editions – determines thus its cultural program that leads to its own ever changing worldview. In principle, such "storages of knowledge" are closely connected to scientific research, although scholars tend to see them as vulgarizations of existing research. Besides, some encyclopaedias have stronger connections with leading research than others. Encyclopaedia usually report on research conducted by others, consequently, they are reports of specialist-written reports; hence the rather reluctant attitude of some scholars towards research involving encyclopaedias. Yet one must recognize that encyclopaedias (1) still reflect views of researchers, and (2) as such deserve to be used as barometers of the state of research at a given moment in time. We can thus examine encyclopaedias from a historiographical angle, considering that because of their specific historical and social position they reflect a world of assumptions and beliefs. Now, high-level research does exactly this, but needs to test explicitly its assumptions and beliefs with the human resources available at a given moment. The historical investigator however behaves as a cynical witness of research, placing the paraphrases and quotes from specialists in a new framework: encyclopaedias and research are thus considered as barometers of the intellectual world.

Seen from this angle, encyclopaedias and research from the past can best be tested with well-targeted questions. In the era of globalization, any researcher can wonder about the type of world view used by former investigators to develop their research questions. In this context, the so called "discovery" of the "New World" by Christopher Columbus seems to be a nice challenge: hence let's examine this "New World" of ancient times from a particular perspective.

What kind of world view(s) emerges from the discourse on the discovery and conquest of (Latin) America by the Spaniards in several West-European encyclopaedias? What models are selected? The discovery of the "New World" has long been treated as a culture shock by many researchers (see Greenblatt 1991; Gruzinski 1999; Cheyfitz 1991; O'Gorman 1958/2006 and others). Therefore, it seems appropriate to address these intercultural issues afresh, e.g. from the linguistic angle: what is or was the role of language(s)/translation in the construction of world views? The multilingual nature of the discovery of a new continent often seems evident to former researchers, but the way of code switching from language 1 to language 2 (or even languages 3 and 4) remains rather obscure while it is supposed to have taken place in a systematic way. Translation must have been an everyday activity and multilingualism the norm for many individuals. But the relative silence on this phenomenon brings us to assume *ab initio* that the chroniclers from our multilingual colonial past believed there was hardly a language problem in this new world of language mixing. Such assumptions may be typical for contemporary business people and for our modern politicians, who avoid mentioning their translators and interpreters. But is Babel really a product of western civilisation?

The analysis of the use of citations in current, scientific work on the subject (Delahaye, forthcoming) shows that the intertextual relationship between these texts and the canonical works from the 16th and 17th centuries is characterized by a number of (usually) language-related problems, such as: so called improvements of oral style and/or of texts considered as primitive or infantile, ways of (not) referring to the language of the canonical text, omissions and the corresponding conventions used to indicate or hide them, modes of quotation leading to manipulations of the quotes, decontextualizations by which quotes are merged into a new co-text and changes of style according to the communication with a specific reader; the term "audience design" as coined by Bell in 1984 and applied to media text design by Holland (2006: 231) could by extension describe some of the selections and re-arrangements that take place in this context, due to the apparently dissimulative character of certain manipulations. These findings show that, despite the great care with which philologists and other scholars treat the primary texts, the reconstruction of the American past remains a precarious and very complex undertaking, and that our actual and factual knowledge of the "New World" through historiography is not self-evident, certainly not in the area of verbal, hence mainly oral communication.

2 Material under investigation

The present study now examines the encyclopaedic discourse popularized for a broader audience and its approach to the authoritative texts as compared to scientific texts for the specialist reader; it tries to determine which models are used in order to construct an image (and which one?) of the "New World". For this purpose, several articles about topics related to the discovery and conquest of America have been examined in three classical encyclopaedias from different language traditions: the *Encyclopaedia Britannica* in its paper supported 2005 edition; the French *Encyclopédie Universalis* in its 5th version on electronic support (CD-ROM, 2002) and the Dutch *Winkler Prins* on electronic support (the CD-ROM was commercialized in 1997 in collaboration with Microsoft's Encarta). All three encyclopaedias offer now also DVD's and online services.

2.1 The *Encyclopaedia Britannica*[1] *(E.B.)*

The 15th edition of the *E.B.* (1974–2005) breaks with the concept of the former editions (from 1/68 on), stating that "an encyclopaedia should not be merely a 'storehouse of facts', but 'a systematic survey of all departments of knowledge'". Its "truly topical and totally nonalphabetical Table of Contents" must give an answer to the defects of the alphabetically organised articles in earlier editions and enables the reader to "make a complete study of a given topic – that is a department of knowledge or field of learning". It has two modes of access: the "Outline of

---

[1] For a brief history of printed encyclopaedias in general, and for the *Britannica* in particular, see Elia 2007: 10–12 and 12–14 respectively.

Knowledge", arranged as a "Circle of learning" (without beginning or end) according to subjects and composed by a team of specialists ("working authorities in the fields of knowledge to be covered, rather than [by] editors"), and the "Index", the "Micropaedia" (with shorter articles) and the "Macropaedia" (with longer ones) in alphabetical order. The "Propaedia" helps the reader to know what he can learn from the *Britannica* concerning one or another area of knowledge, and "was constructed [...] as a table of intents rather than of contents" (*E.B.* 15th ed., Propaedia, pp. 5–8). But even in this circular, never-ending system, the reality or "truth" is in the eye of the beholder; the authors select the topics that "deserve" being treated in the *E.B.*, the sources they use, the length of each article, the suggestions for further reading.

2.2 The (French) *Encyclopédie Universalis*, 2002 (*Universalis*)

The 2002 edition under examination is the 5th one of an encyclopaedia that was first published as late as 1975. It refers to the tradition of Chambers' *Cyclopaedia* (1728) and Diderot and d'Alembert's Grande *Encyclopédie* (1766), but is not intended to function as a return to the past. It claims to be the only real encyclopaedia in the French-speaking community, covering the totality of knowledge at a given moment in time without being exhaustive, and distinguishing itself hereby from the Larousse as a mere "dictionnaire encyclopédique". The *Universalis* states that its entries are chosen by an internal team of experienced publishers, assisted by scientific advisers for each domain. This is obviously a first filter that structures the vision of culture and knowledge at a given moment in time. No doubt that the analysis of its discourse on a particular topic might provide us with fascinating insights in the mobility and complexity of world views.

2.3 The (Dutch) *Winkler Prins*, 1997 (*WP*)

The *Winkler Prins* (the *WP*) is the most authoritative encyclopaedia of the Dutch language. It first appeared in 1870 and was largely written according to the model of the German *Brockhaus* encyclopaedia, that is, like an encyclopaedic dictionary with shorter articles. The *WP* thereby created the encyclopaedic culture in the Low Countries along an internationally recognized model (see also the *Larousse* in France, a "dictionnaire encyclopédique"), as an aggregate of quotations not necessarily fed by only one foreign tradition. For it is quite remarkable that the *WP*, the *Brockhaus*, the *Larousse*, etc., although covering world views and world representations, appear to account for different national traditions. The South American history of the German (French, Spanish, English,) society could possibly bear its own color or banner, and we must keep in mind that the Netherlands also have a colonial past.

The 20th Century has obviously thought about the encyclopaedic challenges. The positivist inspiration of the new structure by the *Grande Encyclopédie* or by *Brockhaus* – for instance – thus generated the expectation that the entire knowledge of a civilization at a particular moment in time, and maybe even all knowledge ever could be covered. Bourdieu (1971: 71) notes that

> [...] le champ des instances de reproduction et de conservation [...] est investi du pouvoir délégué de sauvegarder une orthodoxie culturelle, c'est-à-dire de défendre la sphère de la culture légitime contre les messages concurrents, schismatiques ou hérétiques.
>
> ('the field of reproductive and conservative bodies [and certainly the encyclopaedia, M.D.] is invested with the delegated authority to safeguard a cultural orthodoxy, i.e. to defend the sphere of the legitimate culture against the competing schismatic or heretic messages.')

This idea, namely that an encyclopaedia can give a comprehensive and legitimate vision of the world by means of a structured and organized discourse, is found in each of the encyclopaedias under examination: "a systematic survey of all departments of knowledge" (*E.B.* 2005), "la totalité du savoir [...] sans être exhaustif" ('the totality of knowledge... without being exhaustive') (*Universalis* 2002), and "betrouwbare informatie over bijna alles" ('reliable information on almost everything') (*WP* 1997). Furthermore, all three encyclopaedias aim specifically at the formal education environment as a privileged user (see their respective websites). On the role of education, Bourdieu (1998: 245) observes that

> à travers la délimitation entre ce qui mérite d'être transmis et acquis et ce qui ne le mérite pas, elle [l'école, M.D.] reproduit continûment la distinction entre les œuvres consacrées et les œuvres illégitimes.
>
> ('through the delimitation of what deserves to be transmitted and acquired and what does not, it [the school, M.D.] continuously reproduces the distinction between consecrated and illegitimate works'.)

In the light of this statement and taking into account the self-declared relationship between the encyclopaedias and formal education, we can assume that the encyclopaedias will limit what they call "the totality of knowledge or information", and determine what is worth knowing and what is not. In this sense, they appear as a strong instrument of "interpellation" in Althusser's terms (Robinson 1997: 22–24): their discourse represents the current opinion/ideology of the establishment of Western society and contributes to mould the cultural identity of its users.

3 Methodology

A good method for the investigation of encyclopaedia discourse on the discovery and conquest of America, and of the use of language, translation and source citations, is not immediately obvious. On the one hand, it doesn't seem appropriate to start the examination with a fixed list of entries, for this could steer the research in a specific direction, imposing the mindset of the researcher upon the encyclopaedia and possibly leading to overlook some interesting material. On the other hand, the circular structure of cross-references in the examined encyclopaedias drives the user almost imperceptibly through various options and possibilities such as "related articles", "more options" (including maps and websites), hyperlinks inside articles, multimedia areas and related information on the internet, or shorter and larger articles and cross-references in between articles. Therefore, the investigation has been carried out on the basis of a combined approach, in which a limited number of predefined entries (16)[2] have been followed along some possible routes, just like any user of the encyclopaedia certainly would do. These repeated cross-readings of a subject however have been systematized in the digital versions (*Universalis* and *WP*) in order to ensure that the results of the research would not be based on coincidence. As for the (paper-supported) *E.B.* 2005, the cross-reading has not been carried out as thoroughly as in the former two encyclopaedias since the manipulation of several volumes and different modes of access is much slower and lacks the agility of the digital versions.

According to Elia (2007: 18–21), encyclopaedic discourse (and many other kinds of informative texts) is written in a "formal expository style" which is characterized by "clarity, formality, objectivity and impersonality". Encyclopaedic discourse will thus be marked by "stylistic formality" to avoid ambiguity, by "exactness and accuracy" to avoid fuzziness, it will "decontextualize" and thus be low in deictic references to

---

[2] The approximately 16 lemmas used as starting points were (sometimes in different forms/languages): America, Aztec, chronicle, Columbus, conquista(dor), discovery, Hispaniola, history, historiography, Inca, Indies, Indian, Maya, Spain, World (New).

the physic spatiotemporal settings, and the distance of the time and special setting between sender and receiver will determine the amount of shared context. Or as Venuti (2009: 161) puts it "[w]hen the foreign intertext involves a translation into the foreign language, as is often the case, the problem of decontextualization is exacerbated". Now let's consider on this basis some passages in all three encyclopaedias under investigation.

4 *In medias res*: the encyclopaedic discourse on the "Crónicas de Indias"

4.1 The *E.B.* 2005

Unlike earlier editions, the policy of "monolingualization" is an explicit language strategy of the *E.B.* 2005, as established in the Preface to the Propaedia (p. xvii):

> Britannica authors and editors have been at pains to limit the use of non-English words and phrases and to provide translations or paraphrases of such wherever their use has been unavoidable [...].
>
> [P]lace names and personal names [are rendered] as recommended by the boards of geographic place names in the U.S. and the U.K.

Does this mean that all possibly problematic language issues of former editions have been overcome, at least in relation to our subject? Under the heading "international orientation", the Preface states (p. xiv) that

> articles on subjects spread across the whole of the broad spectrum of knowledge have been assigned to experts, without regard to their place of origin, of residence, or of occupation.

This means that contributions by non-native English scholars must have been revised by "editors" and provided with "translations and paraphrases". With respect to contents, the Preface states (p. xiv) that

> an encyclopaedia is nothing at all if it is not a summary statement of the traditional knowledge of the culture that has produced it.

In other words, the *E.B.* 2005 is a self-declared conservative and authoritative survey of the English-speaking culture and insights on any subject. As to its intended audience,

> all readers of the *Britannica* might be specialists – or have the interest of specialists – in some area of knowledge, [but] they will turn to a general encyclopaedia only as generalists interested in fields outside their own (p. xiii).

In the light of the above mentioned policy, the narrative in the E.B. 2005 and its frequent use of indirect style is a model of overt intertextual processing of discourse that can be compared with the techniques used by Greenblatt (among others) in his *Marvellous Possessions* (1991). This is the case for instance in the paragraph (Micropaedia, p. 609) on the long letter Columbus wrote in 1500 to his sovereigns when he was brought back in chains. After a description of the tone and contents of the letter, and conjectures about the possible reasons for it, the text switches to the indirect style by means of the connector "*Thus*, ...", the change of personal pronouns in "the rotation of the Pole Star gave *him*", verbs of speech in "*he wrote*", the mention of the speakers' name "Columbus" and the use of the third person and the past tense in "had found... and indeed they were widely known".[3] This technique apparently confronts the reader with the very words of Columbus, although this may be just an impression, for the text is entirely written in English; no quotation marks are used, no source references are given besides a rather vague introductory phrase ("The long letter Columbus composed on the journey back and sent to his sovereigns immediately on his return...") and the end of the indirect style quotation is not immediately recognizable. The style of this fragment clearly does not correspond to the "formal expository style", characteristic of an informative text as described by Elia, but is rather a mixture of indirect and indirect free style; who tells what about the episode is not really evident.

The spelling of proper names – and toponyms being often proper names – is a very sensitive item when it comes to detecting the (hybrid) source of a text. Tymoczko (1999: 223) notes that "[t]hey are dense signifiers, signs of essential structures of human societies". In the E.B. 2005, and in spite of its "anglicizing" policy, the

---

[3] "*Thus*, as he approached Trinidad and the Paria Peninsula, the rotation of the Pole Star gave *him*, *he wrote*, the impression that the fleet was climbing. The weather had become extremely mild, and the flow of fresh water into the Gulf of Paria was, *as he saw*, enormous. All this *could* have one explanation only – *they had* mounted toward the temperate heights of the Earthly Paradise, heights from which the rivers from Paradise *ran* into the sea. *Columbus had* found all such signs of the outer regions of the Earthly Paradise in *his* reading, *and indeed they were widely known. He was, then, on this estimate, close to the realms of gold that lay near Paradise. He had not found the gold yet, to be sure; but he knew now where it was.* Columbus' expectations thus allowed him again to interpret his discoveries in terms of biblical and classical sources and to do so in a manner that would be comprehensible to his sponsors and favourable to him." (E.B. 2005, Micropaedia, p. 609)

hybrid character of the sources surfaces now and then in the spelling of proper names, the orthography of toponyms and the language used. An example of confusing proper name spelling is the name *Bartholomew* in 4 different transcriptions: "his brother *Bartholomew*" (p. 605), "*Bartolomé* de las Casas" (p. 605, "the Portuguese explorer *Bartolomeu* Dias" (p. 606) and "*Bartolomeo* Fieschi, captains of ...". Other examples are found in the systematic double spelling of Inca names: "Manco Capac (Manqo Qhapaq), Sinchi Roca (Zinchi Roq'a), Lloque Yupanqui (Lloq'e Yupanki), or in the double orthography of toponyms – i.e. "Veragua (Veraguas)" (p. 605 of the Micropaedia, s.v. *Columbus*), the first being the oldest form (see the fourth Columbian voyage), the latter being a nineteenth century competing form, while only the oldest spelling is used in the rest of the article (pp. 609 and 610). On this subject, Tymoczko (1999: 225) states that "when the information load in a translation is high because of the importation of many names with an unfamiliar foreign phonology and/or orthography, these aspects of naming – recognizability and memorability – become compromised: it becomes hard for the receptor audience to 'keep the names straight' in literary works and historical materials alike".

The language used to quote titles of early texts – examples of which can be found p. 605 in the Micropaedia under the entry "Columbus", in a discussion on the "major written sources" – is also hybrid in nature, as for example in: "Ferdinand Columbus' *The Life of the Admiral Christopher Columbus*, the *Historia de los Reyes Católicos* (c. 1500) of Andrés Bernáldez [...] and the *Historia de las Indias* [...] by Bartolomé de las Casas". While the first title is quoted in English, the second and the third ones appear in Spanish, while both had been published in English translation before 2005.

Furthermore, it must be observed that the text on Pre-Columbian Civilizations (Macropaedia 26, p. 36) discusses "the nature of the sources" and takes into account different semiotic modes of remembrance, not only text, but also quipus and drawings, i.e. "the study of [Francisco] Cusichaq's quipu" by which he "kept records of Spanish exactions" in a "both quantitative and historical dimension", or the "400 pages of pen-and-ink drawings" that Guamán Poma de Ayala added to his "Nueva Corónica y Buen Gobierno". This gives a new dimension to the "translation" and "interpretation" of sources of information.

With regard to the representation of the indigenous people, the *E.B.* 2005 dissociates itself from the 1875 one. Taking the discourse on the Inca civilisation as an example (Macropaedia 26: p. 35: 2b till p. 44), we do not find moral judgements on the character of the Indians, as was the case before. However, typical West-European concepts continue to appear in the description of indigenous features such as *kingdom* or *emperor*, and Inca concepts are treated in different ways, being mentioned now in Quechua with an accompanying explanation in English – "The *ayllu*, a basic social unit identified with communally held land", or "propitiatory cairns (*apacheta*, 'piles of stones')" – then in English marked by capitals to indicate the foreign (and thus translated) character of the concept (*Chosen Women*, or *Sun Temple*). This heterogeneous treatment of indigenous characteristics, in which translation and non translation alternate for the presentation of indigenous terms, is repeated in the bibliography on the Inca, where Spanish chroniclers appear in English editions while the Inca chronicler Guamán Poma de Ayala is mentioned in Spanish ("trans. from Quechua"; in reality, the text is written in Spanish with parts in Quechua). The 19th-century *Volksgeist* has definitely disappeared, while postcolonial interest in the "vision of the conquered" shows on almost every page. Finally, the texts on Pre-Columbian civilisation are interlarded with references to vague sources such as "wrote a chronicler" or "was described by a chronicler", with epistemic modal adverbs such as "probably" and "presumably", and with conjectures on what might have been: "they might have placed some pressure on..."; "the problem would have been..."; "they, too, may have been feeling the effects..;" (Macropaedia 26, p. 37).

Obviously, the "formal expository style" is not prevailing in these articles. Narrative techniques such as indirect and indirect free style do not reify the spatial and temporal distant topic; on the contrary, it novelizes history and obscures the clarity of who tells what about what topic. The hybrid reproduction of proper names, toponyms and text titles, the semiotic variety of the sources mentioned, the confusing treatment of indigenous material, the reference to unidentified sources and the use of epistemic modal adverbs are just as many strategies that counteract the self declared policy of monolingualization. But then, "discourses are by definition never completely monolingual" (Meylaerts 2006: 86).

4.2 Encyclopédie Universalis, 2002

The *Universalis* 2002 is announced as "la plus grande encyclopédie de langue Française [...] pour un public non spécialisé" ('the largest encyclopaedia in French for a non specialized pubic'). In contrast with the *E.B.* 2005, no overt language policy is announced here. The introductory text to the reader makes no allusion to any language issues, not even in relation with subjects from other cultural spheres. It only mentions that the *Universalis* "est le seul ouvrage en langue française à pouvoir justifier aujourd'hui pleinement ce titre" ('is the only work in French that fully can justify its title').

Nevertheless, quotations appear systematically in French, even when the bibliography mentions source texts in several languages (mostly French, English and Spanish). The system of cross-references in the electronic *Universalis* 2002 often leads the reader to a related article, in which the same quotation is rendered in a different (also French) form, proving hereby that translation of quotations is not always an issue. An example is found in the words allegedly written by Columbus in the margin of the *Imago Mundi* by Pierre d'Ailly: in the article on "Amérique, découverte" ('America, discovery'), we read:

> La fin des terres habitées vers l'Occident est assez proche de la fin des terres habitées vers l'Orient, et au milieu il y a une petite mer
>
> ('The end of the inhabited lands to the West is quite close to the end of the inhabited land towards the East, and in the middle there is a small sea')

while in the article on "Christophe Colomb" we find:

> entre la fin de l'Orient et la fin de l'Occident il n'y a qu'une petite mer
>
> ('between the end of the East and the end of the West there is but a small sea')

As in the *E.B.* 2005, some articles use a model of overt intertextual processing of discourse with frequent use of indirect style, i.e. on Columbus:

> Il admirera la simplicité de leurs mœurs, leur libéralité, leur confiance, qui les disposaient, pensait-il, à 'devenir chrétiens'.
>
> ('He will admire the simplicity of their manners, their generosity, their confidence, which prepared them, he thought, to 'become Christians'.')

Or, to quote but one more intertwined example,

> Le jeune humaniste Pierre Martyr d'Anghiera [...] écrivit : 'Colomb vient de découvrir un nouvel hémisphère de la Terre par les Antipodes occidentales.' Cependant, pas plus que le découvreur lui-même, il ne pensait que cet hémisphère fût séparé de l'Asie : on retrouvait

seulement une partie du monde 'Bien connue des Anciens', comme le dit Colomb lui-même. (s.v. "Amérique, Découverte")

('The Young humanist Peter Martyr d'Anghiera [...] wrote: 'Columbus has discovered a new hemisphere of the Earth by the Western Antipodes'. However, just as the discoverer himself, he thought that this hemisphere was not separated from Asia: there was only a part of the world 'Well known to the classics', as stated Columbus himself.')

The transcription of proper names is not always consistent. While most Spanish names are rendered in their Spanish orthography, Columbus appears in the French version as "Christophe Colomb", while his son is mentioned in the same paragraph as "Fernando Colombo", the Italian form of the name (certainly, the *Raccolta Colombiana*, 1892–1896 figures in the bibliography). Another example is the transcription of Magellan as "Magellan" under the lemma "les découvreurs", but as "Pedro de Magalhães de Gadalvo" under the lemma "Portugais et Français au Brésil". Even if these examples do not lead the reader to great confusion, we must recognize that the "recognizability and memorability" (Tymoczko 1999: idem) get compromised.

With respect to content, it is not always clear how selections have been operated. In the article on the Spanish chroniclers ("les chroniqueurs espagnols") for instance, we find – among others – the Milanese Pierre-Martyr d'Anghiera (who wrote in Latin), the Peruvian Inca Guamán Poma de Ayala and the indigenous (Mexican) Hernando de Alvarado Tezozomoc and Fernando de Alva Ixtlilxochitl; obviously, being a citizen of the then Spanish empire, regardless of language and origins, has been the criterion for this category. Another rather striking example of a *sui generis* selection is the omission of Francisco Pizarro, the conqueror of the Incas, in the article on "Les conquistadores". Since this article is part of the lemma on the chronicles of the New World ("chroniques du Nouveau Monde"), the criterion used here has obviously been the authorship of conquistadores. But since the article announces that the scenes of these exploits have been Mexico (conquered by Cortés) and Peru (conquered by Pizarro), the reader is confused when confronted with Pedro de Valdivia, conqueror of Chile, instead of Pizarro, conqueror of "Perou".

Furthermore, the history of the so-called New World is clearly presented from a French perspective: in "chroniques du Nouveau Monde" for instance, there are 4 subdivisions, the first of which, "les découvreurs" ('the discoverers'), surprisingly mentions the French "Paumier de Gonneville" as the first discoverer following

Columbus. Two other subdivisions are about "the French in Canada and in Florida" and "Portuguese and Frenchmen in Brasil". In the fourth subdivision on "les chroniqueurs espagnols", the work of Bartolomé de Las Casas is related with the French Enlightenment and philosophers and authors like Montesquieu and Voltaire, Marmontel and l'abbé Grégoire, the last of whom is quoted as being very positive on Las Casas and claiming his French origins. This selection and interpretation of the material shows a clear "nationalistic French" perspective; in fact, the content corresponding to analogous investigated lemmas is very distant from what we read in the *E.B.* 2005. The factual knowledge corresponding to the "discovery" and "conquest" of America by Spain will be a blue-white-red one for the *Universalis* reader.

Finally, the examination of the discourse on Pre-Columbian civilisation – we again take the Inca as an example – shows that the intermediate language, Spanish, has almost disappeared in favour of Quechua and French. The text systematically mentions Quechua words with their French translation or explanation, the Quechua word sometimes preceding, sometimes following the translation. Only in rare occasions we find tracks of Spanish sources, as for instance in "qui leur valut de la part des Espagnols le surnom d'*orejones* (littéralement 'oreillards')", or "de grandes chasses collectives de *guanacos* ou de cervidés" ('which earned them the nickname 'orejones' (literally 'long-ears') by the Spaniards' or 'great collective guanacos or deer hunts'). As in the *E.B.* 2005, typical West-European concepts such as "l'empereur" ('the emperor'), "prêtres" ('priests'), or "officiants" ('officiants') are used to describe indigenous organisation.

In comparison with the *E.B.* 2005 discourse on the same topic, evidence leads us to conclude that the hybrid nature of the texts is less pronounced in the *Universalis* 2002. Although any mention of pre-established language policy is made, the strategies leading to monolingualization are stronger than in the *Britannica*: quotations appear systematically in French, independently of the sources, proper names of Spaniards don't follow Spanish orthography and the Spanish language as intermediary between the Inca Language/civilisation and the French has almost disappeared. In other words, time has apparently filtered the source texts much more thoroughly in the French tradition than in the English-speaking one. This impression is reinforced when analysing the articles from the viewpoint of their content, since the factual knowledge of the topic under investigation is clearly

"Gallicized". And again, the "formal expository style" is certainly not the general stylistic feature in these historiographical articles.

4.3 *Winkler Prins*, 1997

Dutch translations of the "Crónicas" were rather scarce in the 16th and 17th centuries. Among the early reports that did find their way to Dutch translation was the *Brevísima relación de las Indias* by Bartolomé de Las Casas, a very ideologically coloured text that is seen as one of the main trendsetters of the infamous Black Legend on the alleged perverse, cruel and anti-Christian activities of the Spaniards in the "New World", and as an ideological weapon in the (political and religious) battle of the Low Countries (and their allies) against Spanish rule. A legitimate research question in this context is whether the texts on the discovery and conquest of America in the *WP* are indebted or not to this ideological line, and whether a break is visible between information that can be traced to Las Casas and data from other sources without translation into Dutch.

The digital version of *WP* makes no explicit mention of the sources. It contains no bibliography or source notes with references. When mentioned, both primary and secondary sources appear in the text, for information purposes only, not as a reference to its source material. The references are sometimes very vague, i.e. "volgens de overlevering" ('according to tradition'), an expression that is frequently used without further information and doesn't reveal anything on the underlying canon (written? oral?) but still creates an impression of "auctoritas".

The mention in Spanish of Las Casas' famous work (*Brevísima relación de la Destruyción de las Indias occidentales*) is rather peculiar in view of its many early Dutch translations. Apparently, the Dutch version(s) has not modelled for this article. Furthermore, the text uses almost systematically verbatim formulations between quotation marks, and expressions like "hij beschrijft, benoemt, vermeldt, heeft genoemd" ('he describes, he appoints, he specifies, he has called...') without reference to any source texts, or to a source language, or to the oral/written nature of it. Would it be possible then that this system indicates the use of Dutch models? On the narratological level, some fragments refer vaguely to oral tradition of storytelling, in which the style reminds of 19th century novel and historiography; fiction and non-fiction are here completely intertwined.[4] The reader is literally "transferred" into the 15th century, as if he were part of the "story".

The discourse of the *WP* with respect to the conceptualisation of the New World and its protagonists is rather explicit. In the case of the Spaniards, the hostility of the Low Countries towards their historical "oppressor" is translucent in almost every page. Under the lemma "conquistador" (of "Spaanse veroveraar") for instance, we find a definition that is both a translation ("conquerors/ conquistadores") and a description ("Spanish adventurers and chiefs/Spaanse avonturiers en bevelhebbers"), in which at first it is not clear whether the "chiefs" were also "adventurers". But very soon, no doubt is left about the interpretation of the term: the conquistadores conquered America "not for the king" but "feitelijk voor zichzelf" 'for themselves'. They were thus selfish, not to be trusted, and real fighters. This negative connotation has even remained throughout history, since their descendants kept that name in the following centuries and were openly subversive when, in the 19th century, they rebelled "tegen het Spaanse gezag" ('against Spanish rule'). The same spirit shows in the negative definition of Pizarro, the conqueror of the Inca: "Pizarro is het meest uitgesproken type van de 'conquistador' van die dagen: *ondernemend, koel berekenend en meedogenloos* tegenover de Indianen" ('Pizarro is enterprising, calculating, cold and ruthless against the Indians').

With respect to the conceptualisation of the indigenous peoples, a distinction is made between the Incas ("zachter", 'milder, less cruel') and the Aztecs. The frequent comparisons between these two civilisations in the *WP* are always in

---

[4] "*Vele eeuwen lang hebben de zeelui elkaar het oude verhaal verteld dat* daar waar [...]. *Maar nu, aan het begin van de 15de eeuw, vragen steeds meer mensen zich af of* de oceaan wel beschouwd moet worden als een barrière. *Lijkt de oceaan niet veeleer geschapen om 'Indië' of 'Eldorado' – waar deze gebieden dan ook precies gesitueerd mogen zijn – te bereiken zonder de door de islam beheerste gebieden te moeten doorkruisen? Dat is in ieder geval wel de opvatting van de Portugezen en Spanjaarden* die, gedreven door winstbejag en geloofsijver, op zoek gaan naar nieuw land." ('For many centuries, sailors have told each other the old story of [...]. But now, at the beginning of the 15th century, more and more people wonder if the ocean is to be considered as a barrier. Is it not as if the ocean was rather created to reach 'India' or 'Eldorado' – wherever these areas may be located – without having to traverse the areas controlled by Islam? That is at least the idea of the Portuguese and the Spaniards who, driven by profit and religious zeal, set out to search for new land.')

favour of the Incas. They are often based on the assumption that the reader is familiar with the Inca culture, so it can stand as a model. This idea of the Aztecs as "bad" and the Incas as "good Indians" was widespread until the early 20th century, and thus points back to older sources, perhaps even the *Brockhaus*-text.

The language issue in Latin America is a very complex matter. What solutions are offered by the *WP* to inform the general public about this question? On the one hand, a distinction is made between two types of Spanish, two types of Portuguese: there is "Spanish" and "Spanish (with many borrowings from indigenous languages)", or "Portuguese" and "Portuguese (actually: Brazilian)". On the other hand, there are "indigenous languages", "Indian languages", "Indian Languages" and "non-Spanish language". In other words, there is no uniformity in the names used, but the reader will remember that there is a problem with the Spanish and the Portuguese language in Latin America. Furthermore, the names for indigenous peoples and languages are not univocal. An identical name can refer to a people in one context, and to a language in another one. Incidentally it can be noted that the spelling of native names in the *WP*, (i.e. "Quechua", "Inca", "suyu", "vicoenja" but also "vicuña"), is based on different models: sometimes the Spanish spelling is followed as in "Quechua", not *Kechwa*, sometimes the spelling is phonetic as in "Inka", not *Inca*. In the light of the didactic objectives of encyclopaedias in general and the *WP* in particular, the apparent confusion in the presentation of the language issue in the "New World" must probably be traced back to a multiplicity of sources or intertexts and languages.

The hybrid nature of the present discourse is very high, even in comparison with the *E.B.* 2005 or the *Universalis 2002*. Evidence can be found in the following marvellous collection of hidden translations, both at the level of vocabulary and that of text structure. Different indigenous terms sometimes get a single translation in Dutch ("Coricancha" and "Inticancha"), some definitions are rather incomprehensible due to the distance between cultures and languages, such as "Pachacuti means: Reformer of the country or of the time", in which the words are translated, but not the meaning of the term. Some terms are listed with a kind of epithet without clear meaning in Dutch, as "Sacsahuamán, the 'imperial hawk'". There are different translations for the same phrasing ("reducciones" are sometimes defined as "large villages", then as "Jesuit Missions"). Some terms refer to West-European categories while being used to describe indigenous cultures ("the magistracy", "democratic"). The absence of a clear system may indicate a fragmented use of a variety of sources in different languages and from different epochs. Text structure and wording also can be due to hidden translations, as in "de *vermoording* van De Almagro", a non existing nominalization of the verb *vermoorden* 'to assassinate', or as in the inexistent noun *deemoediging* (for 'deemoed' or 'humility'). In this last case, even the vocabulary and the phrasing of the target language is hybridized according to ungrammatical interventions.

The evidence seems to suggest that the *WP* discourse on the subject examined is probably based to a large extent on several intermediary intertexts and languages. The emerging ideological viewpoint leads us back to the historical, 16th and 17th century political conflict between Spain and the Low Countries, and to the image of the enemy as presented in the famous Black Legend. Even the articles on the indigenous peoples of America are imbued with moral judgements on "good" and "bad" Indians. With regard to the style of the articles, it is certainly not a formal one; on the contrary, some formulations are direct reminiscences to 19th century romantic novel language.

5 Conclusion

The examination of encyclopaedia discourse on the discovery and conquest of America by the Spaniards shows that interpretations and worldviews differ between (West-European) languages and cultures, at least on the level of popularized discourse. Filters have been different over time; intentions have not always been identical. The juxtaposition of English, French and Dutch encyclopaedias enables us to see the impact of language issues on the very nature of the "events" that are told, each from its own perspective.

All three encyclopaedias show a range of heterogeneous "voices" while informing their readers on the "discovery" and "conquest" of the "New World". Intertextuality is apparent in every single article. Some procedures are common to the three discourses, as we could expect: the struggle with the transcription of proper names, toponyms and text titles; the hybrid description/explanation of indigenous cultures, the difficult relation to the sources.

On the contrary, we didn't expect the rather frequent use of indirect and of indirect free style, nor the use of narrative techniques proper of novel writing and the vague references to unidentified or obscure "speakers". According to Elia (2007: 18–21), clarity is very important in informative writing since "readers may have no prior knowledge or former understanding of the topic"; a strong organization is thus needed, through a precise structure. On this basis, it is difficult to qualify the articles under analysis undoubtedly as "informative" texts. They do not generally speaking respond to the requirements of "stylistic formality" because they don't systematically avoid ambiguity. They do mostly meet the demand for decontextualization, except in some cases (see the *WP* and its transference of the reader into the 15th century). The criteria of "exactness" and "accuracy" are often not met since "fuzziness is" not "avoided using precise and unequivocal expressions" as is the case in the three encyclopaedias with respect to factual knowledge such as names, places, titles and even the use of ungrammatical expressions in the target language. And they are unequally meeting the last criterion, "space, time and audience", where Elia states that "the less will remain of the original context in which the discourse has been produced, the more an explicit, precise and context independent textual production will be needed". These variables identified as influencing the formality and comprehensibility of encyclopaedic texts, are often lacking in the articles under investigation.

But can we really deduce from the present analysis who tells what about which topic? Can heterogeneous transcriptions of proper names, of toponyms and of titles illuminate us on the sources used for the texts? Can hybrid orthography be a reliable indication of the intertextual tracks followed by the (written) text? Can marks of hidden translation reveal the models that eventually have been used by modern historiography? We must of course be cautious in affirming this, certainly in the scope of an article. If each feature in particular cannot be an evidence of filiation to (a) specific source(s), the sum of observations may well prove to be a reliable indication of the sources that modelled the hybrid texts.

Now when it comes to the gist of the representation of the topic, the ideological grounds on which the factual knowledge is put forward, we must conclude that we are confronted with three different "stories": while the French *Universalis* follows clearly the nationalistic views in the selection of the topics presented (conquerors, places, source texts), the *Britannica* gives a clearly more postcolonial viewpoint, for instance in its treatment of indigenous culture, even when using western categories to describe foreign culture. The explicit "monolingualization" policy of the *Britannica* could be seen in the light of globalization; it is not clear however from its introduction nor from our analysis if the intended audience is broader than the national scope. As for the *WP*, the viewpoint is a rather scattered one, with on the one hand reminiscences to the 19th century romantic storytelling but on the other one a clear reference to the obsolete historical hatred of the Low Countries against Spain. In short, each encyclopaedia presents its own and *sui generis* narrative of the discovery and conquest of America by the Spaniards, selecting its own highlights, its own favourite sources and passages, and does so with the confidence according to its status as authoritative and didactical source for non specialists. Hence the divergent view of an Englishman, a Frenchman or a Dutchman on the same topics.

It is also striking how kind of a negative consensus seems to support the entire international tradition, notwithstanding the indications about particular national(istic) world views. There is no break between our contemporary experts and their sources (who in fact function as a complex network of selected models): history and historiography seem not be depending neither on languages nor on discourses, not even when they refer to populations that are – on the one hand – familiar with writing and printing, or – on the other hand – fully unfamiliar with it. And there are no indications about any scrupulous awareness of the situation of the storyteller, not even among the contemporaries of the "stream of consciousness". After all, when simulating their historiographical discourse, one might say that the Western doubts about understanding the discourse of other continents, languages, rhetoric and other conventions deserves to be called "candide", in Voltaire's style. There may have been doubts and problems, but not in the area of language and/or discourse.

References

A. Encyclopaedias

Encarta® – *Encyclopedie* © 1993–2002 Microsoft Corporation/Het Spectrum, CD-Rom.
Encyclopaedia Britannica or a Dictionary of Arts and sciences. 1st edition, Edinburgh, Scotland, 1768–1771.
Encyclopaedia Britannica. 9th edition, 1875 ("the scholar's edition").

Encyclopaedia Britannica. 15th edition, 2005.
Encyclopaedia Universalis 2006. Version 11, 2005, logiciel.
Encyclopedia Britannica. http://www.info.eb.com/html/product_online_school_edition.html. Visited August 2009.
Encyclopédie Universalis. http://www.universalis.fr/societe.php. Visited August 2009.
Winkler Prins. http://www.winklerprins.com/info/. Visited December 2010.

B. Secondary sources

Bakhtin, Michael (1981): "Discourse in the Novel." In: Bakhtin, Michael: *The Dialogical Imagination: Four Essays*. Ed. by M. Holquist, transl. by Caryl Emerson and Michael Holquist. Austin: University of Texas Press. 259–422.

––––– (1986): "The Problem of Speech Genres." In: Bakhtin, Michael: *Speech Genres and Other Late Essays*. Ed. by Caryl Emerson and Michael Holquist, transl. by Vern W. McGee. Austin: University of Texas Press. 60–101.

Bell, Allan (1984): "Language Style as Audience Design." In: *Language in Society* 13:2, 145–204.

Bourdieu, Pierre (1971): "Le marché des biens symboliques." In: *L'Année Sociologique* 22, 49–126.

Bourdieu, Pierre (1998): *Les règles de l'art. Genèse et structure du champ littéraire*. Paris: Seuil.

Cheyfitz, Eric (1991): *The Poetics of Imperialism, Translation and Colonization from The Tempest to Tarzan*. London: Oxford University Press.

Compagnon, Antoine (1979): *La Seconde Main, ou le Travail de la Citation*. Paris: Seuil.

Delahaye, Marieke (forthcoming): "Intertextualidad e Historiografía. Las Citas Célebres de las Crónicas de Indias, o el discurso del discurso histórico." In: *Canadian Revue of Comparative Literature/Revue Canadienne de Littérature Comparée*. Edmonton: University of Alberta.

Elia, Antonella (2007): *"Cogitamus ergo sumus". Web 2.0 Encyclopaedi@s: the case of Wikipedia, A Corpus Based Study*. Tesi di Dottorado, Università degli studi di Napoli "Federico II" at http://www.fedoa.unina.it/1818/1/Elia_Lingua_Inglese.pdf. Visited December 2010.

Genette, Gérard (1982): *Palimpsestes. La Littérature au Second Degré*. Paris: Seuil.

Greenblatt, Stephen (1991): *Marvelous Possessions. The Wonder of the New World*. Oxford: Clarendon Press.

Gruzinski, Serge (1999): *La pensée métisse*. Paris: Fayard.

Holland, Robert (2006): "Language(s) in the global news. Translation, audience design and discourse (mis)interpretation." In: *Target* 18:2, 229–259.

Kristeva, Julia (1966): "Word, Dialogue and Novel." In: Roudiez, Leon S. [ed.]: *Desire in Language: A Semiotic Approach to Literature and Art*. Transl. by Thomas Gora, Alice Jardine and Leon S. Roudiez. New York: Columbia University Press. 64–91.

––––– (1984): *Revolution in Poetic Language*. Transl. by Margaret Waller. New York: Columbia University Press.

Lambert, José (2006): *Functional Approaches to Culture and Translation. Selected Papers by José Lambert*. Ed. by Dirk Delabastita, Lieven D'hulst and Reine Meylaerts. Amsterdam and Philadelphia: John Benjamins.

Lambert, José / Van Gorp, Hendrik (1985): "On describing translations." In: Lambert, José: *Functional Approaches to Culture and Translation. Selected papers by José Lambert*. Ed. by Dirk Delabastita, Lieven D'hulst and Reine Meylaerts. Amsterdam and Philadelphia: John Benjamins. 37–47.

Meylaerts, Reine (2006): "Literary heteroglossia in translation." In: Ferreira Duarte, João / Assis Rosa, Alexandra / Seruya, Teresa [eds.]: *Translation Studies at the Interface of Disciplines*. Amsterdam and Philadelphia: John Benjamins. 85–98.

O'Gorman, Edmundo (1958/2006): *La invención de América. Investigación acerca de la estructura histórica del Nuevo Mundo y del sentido de su devenir*. México: Fondo de Cultura Económica. Biblioteca Universitaria de Bolsillo.

Robinson, Douglas (1997): *Translation and Empire. Postcolonial Theories Explained*. Manchester: St. Jerome.

Toury, Gideon (1980): *In Search of a Theory of Translation*. Tel Aviv: The Porter Institute for Poetics and Semiotics, Tel Aviv University.

Tymoczko, Maria (1999): *Translation in a postcolonial context. Early Irish Literature in English Translation*. Manchester: St. Jerome.

Venuti, Lawrence (2009): "Translation, Intertextuality, Interpretation." In: *Romance Studies* 27:3, 157–173.

Pamphlet or Scholarly Work? Book Reviews and Determining the Place of a Translation

Hannu Kemppanen
University of Eastern Finland, Joensuu

Abstract

Analysis of book reviews is a means of studying the reception of translations in a given culture. Discourses used in reviews reflect reactions of individual writers and attitudes of whole social groups towards the reviewed translations. The aim of this article is to introduce a case study of the reception of a Russian-Finnish translation of a non-fiction book on the political history of Finland. The discourses are examined from the point of view of the notions of foreignisation and domestication. The material consists of fifty reviews of Yuri Komissarov's book from 1974 entitled in the Finnish translation *Suomi löytää linjansa* ('Finland finds its course'). The analysis of the reviews showed that there occurred two main discourses: a discourse of acceptance and a discourse of rejection. These two discourses are described from the following point of views: 1) determining the genre, 2) reviewing the language and 3) evaluating socio-cultural effects of translation. The discourse of acceptance defends the place of Komissarov's book as a resistant translation, a text which challenges the canon of history texts written by Finnish authors. The discourse of rejection re-determines the genre of the translated text and excludes it as a foreign element from the canon of history.

1 Introduction

The notion of the book review is of interest to translation research in many respects. It is an institution of written communication through which a considerable part of published books – translated and non-translated works – circulates. When translations are discussed by reviewers, they are evaluated as new issues in the polysystem of written works in the target culture. In the discussion the reviewers prepare the readers for receiving a new book and are expected to commit themselves on the relevance of the translation in this culture. The readers, for their part, have a mental set that Jauss (1982: 24) calls "the horizon of expectations". The expectations can concern style, form, the contents etc. According to Hatim and Mason (1990: 70) "[t]he book review as a genre engages reviewers in a typical expression of attitude towards their subject. In this case the mode of expression is 'evaluative'".

The present study is a part of a larger project where the research group is involved in operationalising the concepts of foreignisation and domestication, introduced by Lawrence Venuti (1995) and discussed by several translation studies scholars.[1] The analysis of book reviews is one attempt to shed light on this fuzzy dichotomy. The earlier studies in the project have dealt with correlation between statistical features and evaluation of translations by subjects in respect to the foreignising vs. domesticating strategy (Kemppanen & Mäkisalo 2010). The study has been preceded also by other related research work on corpus-based translation studies (keyword analysis) and comparative analysis of narrative structures in translated and non-translated history texts (Kemppanen 2004; 2008).

This study aims at describing discourses represented in reviews on a translation of a non-fiction book on Finnish political history. The discourses are examined from the point of view of the notions of foreignisation and domestication. What do the discourses tell about the translator's work or the role of the reviewed translation or the role of the critic him-/herself?

2 The notions of foreignisation and domestication

The concepts of foreignisation and domestication have been discussed by translation scholars in several studies. Among other terms, such as *translator's visibility* or *invisibility*, Venuti (1995, 1998) introduced these issues for describing two opposite translation strategies. His main argument has been a criticism of the Anglo-American domesticating tradition in literary translation. Venuti is a defender of foreignising translation. In his thoughts he has been influenced especially by the German theologian, romantic and translator Friedrich Schleiermacher (2007 [1813]) and the French translation scholar Antoine Berman (2000 [1985]).

---

[1] The project examines possibilities to operationalise the concepts of foreignisation and domestication in three different fields: 1) empirical study of subtitling in audiovisual translation, 2) study of translation of metaphors in newspaper discourse and 3) use of corpus methods as a tool for operationalisation.

Roughly speaking, Venuti's dichotomy continues the discussion on "literal" or "free" translation. Dichotomic divisions of translation strategies have been made according to different principles, reflecting different theoretical approaches to translation. Contradictory strategies (in the sense of a process- or a product-oriented definition of 'a strategy')[2] have been labelled as follows: formal vs. dynamic equivalence (Nida 1964), semantic vs. communicative translation (Newmark 1981), overt and covert translation (House 1977). In Russian tradition, which is less known in Western translation research, the two approaches have until now been examined under the terms *bukvalistskij* and *vol'nyj perevod* – 'literal' and 'free translation' (Borisenko 2007; Lančikov 2007). Gideon Toury (1980), as well, uses two poles for categorisation of different translation strategies. He, however, stresses that his concepts *adequate* and *acceptable translation* describe the product of translation in a continuum.

Venuti's dichotomy differs from the other approaches because of its macro-level focus. He studies translation strategies on the level of whole literatures, not concrete translations. Venuti takes a critical attitude to the domesticating strategy, which, according to him, characterises the Anglo-American translation tradition. Venuti's new approach to translation has met criticism on certain points. The notions of foreignisation and domestication have been criticized because of their obscurity. The dichotomic character of the categorisation of translation strategies has not been accepted by all scholars either (Tymoczko 2000; Boyden 2006). Studies in restricted areas of language use, such as audiovisual translation or translation of children's literature, have shown that choosing a suitable strategy depends on many factors (see Pedersen 2005; Kruger 2007). For example, children as recipients may require the use of domesticating strategy. However, foreign elements in translations of children's literature can be used for educational purposes in multicultural societies (Kruger 2007).

---

[2] The notion of 'translation strategy' is used in different ways. The term can refer to the process of translation and to the product as well. In addition, the same concept has been labelled with different names, such as procedures, methods and tactics (Jääskeläinen 2009: 376). For more detailed analysis of this notion see Jääskeläinen (2009) and Kearns (2008).

3 Reviewing the foreign

Reviewing of translations is an area of increasing interest in Translation Studies. It is often discussed together with the issues of criticism and reception. Maier (2008: 236) sees reviewing and criticism as two related evaluative practices. She states that "the reviewer alerts a reader to new books, describing them and passing judgement as to whether they are worth reading and buying: the critic addresses books that may or may not be new, considering them in detail and usually assuming a reader's familiarity with them." The use of the terms *reviewing* and *criticism* varies in different languages and cultures. In Finland criticism is usually perceived as reviewing literature and art in daily papers and periodicals (Riikonen 2000: 35). According to Stöckell (2007: 456) reviews can be read as documents on reception of translated literature. In addition, they can be taken as texts which build up readers' opinions about good translations.

Reviewing and criticism are mostly connected with literature in the sense of fiction, but as Maier (2008: 236) mentions, they are "evaluative practices concerned with literature in the broadest sense, of not only imaginative writing but also non-fiction". The fact that criticism of non-fiction translations is rarely discussed in translation studies is naturally connected with lack of research on non-fiction translation itself. However, it could be argued that the criticism of non-fiction translation is based largely on the same notions as the criticism of fiction. This argument can be justified by claims concerning common features of these two areas of translation. Observations of translators in their practical work support the idea of common ground. Landers (2001: 103-104) puts it as follows:

> All that has been said about translating narrative fiction applies to translating non-fiction. The same issue of translator–author–reader relationship, the same sensitivity to nuance, the same sense of dedication. There are no uniquely non-fiction translational skills. [...] Translation of non-fiction can be viewed as a subset of translation of fiction, minus some of the more vexatious elements.

Päkkilä (2010) states that the translation process of fiction and non-fiction books consists of stages which have a lot in common: preparation work, making the raw version, editing the translation and finishing the work. Both genres are characterized by narrative features: books have a beginning, a middle and an end. Both fiction and non-fiction books (especially certain subgenres, such as historical narratives) have a plot and sub-plots. Both of them have main characters and minor characters. There are literary elements in non-fiction, and non-fictional elements in fiction.

Despite the fact that non-fiction translation has a lot in common with literary translation, it has also specific features which may have an influence on reviewing translations. Riikonen (2007: 441) stresses that the translator of non-fiction mostly aims at scholarly exactness. In order to achieve this goal he/she uses, for example, terminology originating from Greek and Latin. Riikonen's diachronic study on criticism of translated non-fiction literature in Finland revealed that terminological questions and scholarly exactness have played the most important role in the reviews, but there are cases where the linguistic features have also been criticised, for example the clumsy syntax of the text.

Reviewing of translations has not been discussed extensively in the context of foreignisation and domestication. Venuti (1995) himself does not give any methodological instructions for analysing foreignisation vs. domestication. Munday (2008: 154) considers that on the basis of Venuti's premises about foreignising and domesticating strategies these notions could be studied in several ways, for example, by examining reviews. The analysis may be aimed at the reviews of a certain translation, author or period. Munday states that "the aim would be to see what mentions are made of translators (are they 'visible') and by what criteria reviewers [...] judge translations at a given time and in a given culture."

The role of the reviewer can be seen in different ways. Chesterman (2000: 62–65) categorises three different roles of a critic, depending on the model which is used for describing translations: 1) the static model, 2) the dynamic model or 3) the causal model. The static model is based on the notion of equivalence. The task of the critic is very simple: he or she just states whether the equivalence exists or not. The problem of this model is the fuzziness of the concept 'equivalence' itself. What kind of sameness is required (formal, semantic, functional etc.)?

According to the dynamic model, translation is described as a process taking place in time. The sender sends a message, which is received by the receiver. The translator functions at the same time as a receiver of the original and as a sender of the translated text. In this model the role of the critic differs from the role in the first model. His/her task is to compare the reactions of both the source and target culture readers: do the readers of the translation react in the same way as the readers of the original text? A problem arises again. Do the original and the translation aim at same reactions? Do they have the same skopos? Not always.

The causal model describes causes and effects. The translation itself is a cause and an effect. Chesterman (1998) lists the following translation effects: cognitive effects (in the head of the reader, for example, aesthetic impressions), behavioural effects (in the reader's action, for example, a buying decision of a consumer), socio-cultural effects (changes in the target language, relations between different cultures, attitudes towards different cultures and languages etc.).

Despite the fact that this model also has certain problems, such as the difficulty of measuring the reactions, it is easy to agree with Chesterman (2000: 65) on the preference of the causal model. Evaluation and criticism is a part of the effect which has been caused by the translation. This model stresses the influence of the translation and the translator.

4 Material and methods

The material of the study comprises 50 reviews of the Finnish translation of Yuri Komissarov's (1974) book on Finnish political history entitled *Sovetskij Sojuz – Finljandija: Kurs, ustremlënnyj v buduščee* ('Soviet Union – Finland: A course directed towards the future'). The book was translated by Ulla-Liisa Heino with the title *Suomi löytää linjansa. Neuvostoliittolaisen historiantutkijan näkemys Suomen tasavallan vaiheista* ('Finland finds its course. A Soviet historian's view of the phases of the Republic of Finland') (1974). The reviews were found and photocopied in the archives of Otava Publishing Company in Helsinki.

The reception of this book has earlier been analysed by historians (e.g. Vihavainen 1991), but not from the perspective of translation studies. The translation itself, however, has been used as research material in the corpus-based studies mentioned above (Kemppanen 2004; 2008; Kemppanen & Mäkisalo 2010).

The Russian original of the reviewed book is authored by a pseudonym writer Yuri Komissarov, who later turned out to be the Soviet diplomat Yuri Deryabin. He worked in the Soviet and Russian embassies in Helsinki from the 1970s to the 1990s. He ended his career as the Russian ambassador to Finland (1992–1996). The book represents non-fiction literature on Finnish political history. It has been translated from the manuscript and has never been published in Russian as a book in the Soviet Union or Russia.[3] This fact excludes the theoretical possibility that the reviewers could have compared the source text with the translation. In practice, since most of the reviewers had little or no knowledge of Russian, such a comparison would have been impossible even if the original text had been available.

From the present-day point of view, the reviewing process of Komissarov's book looks quite surprising: a translation of a non-fiction book from Russian, but 50 reviews in newspapers or periodicals! The large number of review articles suggests that in the 1970s there was apparently a demand for literature like this in Finnish society. Most of the articles have been published in newspapers. Their range covers organs of different political parties from left to right, both nationally important papers, such as *Helsingin Sanomat, Aamulehti* and *Turun Sanomat*, and regional ones. Several reviews have been published in the papers of trade unions or organs of certain professional groups (including farmers, factory workers and military staff). Most of the reviews are written in Finnish, except for four of them that have been published in Swedish, which is the other official language in Finland.

The reviewed book is challenging from the translator's point of view. It deals with the target audience's own culture, but the original text has been written by a foreign author. Itkonen-Kaila (1987: 44) states that a translation task like this differs from a usual assignment, where the translator is building a bridge from the source culture to the target culture. In this special case the translator is viewing the things that he or she is more acquainted with than the writer (or the original target audience). Readers may find "books about us" fascinating, because they want to know what the outside world thinks about them. Publishers, as well, may find this category of translations interesting and turn readers' curiosity into sold books.

As Jeremy Munday (2008: 155) states "there is no set model for the analysis of reviews in translation". As a tip for improving the state of affairs he suggests the use of reviews and other paratexts for examining the reception of translations and cultural attitudes to translation in general. Munday foregrounds the cultural theorist

---

[3] Since the 1970s till the post-Soviet era, translation from a manuscript seems to have been standard practice in translating texts on political history from Russian into Finnish. There are only few cases in which the original was published as a book. The reasons for this practice require more detailed investigation.

Gérard Genette (1997) and his work *Paratexts* as a suitable toolkit for further analyses. Genette (1997: 12) divides paratextual elements into two groups: peritexts and epitexts. Peritexts include elements which appear in the same location with the text itself (for example, the title, subtitles, pseudonyms, forewords, dedications, epilogues and framing elements, such as the cover and blurb). Reviews belong to the category of epitexts comprising elements "not materially appended to the text within the same volume but, as it were, circulating freely in a virtually limitless physical and social space" (Genette 1997: 334). In addition to reviews, epitexts include, for example, the following elements: marketing and promotional material, correspondence on the text by the author, and academic and critical discourse on the author and text which have been written by others (Munday 2008: 155).

The research on reviewing can be divided into two approaches according to the type of the material that is used: synchronic and diachronic studies. The synchronic method deals with several reviews of one literal work. Diachronic research focuses on examining reviews of several books of one author in a time span (Jauss 1982). This categorization of methods has been introduced in literary criticism, but can evidently be applied in translation studies as well. The present study is a synchronic research. All the analysed reviews are based on one book and have been released soon after its publication in 1974.

5 Discourses of reception

The analysis of the material revealed the typical genre feature of book reviews referred to earlier in this article – the expression of attitude towards their subject (see also Hatim & Mason 1990: 70). The examined reviews showed a clear division into two main discourses of reception: the discourse of acceptance and the discourse of rejection. These two main discourses will be described in the sections below from the following points of view: 1) determining the genre, 2) reviewing the language and 3) evaluating socio-cultural effects of translation.

5.1 Determining the genre

The genre of a text categorises it into a certain domain of literature. The potential reader of a book gets information about its genre in different ways. Catalogues of books present literature under headings, such as fiction or non-fiction. The genre can be classified in more detail with headings like *biographies and memoires* or *children's books*. The genre of a book becomes clear for the reader also from labelling of shelves in a library or counters in a book store. All this general information and more concrete paratexts, concerning just a certain book, provide the reader with expectations about the genre of a written work.

In the case of Komissarov, the translated book has a subtitle *Neuvostoliittolaisen historiantutkijan näkemys Suomen tasavallan vaiheista* ('The view of a Soviet historian on the phases in the history of the Finnish Republic'). The subtitle follows the main title *Suomi löytää linjansa* ('Finland finds its course') on the cover of the book and on the title page as well. It has been added in the translation process by the translator or/and the publisher. The title of the Russian manuscript reads *Sovetskij Sojuz – Finljandija: Kurs, ustremlënnyj v buduščee* ('Soviet Union – Finland: A course directed towards the future') without any reference to the status of the author.

The analysis showed that determining the genre of the translation is one of the main questions discussed by the reviewers. The discourses on the genre are realised in different ways. One of the realisations is the use of and potential comments on the subtitle of the book mentioned above. The reviews differ from each other in relation to how they react to the subtitle. There were two main ways of handling this subtitle in the analysed reviews: 1) using the same epithet as the publisher plus other epithets, which stress the scholarly value of the book, 2) questioning the subtitle and replacing it with an epithet, which reduces the scholarly value of the book.

Example (1) introduces a case where the reviewer uses the same epithet of the book as the publisher. He makes a positive comment on the trueness of the epithet and gives an additional characterisation of the book, which stresses the approving attitude of the reviewer.

(1) Kustantaja ilmoittaa teoksen olevan "neuvostoliittolaisen historiantutkijan näkemyksen Suomen tasavallan vaiheista". Tämä alaotsikko on oikea, sitä voitaisiin kenties vielä täydentää toteamalla, että yhtä paljon kuin kirja on esitys Suomen tasavallan vaiheista, se on myös teos Suomen ja Neuvostoliiton keskinäissuhteista. (Kansan Uutiset 14.9.1974)

'The publisher states that the book is "the view of a Soviet historian on the phases in the history of the Finnish Republic". This subtitle is correct, it could, perhaps, be supplemented by saying that as much as the book is a presentation of the phases of the Finnish Republic, it is also a work on mutual relations between Finland and Soviet Union.'

In example (2) the reviewer describes Komissarov as being a *researcher*, which preserves the same definition of the genre as the book was given by the publisher. In addition, the reviewer provides a generalisation of the reception of the translated work. The acceptance of the book as a scholarly work and emphasising the positive reactions of critics have the effect of including the translation within Finnish history writing. The reviewer is involved in defending the status of a text of foreign origin.

(2) Neuvostoliittolaisen tutkijan Juri Komissarovin teos, Suomi löytää linjansa, on herättänyt suurta huomiota. Teoksen arviointi on voittopuolisesti myönteistä. (Tiedonantaja, 25.9.1974)

'The book written by the Soviet researcher Yuri Komissarov, Finland finds its course, has aroused great attention. The reviews of the book have been mainly positive.'

In the next example (3) the reviewer makes critical comments on the subtitle of the publisher. The genre of the translation is re-determined with negative comments on the scholarly value of the book. The example illustrates the capacity of a reviewer to influence the reading process. The potential reader gets an idea of a book, which differs from Finnish history writing. Labelling the subtitle as *a smoke screen* and using the phrase *interfering politics of the day* reduce the scholarly value of the translation as a written text in the target culture.

(3) [...] tuntuu ihmeelliseltä, miksi kustantaja on tähän teokseen liittänyt eräänlaiseksi savuverhoksi maininnan neuvostoliittolaisen historiantutkijan näkemyksestä. Meillä historiantutkijat kaihtavat sekaantumista päivänpolitiikkaan, kuten tässä teoksessa tapahtuu. (Turun Sanomat, 8.9.1974)

'[...] it seems curious that the publisher mentions as some kind of smoke screen that this book is the view of a Soviet historian. In Finland historians avoid interfering in the politics of the day, which is what happens in this book.'

Example (4) illustrates a case where the reviewer questions the subtitle of the book by rejecting the text as a scholarly work. The reviewer labels it as *a pamphlet*, which removes the text into another genre than the one suggested by the publisher on the cover of the book. Re-determining the genre and excluding the translation from the category of scholarly texts on the political history of Finland are effective devices for "foreignising the foreign", to put it in Boyden's (2006) terms.

(4) Teos ei ole varsinainen historiantutkimus. [...] se on enemmän luonteeltaan historiallispoliittinen pamfletti tiettyyn ajankohtaiseen tarpeeseen. (Ilta-Sanomat 12.9.1974)

'The book is not a real study of history [...] it is more a pamphlet on history and politics for a current need.'

5.2 Reviewing the language

Another field where the reviewer can influence the reception of a translation is commenting on its linguistic features. Compared to determining the genre, the comments on language use have less influence on the preconceptions of the potential readers. However, the reviewer has an opportunity to emphasise the foreignness or domesticity of the language.

As a whole, the reviews do not deal with the language of the text very much. The main interest is focused on evaluating the contents and the viewpoint of the book. As earlier studies on reception have shown, the review articles rarely discuss the translated texts as translations (see, for example, Puurtinen 2000: 125). Most of the comments on the language concern "the language of the author", as if the translated text were the original. In the analysis of reviews this specific discourse must be taken into account. These comments can give information indirectly about the features of the translation. Direct comments on translation are rare, but they do occur.

The most typical comments on the language concern the language of the text as a whole. Example (5) shows how the reviewer describes the translation as a fluent text. It must be pointed out that the comment on fluency is probably about the book, not about the translation, but since it is adjoined to the information about the translator, it could be interpreted as an indirect assessment of the translation as well. After all, it is not all that clear whether the reviewer is referring to Mr. Komissarov's train of thought or the quality of the translation.

(5) Journalistisen sujuvasti kirjoitettua, Ulla-Liisa Heinon suomentamaa teosta on tervehdittävä ilolla. (Sosialistinen Aikakauslehti 9/1974)

'The book written with journalistic fluency, translated by Ulla-Liisa Heino, must be warmly welcomed.'

Example (6) shows an unusually detailed comment on the translation. Here the reviewer writes about "the successful translation work", although he probably has had no opportunity to see the Russian manuscript and compare it with the target text. The reviewer clearly means by this comment that the quality of the translated text for the most part coincides with his expectations about a Finnish non-fiction text. The present example illustrates a phenomenon which translators may find frustrating: the critic only pays attention to some small details. Such elements in reviews support the observations made in an evaluation test of translations conducted by Kemppanen and Mäkisalo (2010) in which the subjects, translation trainers, were asked which features in various translated texts they found domestic or foreign. The readers of translations pay attention to untypical, foreign elements. It is interesting that the frequency of a certain linguistic element does not need to be very high to evoke a reaction from the reviewer. Checking in the *Comparable Corpus of History Texts* (Kemppanen 2008; Mauranen 2002), where the translation of Komissarov's book – as mentioned above – can be found, reveals that the collocation *Suomessa itsessään* ('in Finland itself') that was criticised by the reviewer (example 6) occurs in the text of 235 pages only five times. The lexical item *itsessään* ('itself') is an unnecessary and untypical element in Finnish. There are other devices for stressing the opposition 'abroad – in Finland itself' in the Finnish language; for example moving the element *Suomessa* 'in Finland' to the beginning of the sentence makes it clear that the following information concerns the state of affairs in Finland as opposed to abroad. The extra element *itsessään* 'itself' is apparent influence of Russian: *v samoj Finlandii* 'in Finland itself'.

(6) Suomentaja Ulla-Liisa Heino on onnistunut käännöstyössä hyvin lukuun ottamatta muutamia muoti-ilmauksia, paria väärää subjektin ja predikaatin viittaussuhdetta sekä siellä täällä vilahtavaa, kummalta kuulostavaa "Suomessa itsessään" -sanontaa. (Kansan Sana 6.12.1974)

'The translator Ulla-Liisa Heino has succeeded in the translation work well except for some vogue expressions, a couple of mistakes in relations of reference between the subject and the predicate, and the strange sounding saying "in Finland itself".'

5.3 Evaluating socio-cultural effects of translation

The analysis brought out that the reviewers reacted actively to the socio-cultural effects of the translation of Komissarov's book. Already the large number of reviews indicates a great interest in the book. The importance of the book is emphasised recurrently in the reviews regardless of the political background of each newspaper or periodical. The material gives a lot of interesting data for further, sociologically oriented analyses. This study focuses only on the most obvious effects of the translation.

Examples (7) and (8) have been picked from articles where the reviewer takes a negative position on Komissarov's book. Both of the reviews label the book as *a pamphlet*. However, both reviewers stress the value of the book as a new point of view in the discussion about Finnish political history. Example (7) has been taken from *Hufvudstadsbladet*, the highest-circulation Swedish-language newspaper in Finland. The reviewer comments on the lack of works of Soviet historians on the Finnish book market. He even criticises education policy in Finland by complaining that the poor knowledge of Russian is one of the reasons for the absence of translations in this field.

(7) De sovjetiska bidrägen har tyvärr inte översatts och i brist på kunskap i ryska har de därför förblivit okända för vidare läsekrets i Finland. (Hufvudstadsbladet 6.12.1974)

'Soviet contributions have unfortunately not been translated and due to the lack of knowledge in Russian they have remained unknown to wider circles of readers.'

The next extract (example 8) is from an article where the reviewer gives critical arguments against the book, but still he finds it useful to get acquainted with another approach to the history of Finland. The author of the article makes it clear that it is important to know what other nations write about us, although the understanding of history differs from that in Finland. The comment on the cultural differences seems very tolerant if you view it against the cultural background of Finland in the 1970s. Compared to today's multicultural society, Finland was still a nation with a narrow view of its own history. The reviewer does not state directly that the new angle on Finnish political history has been made possible through the translation process. However, his comment can be read as recognition of the cultural value of translation.

(8) Mutta kaiken kaikkiaan on hyödyllistä päästä kurkistamaan naapurin ajattelutapaan. On vain luonnollista, että se ei – mitä menneisyyteen tulee – voi olla yhteneväinen omamme kanssa. (Suomenmaa 19.9.1974)

'But, after all, it is useful to be able to take a glance at our neighbour's way of thinking. It is just natural that it cannot – as far as the past is concerned – be congruent with that of our own.'

The last two examples (9) and (10) are taken from articles where Komissarov's book is evaluated extremely positively. They commend it for its social and cultural significance. The review presented in example (9) stresses the alternative character of the translated work. The reviewer questions the canon of Finnish history writing and criticises the power of money in the book market.

(9) Juri Komissarovin kirja Suomi löytää linjansa, tyydyttää tähdellistä tiedontarvetta. Se on samalla vastapaino erinäisten kirjallisten haaskalintujen selittelyille, joita tämänkin syksyn kirjamarkkinat tarjoavat huomattavan suuren mainosbudjetin turvin. (Satakunnan Työ 1.11.1974)

'Yuri Komissarov's book *Finland finds its course* satisfies an important need for information. In addition, it is a counterbalance to the explanations of certain literary vultures, who are again represented on this autumn's book-market with the support of an enormously large advertising budget.'

The last extract (example10) presents a comment where the author of the article points out the value of the reviewed book in filling a gap in Finnish history writing. The act of translation is again somewhere in the background and not mentioned. The reviewer reveals his critical attitude towards Finnish studies on the development of the political relations between Finland and the Soviet Union, and offers the translated book as a potential addition to the canon of Finnish political history.

(10) Suomessa ei ole kirjoitettu yhtenäistä ja keskitettyä esitystä Suomen tasavallan ulkopolitiikasta eikä Suomen ja Neuvostoliiton suhteiden muodostumisesta, särkymisestä ja nykyisen linjan löytymisestä. Minkä tiedämme tai luulemme tietävämme, se koostuu osin ylimalkaisista yleisesityksistä, osin yksityiskohtaisista mutta vain rajattua jaksoa koskevista tutkimuksista. (Palkkatyöläinen 3.2.1975)

'There has not been written any coherent and concentrated presentation on the foreign policy of the Republic of Finland or on the formation and the breaking of the relations between Finland and the Soviet Union, or on the establishment of today's relationship. What we know or think we know, consists partly of approximate general presentations, partly of detailed studies, which, however, concern only limited periods of history.'

6 Conclusions and discussion

The genre of the book review offers a potential field for further research in translation studies. Examining the reception of translations can provide new information about the status of translations in society. As the results of the present study suggest, a translated text functions in different roles in respect to different reviewers. Their reactions vary from clear acceptance to questioning or even rejection.

This study highlighted some pivotal matters represented in the analysed reviews. The attention was focused, firstly, on the evaluation of linguistic features and, secondly, on the socio-cultural relevance of the translation. The analysis revealed that direct comments on translation occurred infrequently. It was, however, possible to draw conclusions about the features of the translated text on the basis of the comments on the language use of "the author". The most typical comments include determining the genre and evaluation of the language on the level of the text as a whole. To some extent there were also comments on more detailed features of the translated text.

The review articles represented clearly the point of view of the reviewers: for or against. In this sense the articles matched the definition of the genre of a book review that was given in the beginning of this paper. They express the attitude of the reviewer towards the literary work which is under evaluation. Although the present study was not focused on the sociological analysis of the reviews, from today's point of view one cannot avoid recognising the interest groups represented in the articles. The division of newspapers and periodicals into left-wing and right-wing issues is eye-catching. Only in rare cases can you find balanced argumentation for and against. Even in these cases the writers reveal their position clearly enough. The analysis shows that reviewing a translated work on Finnish history gave a left-wing critic an opportunity to commit himself on the canon of history texts and make a suggestion for a change in it. Right-wing reviewers, for their part, had a chance to exclude a newcomer from the canon. The analysed reviews provide material for more detailed sociology-oriented translation research.

Apart from the explicit dichotomy between the reviewers with different political attitudes, they are characterised by one common feature as well: Komissarov's book was generally considered as an important contribution to the discussion about Finnish political history. This could be interpreted as a sign of a possible need for changes in the canon of history texts. One might also wonder whether this attitude just refers to the consensus that was typical of the political climate in Finland in the 1970s? It was politically correct both on the Left and on the Right to be interested in the state of affairs in relations between Finland and the Soviet Union. Finland was as a result of the Second World War, the only capitalistic country which had consummated an Agreement on Friendship, Co-operation and Mutual Assistance with the Soviet Union.

From the angle of foreignisation and domestication, the reviewer is able to participate in the process of accepting the translation as a part of the canon or exclude it from the canon. Both discourses used in the reviews – the discourse of acceptance and the discourse of rejection – indicate that the translation of Komissarov's book could be considered as a resistant or a foreignising translation. The defenders of the canon re-determine the genre of the book as a pamphlet, and exclude it from serious academic discussion. The reviewers who criticise the canon and express their support of a new view on Finnish history represented in the translation also regard the text as a resistant translation.

It is clear that the analysis of reviews does not inform us a lot about the details of the translation strategies that have been employed. This can be explained by the nature of reviewing non-fiction translations. Mediating linguistic and cultural details, which often play an important role in the translation of fiction, do not have the same weight in non-fiction translation. That is why the reviews of non-fiction texts concentrate on the evaluation of the contents of the book, its social and cultural relevance. However, this kind of information can help us to know more about the role of non-fiction translation as a means for social change and development of cultures – the translation effects, to use Chesterman's (1998) terms.

References

A. Cited review articles

Kauppila, Erkki (1974): "Neuvostonäkemys Suomen linjanetsinnästä." In: *Kansan Uutiset*, 14.9.1974 (example 1).
Jokinen, Urho (1974): "Huomattava teos Suomen historiasta." In: *Tiedonantaja*, 25.9.1974 (example 2).
Kulha, Keijo, A. (1974): "Tältäkö linjamme näyttää neuvostonaapurin silmin?" In: *Turun Sanomat*, 8.9.1974 (example 3).
Rinne, Matti (1974): "Suomen vaiheita Komissarovin silmin." In: *Ilta-Sanomat*, 12.9.1974 (example 4).
"Neuvostonäkemys Suomen linjasta". In: *Sosialistinen Aikakauslehti* 9/1974 (example 5).
Tikkanen, Seppo (1974): "Suomen linja neuvostosilmin." In: *Kansan Sana* 6.12.1974 (example 6).
Kuhlberg, Svante (1974): "Komissarov om Finlands linje." In: *Hufvudstadsbladet* 6.12.1974 (example 7).
Kuusela, Kalevi (1974): "Neuvostopamfletti Suomen linjoista." In: *Suomenmaa* 19.9.1974 (example 8).
Leino, Juhani (1974): "Neuvostoliittolainen kannanotto: Maittemme nykysuhteet eivät riipu kansainvälien politiikan muutoksista." In: *Satakunnan Työ*. 1.11.1974 (example 9).
Salo, Arvo (1975): "Suomi löysi linjansa, mutta vitkaan ja vastahakoisesti." In: *Palkkatyöläinen*, 3.2.1975 (example 10).

B. Secondary sources

Berman, Antoine (2000 [1985]): "Translation and the Trials of the Foreign." [La Traducion comme épreuve de l'étranger.] In: Venuti, Lawrence [ed.]: *The Translation Studies Reader*. Transl. by Lawrence Venuti. London and New York: Routledge. 284–297.

Boyden, Michael (2006): "Language politics, translation, and American literary history." In: *Target* 18 (1), 121–137.
Borisenko, A. L. (2007): "Ne kriči: 'Bukvalizm!'" In: *Mosty. Žurnal perevodčikov* 14 (2), 25–34.
Chesterman, Andrew (1998): "Cause, Translations, Effects." In: *Target* 10 (2), 201–230.
—— (2000): "Kriitikko ja käännösefektit." In: Paloposki, Outi / Makkonen-Craig, Henna [eds.]: *Käännöskirjallisuus ja sen kritiikki*. Helsinki: Helsingin yliopisto. 62–78.
Genette, Gérard (1997 [1987]): *Paratexts. Thresholds of Interpretation*. [Seuils]. Transl. by Jane E. Lewin. Cambridge, New York and Melbourne: Cambridge University Press.
Hatim, Basil /Mason, Ian (1990): *Discourse and the Translator*. London and New York: Longman.
House, Juliane (1977): *A Model for Translation Quality Assessment*. Tübingen: TBL Verlag Gunter Narr.
Itkonen-Kaila, Marja (1987): "Suomentaja soita ylittämässä." In: *Virittäjä* 91, 441–444.
Jauss, Hans Robert (1982): *Towards an Aesthetic of Reception*. Brighton: Harvester.
Jääskeläinen, Riitta (2009): "Looking for a working definition of translation strategies." In: Inger Mees, M. / Alves, Fabio / Göpferich, Susanne [eds.]: *Methodology, Technology and Innovation in Translation Process Research*. Copenhagen: Samfundslitteratur. 375–388.
Kearns, John (2008): "Strategies." In: Baker, Mona / Saldanha, Gabriela [eds.]: *Routledge Encyclopedia of Translation Studies*. 2nd rev. edn. London and New York: Routledge. 282–285.
Kemppanen, Hannu (2004): "Keywords and ideology in translated history texts: a corpus-based analysis." In: *Across Languages and Cultures* 5 (1), 89–106.
—— (2008): *Avainsanoja ja ideologiaa: käännettyjen ja ei-käännettyjen historiatekstienkorpuslingvistinen analyysi*. Joensuu: University of Joensuu.
Kemppanen, Hannu / Mäkisalo, Jukka (2010): "Operationalizing *the foreign* and *the domestic* in translations: a corpus-based analysis." A paper read in the conference *Methodological Advances in Corpus-Based Translation Studies* at the University of Ghent 9.–10.1.2010.
Komissarov, Juri (1974): *Suomi löytää linjansa. Neuvostoliittolaisen historiantutkijan näkemys Suomen tasavallan vaiheista*. Transl. by Ulla-Liisa Heino. Helsinki: Otava.
Kruger, Haidee (2007): "Towards a paradigm for the study of the translation of children's literature in the South African educational context. Some reflections." In: *Language Matters. Studies in the Languages of Africa* 38 (2), 275–298.
Lančikov, V. K. (2007): "Penthaus iz slonovoj kosti. O stat'e A.L. Borisenko Ne kriči: 'Bukvalizm!'" In: *Mosty. Žurnal perevodčikov* 15 (3), 15–29.
Landers, Clifford E. (2001): *Literary Translation. A Practical Guide*. Clevedon: Multilingual Matters.
Maier, Carol (2008): "Reviewing and criticism." In: Baker, Mona / Saldanha, Gabriela [eds.]: *Routledge Encyclopedia of Translation Studies*. 2nd rev. edn. London and New York: Routledge. 236–241.
Mauranen, Anna (2000): "Strange strings in translated language. A study on corpora." In: Olohan, Maeve [ed.]: *Intercultural Faultlines. Research Models in Translation Studies I. Textual and Cognitive Aspects*. Manchester: St. Jerome. 119–141.
Munday, Jeremy (2008): *Introducing Translation Studies: Theories and Applications*. 2nd edn. New York and London: Routledge.
Newmark, Peter (1981): *Approaches to Translation*. Oxford etc.: Pergamon Press.
Nida, Eugen A. (1964): *Toward a Science of Translating. With Special Reference to Principles and Procedures Involved in Bible Translating*. Leiden: E. J. Brill.
Pedersen, Jan (2007): "How is culture rendered in subtitles?" In: Nauer, S. [ed.]: *Challenges of Multidimensional Translation. Proceedings of the Marie Curie Euroconferences MuTra: Challenges of Multidimensional Translation* – Saarbrücken 2–6 May 2005. http://www.euroconferences.info/proceedings/2005_Proceedings/2005_proceedings.html.

Puurtinen, Tiina (2000): "Lastenkirjallisuuden kääntäminen: normit, luettavuus ja ideologia." In: Paloposki, Outi / Makkonen-Craig, Henna [eds.]: *Käännöskirjallisuus ja sen kritiikki*. Helsinki: Helsingin yliopisto. 106–131.

Päkkilä, Markku (2010): "Kaunokääntäjä tietokääntäjänä." A paper read at the seminar *Kääntäjäpäivä* at the University of Eastern Finland on 10.2.2010.

Riikonen, H. K. (2000): "Käännöskritiikin historiasta: suuntaviivoja ja esimerkkejä." In: Paloposki, Outi / Makkonen-Craig, Henna [eds.]: *Käännöskirjallisuus ja sen kritiikki*. 34–62.

—— (2007): "Suomennoskritiikin vaiheita 1850-luvulta lähtien." In: Riikonen, H. K. / Kovala, Urpo / Kujamäki, Pekka / Paloposki, Outi [eds.]: *Suomennoskirjallisuuden historia 2*. Helsinki: Suomalaisen Kirjallisuuden Seura. 425–451.

Schleiermacher, Friedrich (2007 [1813]): "Eri kääntämismetodeista." [Über die verschiedenen Methoden des Übersetzens]. In Tapani Kilpeläinen (ed.) *Kääntökirja: kirjoituksia kääntämisen filosofiasta*. Translated by Maija Ollikainen. Tampere: Eurooppalaisen filosofian seura. 7–36.

Stöckell, Päivi. 2007. "Käännöskritiikki tänään." In: Riikonen, H. K. / Kovala, Urpo / Kujamäki, Pekka / Paloposki, Outi [eds.]: *Suomennoskirjallisuuden historia 2*. Helsinki: Suomalaisen Kirjallisuuden Seura. 452–458.

Toury, Gideon (1980): *In Search of a Theory of Translation*. Tel Aviv: The Porter Institute for Poetics and Semiotics, Tel Aviv University.

Tymoczko, Maria (2000): "Translation and political engagement, activism, social change and the role of translation in geopolitical shifts." In: *The Translator* 6 (1), 23–47.

Venuti, Lawrence (1995): *The Translator's Invisibility. A History of Translation*. London and New York: Routledge.

—— (1998): *The Scandals of Translation: Towards an Ethics of Difference*. London: Routledge.

# The Taming of a Translation: Microlevel Choices Leading to Macrolevel Thematic Shifts

Ritva Leppihalme
University of Helsinki, Finland

Abstract

Translators' decisions on microlevel translation problems may affect macrolevel thematic webs or networks, causing thematic changes or shifts. In such shifts the clues needed by target readers for their interpretation of the text may be weakened or lost. In the case study examined in this article, there are three types of thematic deviations from standard English novelistic discourse: malapropisms, rhymes and palindromes. It is argued that these deviations are thematic in the source text as they focus the reader's attention on the ultimate relativity of such concepts as backwardness, inversion and otherness, of particular relevance in a postcolonial novel with mostly American characters situated in Africa. The Finnish target text exhibits "taming" or normalization consistent with Toury's (1995) law of growing standardization: the malapropisms are corrected and the rhyming words are mostly rendered by dictionary equivalents and sometimes given a clause structure. Renderings for the most challenging deviation type, the palindromes, are successful technically but rarely manage to transmit the double sense of the reversible word strings. A variety of complementary explanations are discussed, including a possibly relevant cultural difference between source and target readerships.

1 Introduction and aim

Literary translation is well known to involve "thousands of decisions, large and small, [...] on the part of the translator" (Bush 1998: 129). Those decisions, or at least some of them, have long been of interest to translation research and translation criticism. Much of the research and criticism on literary translations focuses on stylistic aspects (e.g. Boase-Beier 2006): certain source-text features (like imagery or foregrounding) are singled out and the researcher looks for similarities and discrepancies between the source and target texts, analysing the material either quantatively or qualitatively. Other studies compare more than one translation, usually retranslations, of the same source text (e.g. Tarvi 2004) or translations of a text into multiple target languages. Scholars may also look for explanations for translators' choices (see Brownlie 2003) and find them for instance in translators' attitudes, in the norms or ideologies involved, or in the effect of a translator's individual voice or fingerprint (Gullin 1998; Baker 2000; Pekkanen 2010). Sociologically inclined researchers may investigate the role played by other agents in the process, like editors and publishers (e.g. Hekkanen 2010). Economic considerations in the publishing industry have their effect on translation decisions and so do translators' time and money concerns.

A perennial theme in studies on literary translation seems to be that translations are "somehow tamer than the original" (Kenny 1998: 520). Toury (1995) has proposed a law of growing standardization, which is supported by many case studies, and scholars working with corpora have found evidence of various kinds of normalization of structures and lexis (that is, substituting what is common for what is uncommon). In this article I examine the translation of creative deviations in a literary text to show what effect the translators' microlevel choices may have on the macrolevel. It is my argument that the translators have not conveyed the function(s) of the source-text deviations to the target text, thereby causing a thematic shift: a "taming" of the thematic deviations and of the whole text.

Shifts or changes of course occur in all translation. This article considers only optional shifts occurring with three types of unusual source-text deviations from English novelistic discourse: *malapropisms, rhymes* and *palindromes*. Deviations are likely to present translation problems and hence could be expected to alert translators to the need to analyse the source-text web of relationships, "the importance of individual items being determined by their *relevance* and *function* in the text" (Snell-Hornby 1988: 69, emphasis added). If an analysis shows that the deviations have an important thematic function on the macrolevel, taming or normalization of these items is clearly not an optimal solution.

I propose that the source text, Barbara Kingsolver's novel *The Poisonwood Bible* (1998), has in addition to its expressive function also a persuasive function[1] and

---

[1] Text types are categorized by Reiss (e.g. 1976), following Bühler (1934) on the functions of language, as expressive, informative and operative. In this paper I prefer the label "persuasive" to operative as I find that the source text, in addition to its expressive function, is constructed to *persuade* its readers of the value of other, different points of view (see below). This function is recognized in much of the

that this latter function or subfunction is less evident in the Finnish target text as a result of certain choices made by the translators regarding the rendering of the deviations. To overlook their relevance and function in the source text when choosing renderings can be expected to destroy some of the thematic web or network that would serve as a basis for reader interpretations. In some earlier work I have studied the way translators have dealt with other challenging source-text elements, like allusions (e.g. Leppihalme 1997; 2005), regionalisms (Leppihalme 2000) and value-adding metaphors (Leppihalme 2007). My interest is both on what translators do with such problems and what the effect of their choices is on target texts and consequently on target readers' chances of interpreting what they read. In other words, my focus is on what function certain elements serve in the text studied and whether the translators' chosen renderings for them also serve that function.

2 The author and the source text

Barbara Kingsolver's novel *The Poisonwood Bible* (1998) is a powerful, provocative and profoundly ambitious literary account of three decades of events in postcolonial Africa, involving many moral and ethical issues. In her "Author's Note" to the novel, Kingsolver, an American writer of fiction, poetry and essays who spent two years in the Congo as a child (Kanner 1998: 1), states: "I spent nearly thirty years waiting for the wisdom and maturity to write this book" (Kingsolver 1998: x). She sees herself "exploring the great, shifting terrain between righteousness and what's right" (ibid.), with the result that the novel has been described as a "compelling exploration of religion, conscience, imperialist arrogance and the many paths to redemption" (BookBrowse.com. 2007: 9). *The Poisonwood Bible* is the story of a troubled family: a Baptist preacher with missionary ambitions and his wife and four daughters arrive in the Belgian Congo in 1959, shortly before that country's independence is announced. Each of the Americans meets the challenges of a foreign culture in his/her own way, but they are also all affected by African political events and American involvement in them. Kingsolver is incensed at the actions of the American government both against the elected first

---

American reader discussion on the source text on the Internet, with participants taking sides on the issues.

African prime minister of the newly independent country and later, and shows some of the consequences on the ground in graphic terms. (She includes the final report of a U.S. Senate select committee to study governmental operations in the brief bibliography at the end of *The Poisonwood Bible*.) She is also critical of attempts to convert people to Christianity and teach them democracy. Briefly, important themes in the novel that it was Kingsolver's "passion to write" (1998: ix) and which lend it "a fierce emotional undertow" (Kakutani 1998: 12) are the need to question preconceived ideas in order to make sense of the world, to struggle for what is right and to condemn what is wrong.

3 Micro-level deviations in the source text: Problems and renderings

It is, then, my argument that in the source text, the frequent malapropisms, rhymes and palindromes are thematic because they help readers interpret the novel and that insufficient attention to their function(s) can result in macrolevel thematic shifts in the target text. In the discussion of individual examples below, some context will be given and the themes will be approached from the reader's interpretive or experiential point of view. As the deviations also have a role in characterization, some comments on this are included in the contextual information.

The material used for this article comes from Books I–III of the novel (pages 1–355 of the source text and pages 9–323 of the target text). A few quotations occurring on later pages are included to further illustrate the themes.

The target text, *Myrkkypuun siemen* 'Poison tree seed' (Kingsolver 1999), translated by Juha Ahokas and Arvi Tamminen, with palindromes rendered by Esa Hirvonen, is described in a Finnish review (Lybeck 2000: 6, 8) as a story of survival with a strong political dimension.[2] The fact that the target text was reissued in paperback five years later indicates that it was favourably received by Finnish readers. But what book did they read?

---

[2] No other signed reviews of the translation were found. See below, Section 4.

3.1 Rachel's malapropisms

The deviations occur in narrative or dialogue. All the American women or girls in the missionary's family function as narrators in turn, each speaking in her own distinctive way. 15-year old Rachel can be read as a caricature of what Barack Obama (1995: 47) in another context called the "blend of ignorance and arrogance that too often characterized Americans abroad". These characteristics are revealed not only by what Rachel says and thinks and how she acts when faced with otherness but also, quite strikingly, by her frequent malapropisms. Malapropism is the "unintentional misuse of a word by confusion with one of similar sound, esp. when creating a ridiculous effect" (*Collins Dictionary of the English Language*, 2nd ed., 1986, s.v. *malapropism*). Some American readers may link Rachel's malapropisms to "Bushisms", slips of the tongue attributed to former president George W. Bush. (See e.g. Miller (2001: 18), who cites such examples as *hostile* for *hostage*.)

Rachel's reactions to her early encounters with Congolese life are negative from the start. "We are supposed to be calling the shots here" (ST 26; ST stands for 'source text), she complains, but all she meets with indicates that "we" are not "in charge of a thing, not even our own selves" (ibid.). She finds everything alienating, and her litany of woes proceeds from one malapropism to another, suggesting to perceptive readers that there *are* other points of view:

(1a) [...] simple things in life I had taken for *granite* (ST 27)
(2a) I knew right then I was in the *sloop* of despond (ST 27)
(3a) Day one in the Congo, and here my brand-new tulip-tailored linen suit [...] was fixing to give up the *goat* (ST 27)
(4a) [...] you'd think she was *Cape Carniveral* launching a rocket ship (ST 53)
(5 a) a *putative* from the law (ST 142)
(6a) a sheer *tapestry* of justice (ST 202)
(7a) a *civilrous* gesture (ST 328)
(8a) a woman's *provocative* (ST 332). (Emphases added here and to all examples below.)

Frequent repetition of this stylistic feature (45 instances noted in the source text material examined) strengthens its thematicity: where readers might at first be understanding of Rachel's lack of tolerance and her disgust of all that is strange to her, every malapropism reinforces the idea of her as uneducated and narrow-minded: ignorant and arrogant.

The Finnish translators do not create deviations in Rachel's Finnish discourse. Practically all her malapropisms are normalized as they are rendered by standard Finnish expressions (TT stands for 'target text'):

(1b) *itsestään selvinä* 'taken for granted' (TT 36)
(2b) *rohkeuteni oli pettämässä* 'my courage was giving way' (TT 36)
(5b) joku *rikollinen* 'some criminal' (TT 141)
(6b) silkkaa oikeuden *irvikuvaa* 'sheer travesty of justice' (TT 192)
(7b) *ritarillinen* ele 'a chivalrous gesture' (TT 301)
(8b) naisen *etuoikeus* 'a woman's prerogative'(TT 305)

There is an occasional – very rare – omission of a malapropism as opposed to its correction: (4a) *Cape Carniveral* is rendered simply as *avaruusasemalla* 'at a space station' (TT 60; in this example there is also the neutralization of the metaphor of a busy woman in a kitchen being herself a space station). There are also some misunderstandings in the target text: for example *to give up the ghost* is an expression meaning 'to die, to expire', but the malapropism in (3a) with *goat,* combined in the context with goat meat cooked to welcome the newly arrived American family (ST 30), leads the translators astray:

(3b) valmistauduin *nauttimaan vuohiateriasta upouudessa* [...] *puvussani* 'I was preparing to enjoy a meal of goat meat wearing my brand-new [...] suit' (TT 37)

What this repeated alteration of the author's technique results in is loss of thematicity and also loss of humour, "the comedy of colliding cultures" (Klinkenborg 1998: 5). Rachel's role as a representative of "Americans abroad" is flattened, and she comes across only as a resentful and rather boring young girl.

When Rachel's Finnish in the target text for once does retain a deviation, it is largely ineffective as the loanword she then uses is hardly ever found in Finnish outside academic texts on political science; misuse of this low-frequency item is therefore unlikely to reward most target readers:

(9a) "[I]f we don't boil our water for thirty full minutes we'll get *plebiscites* and what not" (ST 248) 'parasites'
(9b) "Jos emme muista keittää vettämme ainakin puolen tunnin ajan, saamme *plebiskiittejä* ja ties mitä." (TT 232)

In order for criticism of a translator's strategies to be fair, alternative solutions also need to be weighed. With malapropisms, it is not too difficult to propose alternatives because unfamiliarity and confusion with *sivistyssanat* 'educated words' (i.e. low-frequency loanwords) is a feature that Finns also recognize and find amusing. Furthermore, there are compound words and idioms in Finnish which are not always transparent. The translators could therefore have given Rachel's Finnish various sorts of humorous twists of both loanwords and Finnish compounds and idioms had they wished to convey the effect of Rachel's malapropisms and retain their function. Imitating the source-text technique, in other words altering Finnish "educated words" slightly, is the obvious solution where the ST word (or a part of it) has a cognate in Finnish. For example e*piscopotamians* (ST 182) could be rendered as *episkopaanut* (*paanu* 'shingle') or *episkopaavit* (*paavi* 'pope') and *splectacular* (ST 56, 144) as *splektaakkelimainen*. The translators' chosen solutions for these examples again in no way depart from Standard Finnish: the target text has *episkopaaleja* 'Episcopalians' (TT 175) and replaces *splectacular* by *dramaattinen* 'dramatic' (TT 59, 143). Example (9a) above, "we'll get *plebiscites* and what not" (ST 248), might be rendered as *siitä saa paratiiseja* 'we'll get paradised', playing on the words *parasiitti* 'parasite' and *paratiisi* 'paradise'.

Where credible target-language malapropisms are not available, lexical elements could be combined to produce non-existent compound words and phrases suggesting – like malapropisms – that the speaker is outside her "comfort zone" when using them (for instance *lainrikokselinen, oikeuden irtokuva, naisen edesoikeus* for examples 5a, 6a, and 8a above). Example (4a) could be rendered as *Cape Carneval* as the word *karnevaali* 'carnival' is well known in Finnish.

3.2 Adah's rhymes

Before she takes her first turn as narrator, Rachel's young sister Adah is presented as gifted but brain-damaged (ST 23–24); she refers to herself as a "half-brain" (ST 35), later specifying: "I was born with half my brain dried up like a prune" (ST 39). Her congenital condition is hemiplegia combined with some type of aphasia. This condition, while obviously created for literary purposes in the novel, was immediately recognized by the experienced Finnish physiotherapist consulted during the preparation of this article. The cause of the condition is often a stroke or brain hemorrhage before birth. The physiotherapist noted that patients with similar conditions are usually of normal or even high intelligence and may compensate for their handicap by developing unexpected talents; indeed, while the child Adah does not speak to others, in her internal discourse she shows evidence of a literary talent and a fondness for often bitter language play. Her striking rhymes and palindromes are comic but they are also often thematic. And as Klinkenborg (1998: 5) notes, once the comedy ends, the tragedy begins:

(10a) A lightning that cannot strike twice, our lesson learned in the hateful speed of light. *A bite at light at Ruth a truth* a sky-blue presentiment and oh how dear we are to ourselves when it comes, it comes, that long, long shadow in the grass (ST 416, emphasis added).

Adah's rhymes suggest both brain damage and rap music:

(11a) *Sunrise tantalize, evil eyes hypnotize:* that is the morning, Congo pink (ST 35)
(12a) *overjoyed, null and void, Mongoloid* (ST 66)

Example (11a) represents her early reactions to the Congo, and especially the *evil eyes* are strongly thematic, recurring many times in connection with snakes and the perilous jungle. Example (12a) refers to the narrow escape Adah had from being placed "in Special Ed with the mongoloids" (ST 66). Critically observing her father, she later notes that his deficiencies are deficiencies of *words*: impatient with translation, he tries to reach people in his "wildly half-baked" Kikongo (ST 243). Adah comments:

(13a) In the beginning was *the word the herd the blurred the turd the debts incurred the theatrical absurd* (ST 242).

It is obvious that the rhymes are a translation problem difficult to solve satisfactorily by literal translation because words rhyming in the source language are most unlikely to have rhyming equivalents in the target language. Furthermore, Finnish words with their inflections are usually longer than English words, and so the rap-like rhythm is likely to be lost. Example (11a) gets a more or less literal translation dispensing with rhymes, and the two pairs of the utterance are seen as two clauses:

(11b) *Nouseva aurinko houkuttelee, paha silmä hypnotisoi* 'The rising sun attracts, the evil eye hypnotizes' (TT 41).

Example (12b) also dispenses with rhyming words (though there is one half-rhyme of sorts) and again rephrases the line as a clause:

(12b) Suunniltaan ilosta, turhanaikainen ja *tyhjä*, on mongoloidi *tyhmä* 'Overjoyed, useless and empty, the Mongoloid is stupid' or '[...] is the stupid Mongoloid' (TT 70).

In (13b), the translators try harder:

(13b) Alussa oli *sana, kana, tana,* kuin teatraali*sena* absur*dina* vel*kana* 'In the beginning was the word, the hen, [...] like a theatrical absurd debt' (TT 227)

Tana, missing in the gloss, defeats literal translation as it suggests either a firm stance, like a soldier with a levelled bayonet (*pistin tanassa*), or a euphemistic variant of the swearword *saatana* 'Satan'. The essive cases in the latter part of (13b) do not lead to satisfactory rhymes as the line does not scan: the stress falls on the wrong syllables. The effect of the translators' efforts falls flat, especially as the playfulness of the rhyming words unrelated by meaning is again submerged under an attempt to create syntactic sense.

A better rhyming rendering is given for:

(14a) It rained cats and *dogs frogs bogs* then it rained snakes and lizards (ST 67)

where the translator achieves both contextual sense and rhyme without overdoing it:

(14b) Satoi kissoja ja koiria, *sammakoita, lutikoita,* sitten satoi sisiliskoja ja käärmeitä 'It rained cats and dogs, frogs, lice, then it rained lizards and snakes' (TT 72).

Perhaps a freer, more creative way of rendering the rhymes could have led to solutions suggesting mischievous delight in playing with words and inspiring readers to look for unexpected connections. Starting with words rhyming in the target language and paying attention to rhythm could give for example: *Aamun työ, meidät lyö, viidakossa silmät syö* 'Morning work, beats us all, in the jungle eats the eyes' for example (11a) above while a similar strategy for (12a) could give *Iloinen, köykäinen, vammainen* 'Happy, lightweight, retarded' or *Hyvä niin, nollattiin, mollattiin* 'Okay, seen as worthless, abused'. The rhymes on *word* in example (13a) might be rendered as: *Aluss' oli sana, kaikkein kuultavana, isä huutavana* 'In the beginning was the word, by all it could be heard, father yelling'. But it must be remembered that these suggestions are by no means offered as optimal renderings, only as illustrations of a different technique of coping with the source-text deviations constituted by Adah's only seemingly senseless rhymes.

3.3 Adah's palindromes

Strictly speaking, palindromes are words and phrases that can be read in either direction, yet producing the same word or phrase, like English *level* or Finnish *saippuakauppias*. Other words and phrases may produce different words or phrases when read backwards: *live/evil, rats/stars, maps/spam,* etc. and these are often called semi- or half-palindromes. One more type of palindrome reverses words rather than letters: *book different a is it* (ST 66). All three types are used in *The Poisonwood*

Bible but for convenience' sake in this article they will all be referred to as palindromes – an umbrella category.

There are dozens of palindromes in Adah's narratives, some resembling English: *Draw a level award* (ST p. 66), others not: *Ti morf sgniht wen nrael nac uoy* (ST 67) 'you can learn new things from it', *it from things new learn can you* (ST 66). They keep reminding readers that "[e]verything you're sure is right can be wrong in another place. Especially *here*" (ST 572, original emphasis).

The source-text palindromes function as a thematic element as doing things right, or doing them back to front, thinking in the right way or the wrong way, being thought a backward child or a backward nation, come up again and again in the novel, questioning the appropriateness of such labels. Their function is to persuade readers that their preconceived ideas may not be the only way to see things: that in Africa, things are often puzzling and may be different from what is familiar. Palindromes, when reversed, make a new kind of sense. Adah notes: "When I finish reading a book from front to back, I read it back to front. It is a different book back to front, and you can learn new things from it" (ST 66). This change of sense that occurs with a change of direction of reading makes for a nearly overwhelming translation problem. The thematic function of the palindromes is weakened as the technical difficulty of getting *some* sense into them for the target text obscures the need for the right *kind* of sense. Obviously, when the letters of English words and phrases are reversed, it is highly unlikely that reversing their Finnish dictionary equivalents will result in anything like the required sense: reversing the letters of *God* gives *dog*, but reversal of Finnish *Jumala* 'God' does not mean anything at all in Finnish.

Still, Esa Hirvonen, the translator of the palindromes in the target text, often manages to create quite neat Finnish renderings. For example, where Adah mentions Edgar Allan Poe and his Raven and quotes in half-palindrome: *Erom Reven* 'Never more' (ST 64), Hirvonen is not fazed by the allusion but produces *Naakni Olli, mie*, a reversal of *ei milloinkaan* 'never more' (TT 69).[3] Sometimes he provides a short (and therefore easy to unravel) palindrome: *Poor Dan is in a droop* (ST 67) gets rendered briefly as *Ikävä väki* 'Dull people' (TT 71). Yet mostly his reversals are longer than the source-text ones (and so require more effort to "back-

---

[3] *Never more* could also be rendered e.g. as *ei koskaan enää* or *ei ikinä enää* if a translator did not recognize the allusion to Poe's poem.

reverse"), and sometimes they are cruder than those in the source text. Where Adah writes on the cover of her notebook *Elapsed or esteemed, all Ade meets erodes pale* "as a warning to others" (ST 67), the translator chooses to vulgarize this as *Akkako siis ilona hiedan, Ada ihan olisi iso kakka* (TT 71). A literal translation of this is roughly, 'So is the old woman a joy for the sand? Ada'd be a big shit'. For Adah to write this on her own notebook is unmotivated, and if she did, it would hardly convey a "warning to others".

At times the thematic meaning is completely lost: Adah has a crippled talking parrot whose breast is "weighed down with the words of human beings" (ST 157). She tries to train the bird to be independent (note the thematicity of this in connection with the Congo) and wants him to learn that "fruit is not a thing he must rely on the hands of mankind for, but grows on trees" (ST 157). This suggests another palindrome to Adah: *Treason grows but for kind man* (ibid.). Treason comes to the Congo with independence as readers will eventually learn, and kind men are in short supply, but the translator's rendering misses the point completely: *Hede-elämä kasvaa puusta hedelmää* (TT 154). This is barely understandable in a botanical sense ('stamen life has fruit grow from the tree') and is devoid of any political reference or allusion to treason.

At other times the palindrome translator appears to trust that target readers will know enough English to cope with an undertranslated passage. Two examples:

(15a) For my twin sister's name I prefer the spelling *Lee* as that makes her [...] *the slippery length of muscle* that she is" (ST 67)

For *slippery length of muscle*, read *eel*, which is a half-palindrome of *Lee*. The translator renders this literally as *ankerias*:

(15b) Kaksossisareni nimen kohdalla pidän kirjoitusasusta Lee, sillä se tekee hänestä [...] *liukkaan ankeriaan*, mikä hän onkin 'For my twin sister's name I like the spelling Lee for that makes of her [...] a slippery eel, which is what she is' (TT 71).

The full meaning of this is understandable to Finnish readers only through back-translation into English as a non-English speaker can have no idea of any link between *Lee* and *ankerias* 'eel'.

When the local language Kikongo enters the game, Adah comments:

(16a) Many Kikongo words resemble English words backward and have antithetical meanings: *Syebo* is a horrible, destructive rain that just exactly does not do what it says backward (ST 85).

Syebo backward is of course 'obeys' and the translator adds a gloss to his otherwise literal translation:

(16b) *syebo* on hirvittävä, tuhoisa sade, joka ei varsinaisesti tee sitä, mitä sanoo takaperin, *eli tottele* '[...] i.e. obey' (TT 88, first emphasis original).

This, too, only makes sense if target readers can work out and understand the English word.

Kingsolver also criticizes certain aspects of Christianity. The *poisonwood* in the title of the novel reflects the missionary father's way of mispronouncing the Kikongo word *bangala* 'precious, dear' as *bängala* 'poisonwood tree' and so – mistrusting his interpreters – changing the message at the end of his sermons: *Tata Jesus is bängala!* (ST 312). It is also an allusion to various Bible editions known by their errors or misprints. Errors, too, are thematic: "We came in stamped with such *errors* we can never know which ones made a lasting impression" (ST 603; emphasis added). Kingsolver presents the father's attempts to exert religious control over the village as a series of misdirected and futile efforts, doomed to fail, and this effect is mirrored in Adah's recollection of her early Sunday school experiences:

(17a) From that day on, I stopped parroting the words of *Oh God! God's love!* and began to cant in my own backward tongue: *Evol's dog! Dog ho!* (ST 197).

This turning of her back on the religion that she has been taught gets vulgarized in the translation, losing its thematicity:

(17b) Siitä päivästä alkaen lakkasin hokemasta kuin papukaija *Suola Jeesuksellain, onni, autuus!* ja aloin pamlata omalla takaperoisella kielelläni: *Suutu ain, noin alles kusee jalous!* (TT 188) 'From that day on I stopped repeating like a parrot: *My Jesus has the salt – happiness and bliss!* and began to talk in my own backward tongue: *Go on, get mad, noble feelings make you wet your bed*'

The beginning of the target-text palindrome does sound somewhat like a metaphorical line of a Christian hymn, but the second part is much cruder than needed (the gloss avoids a stigmatized word in the target-text rendering) and totally obscures the point about the absence of love in the brand of Christianity that Adah knows. As an alternative, one could perhaps propose *Oi Herra! Herran armo!* 'Oh Lord! The Lord's mercy!', reversed (true, without semantic sense in Finnish) as *Omran arreh! Arre hio!* which has the advantage of brevity and avoids the vulgarity of the published line.[4] Alternatively, the type of palindrome that reverses words not

---

[4] It was suggested in the discussion following the presentation of this paper at the conference "Translation Studies: Moving In – Moving On" in Joensuu (2009) that

letters might be chosen. Even this is difficult as with its inflectional suffixes, Finnish allows for a freer word order but less variation in sense if the word order is altered.

4 Discussion

The examples above show that the translators have not prioritized the themes of the novel when coming to a decision on how to solve the translation problem of microlevel thematic deviations – the malapropisms, rhymes and palindromes – in the discourses of two of the narrators. The question arises, why not?

Kenny's corpus-based study (2001) shows that normalization frequently occurs in translation. According to her, creativity in translation is affected both by how translators see their brief and how closely the resources of the two languages match. Øverås (1998: 569) argues that neutralization of metaphorical expressions reduces processing effort and so increases the readability of the target text. This might apply to other possibly puzzling features as well, like those discussed in this article. All of these factors can have played a role in the translation process that resulted in the target text examined.

It is hardly productive to interview translators on work carried out more than a decade ago. I have not approached the translators to interview them and so have no information on how they saw their brief, nor on why more than one translator was involved or how the two principal translators divided the work. The two translators in charge of most of the target text, Juha Ahokas and Arvi Tamminen, are both experienced translators of mostly popular fiction. Juha Ahokas is credited with 106 published translations into Finnish since 1994 in *Fennica*, the National Bibliography of Finland (but note that the bibliography lists reprints as separate items). His translations include works by such authors of crime novels as Edward Bunker, James Elroy and Denise Mina and science fiction by Dan Simmons. Arvi Tamminen's career as a translator is even longer: since 1972 he has had 96 translations published, mostly from English but also from Swedish and Norwegian,

---

Dog ho! may be read as containing the word *whore*, sometimes spelled as *ho,* and that therefore the vulgarity of the target-text rendering may be less inappropriate than is claimed here.

according to *Fennica*. Many of his translations include crime and science fiction by such authors as Jan Guillou, Philip K. Dick and Karin Fossum, as well as Westerns by the Norwegian author going by the pseudonym Louis Masterson. Tamminen has also translated older literary texts, for example by Joseph Conrad and Nathanael Hawthorne. Both of these are in a sense relevant in connection with Kingsolver's novel – consider Conrad's *Heart of Darkness* (1902) and the comparison of her novel to a "Hawthornian tale of sin and redemption" (Kakutani 1998: 1).

The translator of the palindromes is Esa Hirvonen, a published palindrome poet. His book of palindrome poetry, *Takana kapakan akat,* was published in 2002. Hirvonen's rendering of the source-text palindromes was greeted with enthusiasm by the anonymous writer of an online site, *Viikon kulttuurivinkki* (2004) (a weekly hint on what is worth checking out in the cultural sphere in Finland), who called it "a so far unsurpassed achievement" and "worth raising your hat to" (my translation). But the commentator did not address the function of the palindromes on the macrolevel of the novel, limiting his/her enthusiasm to the technical achievement alone.

Judging by the target text and the information on the translators' careers, it is likely that the translators were used to working quickly without spending much time in advance on analysis of the source text and were doubtless expected by the publisher to produce the target text on schedule. The preparation and analysis that scholars view as a necessary part of the translation process (e.g. Snell-Hornby 1988: 69–70) may be seen as a time-consuming, unpaid activity by practitioners, and therefore be disregarded in the process. The translators may have missed some of the malapropisms and thought of others as misprints or the author's errors and so corrected them, regarding it as the translator's responsibility to iron out mistakes. Readability, in the sense of avoiding what might puzzle target-text readers, may also have been an issue. The translators appear not to have had an ear for the music of Adah's rhymes, preferring lexical to rhythmic faithfulness. They realized that the translation of the palindromes required an expert and presumably persuaded the publisher of this need. But in all likelihood, when producing his Finnish palindromes for the target text the palindrome poet was not invited, or paid, to consider the over 600 pages long source text as a whole. Rather, his task is likely to have been to focus on the palindromes alone.

One way of dealing with the problem of retaining the function of the deviations might have been a translators' preface or postscript outlining the problem and perhaps presenting some examples and alternative translations for readers to consider. The paratext could also have explained why normalization was ultimately adopted in preference to other solutions.

The comparison of the English creative deviations and their Finnish renderings above also shows that the three types of deviations considered differ in the degree of difficulty they present to translators. Malapropisms are a recognized type of language play in both language cultures; that the translators did not to create any cannot be due to a lack of resources in the target language. Rhymes are more difficult because the lexical resources of the two languages differ: monosyllabic English rhymes more easily and needs less space to convey information than Finnish with its usually longer words. Palindromes are the hardest to recreate as only very rarely would reversed letters or words in target language items retain the source-text meaning.

A shift in functions between source and target texts often occurs because of the differences between source and target cultures. One text's intertextual allusions, for example, will not resonate in the target culture where the source of the allusions is unknown (Leppihalme 2005). In the present case study, one possibly relevant difference concerns readers' attitudes to and familiarity with postcolonial issues of ideology and power, which are clearly present in Kingsolver's novel. Translations of postcolonial literature are published in Finland though few of them are best-sellers or even attract much attention. Critical reviews of such literature are few and far between and rarely analyse the translation itself in any detail. The influential newspaper *Helsingin Sanomat* has an online archive of book reviews (www.hs.fi/kirjat), with over 10,000 items listed since 1997. A search for novels by Kingsolver brings up none. Pouttu-Delière (2008: 4–5) reports that the publisher of the Finnish translation of another award-winning postcolonial novel, Edwige Danticat's *The Farming of Bones* (1998, Finnish translation 2001), eventually invalidated over half of the printed translation as it did not sell sufficiently well.

It is difficult to estimate to what extent readers in Finland who read translated literature are comparable to readers in former colonial powers. In other words, how likely are Finnish readers to take sides, to feel anger, guilt or remorse, and how much does this affect their reading experiences? Kingsolver expects such emotional responses from her American readers as can be seen from her question (Kanner 1998: 3): "Given that this is what we did as a nation in Africa, how are we to feel about it now?" A function of her text, as argued above, is to persuade readers to rethink their attitudes to otherness. A recent survey of the attitudes of 1,200 Finns in order to gauge their awareness of the past suggests (Torsti 2010) that Finns are more conscious of their past than Americans, but the survey, only initial results of which have been reported so far, was limited to attitudes to events in the 20th century. It is beyond the scope of this article to address the question whether any part of Finnish history qualifies as colonial history. A general view among historians seems to be that during the centuries of Swedish rule (up to 1809) Finland was regarded as part of the Swedish kingdom and not a colony (see e.g. Engman 2009: 23–25). In the period 1809–1917 Finland was an autonomous grand duchy under the Russian czar. A provocative column in *Helsingin Sanomat* (Huuskonen 2010) recently suggested that after joining the EU in 1995, Finland should be seen as a colonial power herself as she now profits economically from the earlier exploitation of colonies by member states that once were colonizers; this was rebutted by practically every member of the public whose opinions were published on the newspaper's website. Their arguments linked the discussion to an on-going debate about currently increasing numbers of (especially African) immigrants in Finland. In other words, the commentators argued that Finland had never been a colonizer, had not profited from colonialism elsewhere and should therefore not be expected to make amends for other countries' past actions by allowing economic refugees into the country. Some of the commentators did take the view that Finland had been a colony herself in the past but this was usually said without heat and was rebutted in other comments.

If we can assume that in Finnish historical consciousness, there is not much guilt for past sins committed in colonized countries and therefore less likelihood of an emotional response to postcolonial literary texts, this might contribute to explaining why the target text of *The Poisonwood Bible* appears to bypass aspects and themes which are probably more highly charged emotionally in the source culture.

5 Conclusion

The creative source-text deviations in *The Poisonwood Bible* considered in this article function on two levels. On one, they characterize the narrators who use them; on the other, they help construct part of the thematic network of the novel. The malapropisms reveal the arrogance and ignorance of (some) Americans abroad. The rhymes and the palindromes, at first puzzling to readers, may encourage them to find new ways of looking at the world, seeing things differently, acknowledging that familiar established values may not be appropriate everywhere, and that we may need to reconsider *who* is backward, how right differs from righteousness and what is justice, or betrayal, or sin.

In the Finnish translation of the novel these themes do of course appear when they are expressed explicitly in the narrative or dialogue. But when the subtler and possibly more persuasive microlevel deviations discussed above are removed or normalized in the translation, thematic shifts occur. There are practically no malapropisms in the target text. The rhymes are given literal translations that rarely scan, and lists of words may be transformed into clauses. The palindromes do not really reward readers for their efforts as those recreated for the translation seldom provide clues to the themes of the novel. Efforts at compensation were not noted. How grave these losses are is hard to gauge accurately in the absence of critical reviews of the target text. But it is evident that the thematic network so carefully constructed by the author has lost many of its links in the "taming" process. Target-text readers cannot pick up the author's clues and use them for their interpretation of the text if the clues are not there.

The results of this case study are in line with Toury's law of growing standardization (1995): the creative deviations are "modified, sometimes to the point of being totally ignored, in favour of [more] habitual options" (1995: 268). This applies particularly to the first two types of deviations. Possible explanations proposed in this article include the production team's probable need to get the translation done without delay, translators prioritizing readability and therefore taming elements that might puzzle readers; certain differences between English and Finnish potential for creative deviations of the types considered here, and cultural differences between readers in the United States and Finland.

Acknowledgements

I thank Karla Pesonen-Wikman for information on disabilities resembling that of the character Adah and Caroline Leppihalme for her lively stories, which have helped me visualize a child's life in the Congo.

References

Baker, Mona (2000): "Towards a Methodology for Investigating the Style of a Literary Translator." In: *Target* 12(2), 241–265.
Boase-Beier, Jean (2006): *Stylistic Approaches to Translation*. Manchester: St. Jerome.
BookBrowse.com (2007) = Author Biography of Barbara Kingsolver. Last updated on 16 May 2007. Online. www.bookbrowse.com/biographies/index.cfm?author_numbe. Visited April 2009.
Brownlie, Siobhan (2003): "Investigating Explanations of Translational Phenomena." In: *Target* 15(1), 111–152.
Bush, Peter (1998): "Literary translation, practices." In: Baker, Mona [ed.] (1998): *Routledge Encyclopedia of Translation Studies*. London and New York: Routledge. 127–130.
Bühler, Karl (1934): *Sprachtheorie: Die Darstellungsfunktion der Sprache*. Jena: G. Fischer.
Collins Dictionary of the English Language, 2nd ed. (1986). London & Glasgow: Collins.
Conrad, Joseph (1902/1976): *Heart of Darkness*. Harmondsworth: Penguin.
Danticat, Edwige (1998): *The Farming of Bones*. New York: Soho Press.
—— (2000): *Veressä viljava maa*. Trans. Leena Tamminen. Jyväskylä: Gummerus.
Engman, Max (2009): *Ett långt farväl: Finland mellan Sverige och Ryssland efter 1809*. Stockholm: Atlantis.
Fennica. National Bibliography of Finland. https://fennica.linneanet.fi. Visited January 2010.
Gullin, Christina (1998): *Översättarens röst*. Lund: Lund University Press.
Hekkanen, Raila (2010): *Englanniksiko maailmanmaineeseen? Suomalaisen proosakirjallisuuden kääntäminen englanniksi Isossa-Britanniassa vuosina 1945–2003* ['World-famous if Englished? The translation of Finnish literary prose into English in Great Britain 1945–2003']. Doctoral dissertation, Department of Modern Languages, University of Helsinki. http://helda.helsinki.fi/handle/10138/19296.
Helsingin Sanomat Archive of book reviews. www.hs.fi/kirjat. Visited March 2010.
Hirvonen, Esa (2002): *Takana kapakan akat: palindromirunoja*. Turku: Savukeidas.
Huuskonen, Matti (2010): "Siirtomaavalta Suomi." In: *Helsingin Sanomat* 1 Feb. 2010, A6.
Kakutani, Michiko (1998): "'The Poisonwood Bible': A family a heart of darkness." www.times.com/books/98/10/11/daily/kingsolver-book-review. Visited March 2010.
Kanner, Ellen (1998): "Barbara Kingsolver turns to her past to understand the present." Interview with Barbara Kingsolver. www.bookpage.com/books. Visited March 2010.
Kenny, Dorothy (1998): "Creatures of Habit? What Translators Usually Do with Words." In: *Meta* 43(4), 515–523.
—— (2001): *Lexis and Creativity in Translation: A Corpus-based Study*. Manchester: St. Jerome.
Kingsolver, Barbara (1998): *The Poisonwood Bible*. Paperback edition (1999). London: Faber & Faber.

—— (1999): *Myrkkypuun siemen*. Trans. Juha Ahokas & Arvi Tamminen, with palindromes rendered by Esa Hirvonen. Helsinki: Like.

Klinkenborg,Verlyn (1998): "Going Native." In: *New York Times* Oct. 18, 1998. www.nytimes.com/1998/10/18/books/goingnative.html. Visited January 2010.

Leppihalme, Ritva (1997): "The re-writing of a well-read man, or what happened to Wexford." In: Mauranen, Anna / Puurtinen, Tiina [eds.] (1997): *Translation, Acquisition, Use*. Jyväskylä: Jyväskylä University Press. 61–69.

—— (2000): "The two faces of standardization. On the translation of regionalisms in literary dialogue." In: *The Translator* (6) 2 (Special issue on translation evaluation guest-edited by Carol Meier), 247–269.

—— (2005): "Faithfulness versus fluency: Counting the cost." In: *Across Languages and Cultures* 6 (2), 221–241.

—— (2007): "Value-adding metaphors: On creativity in translation." In: Jääskeläinen, Riitta / Puurtinen, Tiina / Stotesbury, Hilkka [eds.] (2007): *Text, Processes and Corpora: Research Inspired by Sonja Tirkkonen-Condit*. Joensuu: Joensuu University Press. 129–144.

Lybeck, Jari (2000): "Matka pimeyden sydämeen ja takaisin." In: *Turun Sanomat*. Verkkolehti 12 Feb. 2000. Online. www.turunsanomat.fi/kulttuuri/?ts=1,3:1005:0:0,4:5:0:1:2000. Visited May 2009.

Miller, Mark Crispin (2001): *The Bush Dyslexicon*. London: Bantam Books.

Obama, Barack. (1995/2007): *Dreams from My Father. A Story of Race and Inheritance*. Edinburgh: Canongate Books.

Pekkanen, Hilkka (2010): *The Duet between the Author and the Translator: An Analysis of Style through Shifts in Literary Translation*. Doctoral dissertation, Department of English, University of Helsinki. Helsinki: Helsinki University Print. http://oa.doria.fi/handle/10024/59427.

Pouttu-Delière, Päivi (2008): *Parsley, Pési and Perejil: On the Finnish translation of Edwige Danticat's culturally and linguistically hybrid novel* The Farming of Bones. Unpublished Master's thesis, University of Helsinki, Department of English.

Reiss, Katarina (1976): *Texttyp und Übersetzungsmethode. Der operative Text*. Kronberg: Scriptor.

Snell-Hornby, Mary (1988): *Translation Studies: An Integrated Approach*. Amsterdam and Philadelphia: John Benjamins.

Tarvi, Ljuba (2004): *Comparative Translation Assessment: Quantifying Quality*. Doctoral dissertation, Department of English, University of Helsinki. Helsinki: Helsinki University Print.

Torsti, Pilvi (2010): "Mitä ihmiset ajattelevat historiasta ja mitä väliä sillä on? Historiatietoisuus Suomessa -tutkimushanke osana historiatietoisuuden tutkimustraditiota" ['What do people think about history and what does it matter? The project 'Historical Consciousness in Finland' as a part of the tradition of research on historical consciousness']. European Research Network lecture, Helsinki, 4 March 2010.

Toury, Gideon (1995): *Descriptive Translation Studies and Beyond*. Amsterdam and Philadelphia: John Benjamins.

Viikon 25-2004 kulttuurivinkki[TM]. www.warthog.fi/vuosi2004/kulttuurivinkit/vinkki25-2004.html. Visited January 2010.

Øverås, Linn (1998): "In Search of the Third Code: An Investigation of Norms in Literary Translation." In: *Meta* 43 (4), 557–570.

The Translation of Book Titles: Theoretical and Practical Aspects

Maurizio Viezzi
University of Trieste, Italy

Abstract

While exhibiting a fair amount of variability, the practice of book title translation is often characterized by a lack of semantic equivalence between a source title and the corresponding target title. The reason lies in the nature and functions of titles. Titles are names – they are the names of cultural products and are chosen with a view to functions to be pursued and fulfilled. When translating a title, functions to be pursued and fulfilled are not considered with reference to the source title, but rather with reference to the target culture. This may lead to target titles whose semantic content is to some extent different from or even independent of the semantic content of the corresponding source title. Such a process – based not on *semantic* equivalence, but on what Rabadán (1991) calls *translemic* equivalence – may legitimately be called translation and a source title and its target title may be said to be mutual intertranslations as they are names of the same cultural product.

1 Introduction

The practice of book title translation exhibits a fair amount of variability across time, space and genres – titles are not translated now as they were centuries ago, different traditions exist in different countries, different approaches are generally used for literary and non-literary works. However, when comparing 20th- and 21st-century fiction titles and their translations in the Western world, a trend clearly emerges: there is often a lack of semantic equivalence between a title and its translation or, to use a couple of terms that will be employed throughout this paper, between a source title and the corresponding target title. This results from a strategy that may be regarded as an extreme form of adaptation. A few examples from a virtually endless list may serve to illustrate this point: Ian McEwan's *The Innocent* was published in Italy under the title *Lettera a Berlino* [Letter to Berlin], the first book in Stieg Larsson's *Millennium Trilogy*, *Män som hatar kvinnor* [Men who hate women] is known in the English-speaking world as *The Girl with the Dragon Tattoo*, in France Agatha Christie's *A Caribbean Mystery* was published as *Le major parlait trop* [The major spoke too much] etc. Literal or quasi-literal translation of titles, i.e. translation that exactly or almost exactly reproduces the semantic content of the source title, is a practice that still exists, of course, but it is not or not necessarily the strategy of choice.[1]

Drawing on an extensive corpus of titles collected by this author over the years, the paper will address two questions.[2] The first: what are the reasons why the deliberate choice is often made to devise target titles that do not convey the semantic content of the corresponding source titles? The second: when there is no semantic equivalence between source title and target title, is the word "translation" still justified? In other words, when the source title and the target title are semantically unrelated, is translation the link between the two?

2 The nature and function of titles

In order to answer the first question it may be useful briefly to consider the nature and functions of titles.[3] Titles are names, proper names, they are the names of cultural products such as books,[4] films, operas, records, songs, paintings, poems etc. Titles may be used as names of real or fictional referents. For example, *Death of a Writer* is the title of a real book by Michael Collins, whereas *I'm Sick of Following My Dreams: I'm Just Going to Ask Them Where They're Going & Hook Up With Them Later* is the title of a fictitious autobiography mentioned in *Death of a Writer*. A title like *I Married a Communist* is both: it is the title of a real book by Philip Roth where mention is made of a fictitious book with the same title.

---

[1] Lack of semantic equivalence between source title and target title is also common, indeed even more common, in film title translation, in particular in countries such as Spain and Italy (cf. Pascua Febles 1994, Fuentes Luque 1997 and 1997–98, Viezzi 2004a).

[2] The corpus includes source and target titles of books (mainly novels) and films in English, Italian, French and Spanish. At the time of writing the total number of titles exceeds 40,000.

[3] Investigating the nature and functions of titles is the goal of *titrologie* or titology, a little-known academic discipline initiated by the Dutch scholar Leo H. Hoek with two seminal books dating back to the early 1970s and 1980s (Hoek 1973 and 1981).

[4] "Le titre, c'est bien connu, est le 'nom' du livre" (Genette 1987: 78).

Titles are indicators. They provide information about the cultural products themselves, about the period to which they belong, about the linguacultural system in which they are produced or for which they are destined.

Titles may be regarded as a genre, with specific defining features. For example, in titles verbal forms are rather rare and definite articles are much more frequent than indefinite articles; furthermore, titles tend to be synthetic rather than analytic and generally take the form of captions rather than narratives (Viezzi 2006).

Titles come in a variety of forms. They may be very short (e.g. *V.* by Thomas Pynchon) or very long (e.g. *Karl der Große und die theologischen Herausforderungen seiner Zeit. Zur Wechselwirkung zwischen Theologie und Politik im Zeitalter des großen Frankenherrschers* by Helmut Nagel). They may consist of special characters or signs (e.g. *ε* by Jacques Roubaud or *?* by Victor Hugo) or figures (e.g. *666* by Truman Dayon Godwin or *1984* by George Orwell, and the different status of the two figures is immediately clear). Their structure may be varyingly complex, as is shown by the following Pink Floyd titles: *The Wall, The Final Cut, The Piper at the Gates of Dawn, Is There Anybody Out There?*

Titles are names and, even more importantly, they "are names for a purpose" (Fisher 1984: 288). They fulfil functions and are devised with a view to functions to be pursued and fulfilled. Several functions or sets of functions have been identified and discussed by authors such as Hoek (1973, 1981), Rothe (1986), Nord (1990, 1994a, 1994b, 1995), Pascua Febles (1994), Fuentes-Luque (1997, 1997–98), Weinrich (2001), Viezzi (2004b). On the basis of their research, in particular on the basis of the very influential work done by Nord, and after further analysis of the topic it is here suggested that ten main functions may be associated with titles. Three of them may be regarded as essential, in that they are necessarily fulfilled by any title, whereas seven may be considered optional, in that they may or may not be pursued and may or may not be successfully fulfilled.

The first essential function is the *naming* function: a title necessarily is the name of a cultural product. The second essential function is the *phatic* function: a title necessarily establishes some kind of contact with the potential reader or spectator and with the public at large. The third essential function is the *informatory* function: a title necessarily informs the potential reader or spectator and the public at large about the existence of a cultural product bearing that name. As has been said, by the simple fact of being a title, any title fulfils the three functions.

The first optional function is the *distinctive* function: a title may distinguish a given cultural product from any other cultural product. For one reason or another the distinctive function is not always pursued: for example, three films entitled *Fuori di testa* [Insane] were distributed in Italy over the period 1982–1991, and any well-stocked library will contain a number of different books entitled *(The) Story of My Life* (by Helen Keller, by Anne Cassidy, by Jay McInerney etc.). The second optional function is the *descriptive* function: a title may provide information about the cultural product, its content, its characters, some of its features etc. A title like *My Son's Story* by Nadine Gordimer tells the potential reader that the novel is about the narrator's son; a title such as *Equal Music* by Vikram Seth gives no clue about what the book is about, although one may imagine music to have some role in the story; a title like Peter Robinson's *All the Colours of Darkness* is totally non-descriptive. The third optional function is the *expressive* function: a title may express the author's opinion or feelings about the cultural product or its content. For example, with a title such as *The Strange Case of Dr Jekyll and Mr Hyde* Robert Louis Stevenson tells the potential reader that the case in question is, indeed, strange. The fourth optional function is the *suggestive* function: a title may suggest to the reader how the cultural product is to be interpreted or understood. For example, a title such as George Orwell's *Homage to Catalonia* tells the reader that the text is to be interpreted as a homage and not as anything else. The fifth optional function is the *seductive* function:[5] a title may (try to) attract the potential reader or spectator. As is obvious, economic considerations make the seductive function crucially important. Several strategies or tools may be used in this respect, such as intriguing references to sex (e.g. *Strip Tease* by Carl Hiaasen), mystery (e.g. *You Only Live Twice* by Ian Fleming), the name of a popular character (e.g. Georges Simenon's *Maigret et la vieille dame* [Maigret and the old lady]) etc. The sixth optional function is the *intertextual* function: a title may refer to some other title or text. For example, *Three Men on the Bummel* by Jerome K. Jerome is a clear reference to a previous novel by the same author (*Three Men in a Boat*) and John Le Carré's *Tinker, Tailor, Soldier, Spy* refers to a well-known English rhyme. Finally, the seventh optional function is the

---

[5] It was Pascua Febles (1994) who introduced the term *función seductora* (seductive function) to refer to what Nord had called appellative function. Pascua Febles' term seems better to capture the real nature of this function.

poetic function: a title may pursue a poetic effect, for example through alliteration, as is the case in Jane Austen's *Pride and Prejudice* or *Sense and Sensibility*.

3 Titles and translation

Titles tend to be translated. Not all of them and not always, though. When a book is translated, its title is generally translated as well: Ian McEwan's *Saturday* is *Sabato* in the Italian edition and *Samedi* in the French edition. However, this is not always the case: that same McEwan book was published in German with the original English title, *Saturday*. The titles of sub-titled films are usually not translated, whereas the titles of dubbed films are, although in some countries the practice of retaining the original foreign-language title has become rather common (cf. Jiménez 1997, Viezzi 2004b).[6] Opera titles are often translated even when the librettos are not: in Italy Mozart's *Die Zauberflöte* is *Il flauto magico* even when it is performed in German. Records are not translated and their titles are not translated either: Pink Floyd's *The Dark Side of the Moon* or Chico Buarque's *Construção* remain the same everywhere. Paintings are obviously not translated but their titles usually are: for example, outside the Dutch-speaking world Van Gogh's *De Aardappeleters* is known as *Les mangeurs de pommes de terre*, *The Potato Eaters*, *I mangiatori di patate*, *Die Kartoffelessers* etc.

When a title is translated, the issue of which functions to pursue and how is addressed with reference to and in the framework of the target culture because it is there that functions will have to be fulfilled. Functions pursued through the source title in the source culture may be regarded as irrelevant to the target culture and therefore ignored; conversely, other functions may become a priority, which paves the way for the choice of target titles whose content is to some extent different from or even independent of the content of the corresponding source titles. Even

---

[6] The use of a foreign-language film title may have something to do with globalised merchandising, advertising etc., but, as will be seen later, seductive considerations are not irrelevant. It is also worth noting that the concomitant use of non-translation (for film titles) and adaptation (for book titles) may be rather confusing. For example, *Mystic River*, the novel by Dennis Lehane, was published in Italian under the title *La morte non dimentica* [Death does not forget], whereas *Mystic River*, the film by Clint Eastwood based on Lehane's novel, was distributed in Italy (and in Italian) as *Mystic River*.

when the same functions are pursued, the semantic content of the source title may be regarded as inadequate and therefore replaced by a different semantic content. As Nord says (1990: 153), when there is conflict between functions pursued and fidelity, the latter may be sacrificed.

As noted in the Introduction, what may be called literal translation or quasi-literal translation, i.e. a more or less accurate reformulation of the semantic content of the source title, is by no means unusual: for example, Paul Auster's *The Book of Illusions* is *Le livre des illusions* [The book of illusions] in French and *Il libro delle illusioni* [The book of illusions] in Italian. However, literal or quasi-literal translation is just one option and not necessarily the most common, in particular for some genres in some countries.[7] A function-oriented approach, whereby the emphasis is on functions to be pursued and not on semantic equivalence to be realised, often leads to different choices, as demonstrated by the examples discussed below.

David Lodge's *Small World* was published in Italy under the title *Il professore va al congresso* [The lecturer goes to the conference]. A literal translation of *Small World* into Italian, something like "Piccolo mondo" or "Mondo piccolo", would have elicited an immediate association with other texts and other authors (Antonio Fogazzaro's *Piccolo mondo antico* and Giovannino Guareschi's *Mondo piccolo*). Hence the need to find something else in order to fulfil the distinctive function. Interestingly, the target title in question turns out to be descriptive (the novel is about academics and conferences) while the source title is not.[8]

Two further examples of attention paid to the descriptive function to the detriment of semantic equivalence are P.D. James' *Original Sin*, published in Italy under the title *Morte sul fiume* [Death on the river] and Ian McEwan's *The Child in Time* published in France as *L'enfant volé* [The stolen child]. In each case a rather opaque title has been replaced by a title providing some information about the novel's content: the former is about a murder in a building on the banks of river Thames, the latter is about a little girl kidnapped. Curiously, the French translation of the

---

[7] Mention has already been made of film titles in Spain and Italy. In the latter, another significant example is crime fiction.
[8] Such an occurrence is not unusual – verifying the explicitation hypothesis (cf. Séguinot 1988: 108) in title translation could be a promising line of research for the future.

former and the Italian translation of the latter are literal or quasi-literal: *Péché originel* [Original sin] and *Bambini nel tempo* [Children in time].

Intertextual considerations were involved in the choice of translating André Malraux's *L'espoir* [Hope] as *Man's Hope* after the same author's *La condition humaine* [The Human Condition] had been published under the title *Man's Fate*. The choice was criticized by Genette (1987: 67) as it seemed to suggest an unjustified analogy between the two novels. Actually the choice may have been inspired not by some form of literary criticism, but rather by a desire to attract the reader through an intertextual reference.[9]

As has been said, the seductive function is crucially important for the economic success of a cultural product, in fact much more important than semantic equivalence, and may be pursued in several ways: with a reference to a well-known character, as was the case with Agatha Christie's last Miss Marple mystery, *Sleeping Murder*, translated into Italian as *Addio, miss Marple* [Farewell, miss Marple]; or with a reference to a well-known character accompanied by a reference to death or blood or crime etc., as in Manuel Vázquez Montalbán's *La soledad del manager* [The manager's loneliness] published in Germany under the title *Carvalho und der tote Manager* [Carvalho and the dead manager]; or with a reference to exotic lands (which is apparently very seductive for a German readership), as in *Die Flucht nach Manoa* [Flight to Manoa], the German translation of Alejo Carpenter's *Los pasos perdidos* [The lost steps] etc.

The seductive function also seems to have had a role in the first book of the Harry Potter series. The title is *Harry Potter and the Philosopher's Stone*, but for the American edition it was changed into *Harry Potter and the Sorcerer's Stone* – an example of intralingual title translation probably responding to the need to make the Harry Potter product more attractive to the American public.

An interesting case of semantic equivalence largely being ignored is the series of novels written by the American crime writer Sue Grafton. Grafton has undertaken to write what she calls the Alphabet of Crime and all her titles have the same structure: *A is for Alibi, B is for Burglar, C is for Corpse, D is for Deadbeat* etc. (she has now reached the letter U which means that she is not far from the end). In all

---

[9] Fuentes Luque (1997–98) provides examples of this strategy being used to translate American film titles into Spanish.

countries the translated titles have retained the same structure with little or no attention paid to the actual meaning of the words used in the original titles, equivalence of form prevailing over equivalence of semantic content: for example, the second book in the series is *B come bugiardo* [B is for liar] in Italian, *B comme brûlée* [B is for burnt] in French, *B de bestias* [B is for beasts] in Spanish.

Mention has been made of the increasingly frequent practice of using the original foreign-language titles for dubbed films. For translated books the practice is less widespread, but significant examples of what, following Ballard (2001: 18), may be called translation degree zero ("le degré zéro de la traduction du signifiant") are easily found. In 2005, for example, Don DeLillo's *Running Dog* was published in Italian with that same title. It is interesting to note that fourteen years earlier DeLillo's book had been published with an Italian title (*Cane che corre*, a literal translation of *Running Dog*). It is impossible to know for certain why the publishing house decided to use the English title. However, English words are often used in Italy to convey a sense of being modern, up-to-date, state-of-the-art, high-level etc. In all forms of public communication, from politics to advertising to business communication, the English language is used as a marketing tool. In the choice of an English title, therefore, it is easy to recognize some kind of seductive strategy at work.[10]

Changing translated book titles, as was done with DeLillo's book, is not rare at all. For example, Italo Svevo's *La coscienza di Zeno* [Zeno's conscience] was first translated into English as *The Confessions of Zeno* and then as *Zeno's Conscience*, and the same author's *Senilità* [Senility] was first published as *As a Man Grows Older* and then as *Emilio's Carnival*. In Italy, J.D. Salinger's *The Catcher in the Rye* was first published under the title *Vita da uomo* [A man's life] and then under the title *Il giovane Holden* [Young Holden], with the latter prevailing and the former long since forgotten. The Italian record in this respect probably belongs to Agatha Christie's *The Mysterious Affair at Styles*, which has been published under no fewer than nine different titles.[11] Different reasons may explain the decision to change a title. Georges Simenon's first novel, *Pietr-le-Letton* [Pietr the Latvian], was first published in Italy under the

---

[10] For a discussion of the use of language as a marketing tool, see Viezzi (2010).
[11] *Un delitto a Styles Court, Il misterioso "Affare Styles", Morte misteriosa a Styles Court, Il misterioso affare di Styles, L'affare misterioso di Styles, Il mistero di Styles Court, L'affare Styles, Omicidio premeditato, Poirot a Styles Court*: a sort of exercise in variations on a theme.

title *Pietro il Lettone* [Pietro the Latvian], at a time when it was customary to give an Italian form to foreign names (e.g. *Carlo* Marx, *Giulio* Verne); then it was published under the title *Maigret e il Lettone* [Maigret and the Latvian], probably to use the name of the famous character as a source of attraction; now the latest edition bears the title *Pietr il lettone* [Pietr the Latvian], with the name restored to its foreign form, as is the practice these days when an Italianized form would be resented by the public. *Maigret chez le coroner* [Maigret at the coroner's] was first published with the title *Maigret va dal giudice* [Maigret goes to the judge] and then with the title *Maigret va dal coroner* [Maigret goes to the coroner]: a clear attempt to make the book more attractive by hinting at an unusual-for-Maigret setting. Whatever the real reasons, however, one has the impression that changes have more to do with the attempt to increase the impact on the potential reader rather than with the attempt to devise a "better" title for the book, i.e. they seem to be potential-reader-oriented rather than source-text-oriented.

Examples could be provided endlessly, showing unmistakably that translating a title means choosing a title for a given linguaculture while taking into account specific needs or specific functions to be fulfilled in that linguaculture. In such an operation the source title is just one possible source of inspiration (cf. Viezzi 2005: 169) and semantic equivalence is just one possible option. In other words, the translation of book titles seems to be a perfect example of implemented *Skopos* theory or, to refer to the title of a book by Christiane Nord, a perfect example of translating as a purposeful activity.

4 Title translation and equivalence

Those who are in charge of translating a title, therefore, do what they deem appropriate to fulfil the functions they wish (or are instructed) to fulfil, even at the cost of ignoring semantic equivalence, even at the cost of producing a title that bears no resemblance whatsoever to the original title. Is this translation? Juliane House (2001: 43) says that "translation is essentially an operation in which the meaning of linguistic units is to be kept equivalent across languages". The penultimate novel by P.D. James, *The Lighthouse*, was published in Italy under the title *Brividi di morte per l'ispettore Dalgliesh* [Death shivers for Inspector Dalgliesh]. Is this translation? Is there any kind of equivalence between the two titles? According to House's definition this is not translation because clearly the *meaning* of linguistic units has not been kept equivalent across languages: there is no linguistic link between a lighthouse and a shivering inspector. But House's definition is just one definition and there is no need for translation to be defined in such a traditional, conservative and restrictive way. The co-founder of *Skopos* theory, Hans Vermeer (1996: 15), advocated the "necessity or advisability of redefining the concept of 'translating' and 'translation'", declared himself "in favour of a broader concept of translating, translation and translator" (Vermeer 1996: 34) and suggested that "in an extreme case it may [...] be preferable not to translate the source-text at all, but to 'design' a new text, partly or as a whole, under target-culture conventions" (*ibid.*). Which is what happens more often than not with title translation: target titles are primarily chosen or designed with target-culture (rather than source-title) considerations in mind. *Skopos* theory implemented indeed.

The operation leading from a title such as *The Lighthouse* to a title such as *Brividi di morte per l'ispettore Dalgliesh* may thus legitimately be called translation if only translation is defined broadly enough to accommodate something more than strict "linguistic" or semantic equivalence, and there is no reason why this should not be the case. There is something more, though, closely related to titles being names. Just as *Cologne* in English and *Köln* in German "are mutual intertranslations *just because they name the same thing* in their respective languages" (Wilson 1978: 97, italics in the original), *The Lighthouse* and *Brividi di morte per l'ispettore Dalgliesh* may be said to be mutual intertranslations because they refer to the "same" novel, they are names of the "same" cultural product.[12] The link between the two is what Rabadán (1991) calls *equivalencia translémica* (translemic equivalence): the unique relationship characterizing any pair of source and target texts above the mere "linguistic" level. In linguistic, semantic terms the two are not equivalent, as any *ordinary* dictionary would confirm; in *translational* terms and within a clearly defined context of use they are perfectly equivalent, as any dictionary of *literary works* would show: what is called *The Lighthouse* in English is called *Brividi di morte per l'ispettore Dalgliesh* in Italian.

---

12   It is true that one title refers to the English text and the other to the Italian text and it is also true that by definition the two texts are not identical and therefore are not the same. However, both refer to P.D. James' penultimate novel, and P.D. James' penultimate novel is by definition one.

While it may be used as a category to describe the superficial relationship between a source title and the corresponding target title, semantic equivalence is basically irrelevant: a target title is just a title and its status and effectiveness have little to do with its being semantically equivalent to its source title. Target titles such as *La miglior vendetta* [The best revenge], *Le lieu du crime* [The crime scene] and *Keiner werfe den ersten Stein* [Let no one cast the first stone], the Italian, French and German translations of Elizabeth George's *Payment in Blood*, are not intrinsically worse (or better) than target titles such as *Il terzo gemello*, *Le troisième jumeau*, *Der dritte Zwilling*, the (literal) Italian, French and German translations of Ken Follett's *The Third Twin*.

Going back to the P.D. James titles, a comparison reveals that the English title is moderately descriptive as the crime scene is a lighthouse, whereas, more ambitiously, the Italian title addresses both the descriptive and the seductive functions, with the use of the name of what is a well-known character in P.D. James' universe and with its direct and indirect references to illness or fear and death (in the story inspector Dalgliesh actually falls ill and his life seems to be in danger). What differentiates the two titles in terms of functions pursued, and intended effect, would seem to be much more significant and interesting than what differentiates them in terms of semantic content.

5 Conclusion

Title translation is a rather neglected area in translation studies. Yet it would seem to deserve closer scholarly attention as it is both interesting, on account of information it directly or indirectly conveys about linguacultural systems, and important, on account of the impact translated titles have on language use.

As has been shown, title translation is characterized by a variety of strategies leading to a variety of outcomes. While it may be difficult clearly to identify regular patterns making it possible reliably to predict how any given title will be dealt with, what emerges from an analysis of titles and their translations is that translating a title often means *devising* a new title; it often means thinking of how to *find* a title for a cultural product destined for another culture and another communicative situation; it often means undertaking a process that is very much target-oriented rather than source-oriented. Which explains why little or no trace of the source title is often found in the corresponding target title and makes title translation a fascinating research field.

References

Ballard, Michel (2001): *Le nom propre en traduction*. Gap et Paris: Ophrys.
Fisher, John (1984): "Entitling." In: *Critical Enquiry* 11, 2, 286–298.
Fuentes Luque, Adrián (1997): "Funcionalidad y fidelidad en la traducción de los títulos de las películas." In: Félix Fernández, Leandro / Ortega Arjonilla, Emilio [eds.] (1997): *Estudios sobre traducción e interpretación*. Málaga: CEDMA. 419–424.
Fuentes Luque, Adrián (1997–98): "La traducción de los títulos de películas y series de televisión ('¿Y esto ... de qué va?')." In: *Sendebar* 8/9, 107–114.
Genette, Gérard (1987): *Seuils*. Paris: Éditions du Seuil.
Hoek, Leo H. (1973): *Pour une sémiotique du titre*. Urbino: Centro Internazionale di Semiotica e di Linguistica, Università di Urbino.
—— (1981): *La marque du titre. Dispositifs sémiotiques d'une pratique textuelle*. The Hague, Paris and New York: Mouton.
House, Juliane (2001): "Translation Quality Assessment: Linguistic Description versus Social Evaluation." In: *Meta* 46, 2, 243–257.
Jiménez, Oscar (1997): "Breves notas sobre la traducción al español de los títulos de largometrajes en inglés." In: Arias Torres, Juan Pablo / Morillas, Esther [eds.] (1997): *El papel del traductor*. Málaga: CEDMA. 443–450.
Nord, Christiane (1990): "Funcionalismo y lealtad: algunas consideraciones en torno a la traducción de títulos." In: Raders, Margit / Conesa, Juan [eds.] (1990): *II Encuentros Complutenses en torno a la traducción*. Madrid: Editorial Complutense. 153–162.
—— (1994a): "Translation as a process of linguistic and cultural adaptation." In: Dollerup, Cay / Lindegaard, Annette [eds.] (1994): *Teaching Translation and Interpreting 2. Insights, Aims, Visions*. Amsterdam and Philadelphia: John Benjamins. 59–67.
—— (1994b): "Las funciones comunicativas y su realización textual en la traducción." In: *Sendebar* 5, 85–103.
—— (1995): "Text-Functions in Translation: Titles and Headings as a Case in Point." In: *Target* 7: 2, 261–284.
Pascua Febles, Isabel (1994): "Estudio sobre la traducción de los títulos de películas." In: Raders, Margit / Martín-Gaitero, Rafael [eds.] (1994): *IV Encuentros Complutenses en torno a la traducción*. Madrid: Editorial Complutense. 349–354.
Rabadán, Rosa (1991): *Equivalencia y traducción. Problemática de la equivalencia translémica inglés-español*. León: Universidad de León.
Rothe, Arnold (1986): *Der literarische Titel*. Frankfurt am Main: Klostermann.
Séguinot, Candace (1988): "Pragmatics and the Explicitation Hypothesis." In: *TTR : traduction, terminologie, rédaction*, 1, 2, 106–113.
Vermeer, Hans J. (1996): *A Skopos Theory of Translation (Some arguments for and against)*. Heidelberg: TEXTconTEXT.
Viezzi, Maurizio (2004a): "Cinema e lingua: i titoli dei film." In: Cardinaletti, Anna / Garzone, Giuliana [eds.] (2004): *Lingua, mediazione linguistica e interferenza*. Milano: FrancoAngeli. 255–270.

—— (2004b): *Denominazioni proprie e traduzione*. Milano: LED.
—— (2005): "Oltre l'equivalenza: titoli e traduzione." In: Kocijančič Pokorn, Nike / Prunč, Erich / Riccardi, Alessandra [eds.] (2005): *Beyond Equivalence – Jenseits der Äquivalenz – Oltre l'equivalenza – Onkraj ekvivalence*. Graz: ITAT, Universität Graz. 159–172.
—— (2006): "Forme verbali nei titoli: aspetti funzionali e traduttivi." In: Calogiuri, Antonella [ed.] (2006): *Verbo e dintorni fra inglese, italiano e dialetto*. Lecce: Manni. 47–70.
—— (2010): "Il lato oscuro della globalizzazione." In: Lee-Jahnke, Hannelore / Prunč, Erich [eds.] (2010): *Am Schnittpunkt von Philologie und Translationswissenschaft*. Bern: Peter Lang. 357–369.
Weinrich, Harald (2001): "I titoli e i testi." In: Prandi, Michele / Ramat, Paolo [eds.] (2001): *Semiotica e linguistica. Per ricordare Maria Elisabeth Conte*. Milano: FrancoAngeli. 49–62.
Wilson, Neil L. (1978): "Concerning the Translation of Predicates." In: Guenthner, Franz / Guenthner-Reutter, M. [eds.] (1978): *Meaning and Translation*. London: Duckworth. 95–105.

Some Insights into the Factors Underlying the Translation of Phraseology in the COVALT Corpus[1]

Josep Marco
Universitat Jaume I, Castelló, Spain

Abstract

The starting-point of this article is the outcome of a previous study on the translation of phraseology in the English-Catalan component of COVALT (Valencian Corpus of Translated Literature), according to which the target texts in the corpus can be said to be more *phraseological* than their corresponding source texts. The aim of the present article is to find out what factors impinge on the translation of phraseology, with special attention to two particular (previously hypothesised) ones: stylistic motivation and translator expertise. A questionnaire was designed and administered to three translators some of whose translations are part of our corpus. Answers to the questionnaire not only confirmed the two factors just mentioned but helped to uncover others, which could be grouped under five different headings: the translator's knowledge, skills and attitudes; cross-linguistic differences; the target text's readability and comprehensibility; stylistic consistency; and expressivity (a stylistic value often associated with phraseology).

1 Background

1.1 Corpus-Based Translation Studies and the COVALT Project

The COVALT research group set out some years ago to build a corpus which could be regarded as representative of the practice of contemporary literary translation into Catalan in the area of Valencia. Our aim in building the corpus was basically descriptive: we intended to uncover the main features of translated texts *vis-à-vis* their corresponding source texts and thus to determine what translation

---

[1] Research funds for this article have been provided by two research projects: FFI2009-09544, funded by the Spanish Ministry of Science and Innovation, and P1·1B2008-59, funded by the *Caixa Castelló – Bancaixa* Foundation, within the framework of an agreement with the Universitat Jaume I.

techniques had been used in the solution of a number of given problems. Some years after the inception of the project there emerged COVALT (Valencian Corpus of Translated Literature), a multilingual corpus – still under construction but almost completed – made up of two components: (1) translations into Catalan of narrative works originally written in English, French and German published in the autonomous region of Valencia from 1990 to 2000, and (2) their corresponding source texts. The English-Catalan component of COVALT currently holds 32 source texts by 20 different authors and 33 target texts (there are two translations of Jack London's *The Call of the Wild*) by 21 different translators. Taken all in all, the English source texts contain 890,486 words, and their Catalan translations, 930,625 words. The German-Catalan component is made up of 18 source texts by 14 different authors amounting to 447,195 words and 19 target texts (again, one source text features two translations) by 11 different translators or translator teams amounting to 540,673 words. Finally, the French-Catalan component includes 29 source texts by 25 different authors amounting to 607,463 words and 29 target texts by 22 different translators amounting to 593,477 words.

It might be argued that both corpus composition and our main object of study were not trendy when its compilation started (the early 2000s), as Baker (e.g. 1993, 1995) and other influencing scholars had recurrently called for the construction of comparable corpora along the lines laid by the Manchester-based English Comparable Corpus. However well justified that kind of corpus may have been in the context of the research goals it served, we felt that the source text was too important a factor in translation practice to be left out of the picture. Therefore, we stuck to the traditional coupling of source text and target text because we were more interested in the dynamics of translation (what happens to the source text, or to particular segments of it, when it becomes the object of translation) than in a(n arguably) static picture of translated *vis-à-vis* non-translated text. But that does not mean that we are not interested in that kind of picture *at all*. In fact, we eventually came to realise (with the invaluable help of many of the contributions to Mauranen and Kujamäki 2004 or of Bernardini 2005) that both kinds of corpora were far from incompatible and could in fact complement each other to achieve certain research goals. As a result, we have recently started building a third component comparable to COVALT – a monolingual corpus made up of literary narrative works originally written in Catalan and published in the region of Valencia between 1990 and 2000.

One of the most valuable contributions of Baker's mid-nineties articles undoubtedly was the new emphasis laid on the notion of *translation universal*. However much we may want, or need, to relativise the notion, it cannot be denied that it has given a sense of direction to much corpus-based translation research over the last ten to fifteen years. Even though we were not using the comparable corpus methodology advocated by Baker, we were perfectly willing to take the notion of universal on board, for two reasons. Firstly, because it was challenging, as it implied that certain features of translated text were so distinctive that they might be regarded as universal, even if the scope of the notion must be restricted as much as necessary and the notion itself put forward as a probabilistic tendency (Toury 2004) rather than as an absolute. And secondly, because the idea of piling up evidence from different quarters (including the Catalan-speaking area) towards the validation of an allegedly universal hypothesis was appealing in very obvious ways – it makes individual research efforts collaborative, and it prevents them from falling into isolation and (what is worse) irrelevance.

1.2 Phraseology

Analysis of COVALT (the parallel corpus, without the comparable element, which is not yet fully available) has centred so far on a particular stylistic feature of literary texts – the use of phraseology. Phraseology is an area of linguistic study which has gained strength over the last twenty years and has even acquired a certain degree of autonomy within linguistics. As I argued elsewhere (Marco 2009: 844), "the study of phraseology, after years of being a minor concern for linguists, has become the aim of a linguistic discipline in its own right and arouses interest all over the world". So phraseology refers both to the discipline and to its object of study, which can be broken down into discrete units called (among other terms used) *phraseological units* or *phrasemes*. Phraseology, like virtually all humanistic disciplines, is beset by conceptual and terminological confusion; in order to avoid this kind of problem, in the present study I will stick to the term *phraseological unit* (PU), which is widely used and is not tied to a particular national tradition.

According to Van Lawick (forthcoming), phraseological units have traditionally been defined as units made up of at least two lexical items whose overall meaning is not always the result of adding up the meanings of their constituents. Since they are frequently used, they are conventionalised as prefabricated chunks and stored as such in memory. Moreover, they display some formal restrictions. These (polilexicality, non-compositionality, frequency of use, fixedness, restrictions) are some of the features commonly associated with phraseology. They do not exhaust the potential of the notion, but they go a long way towards its characterisation. Moreover, as observed by Fleischer (1982), not all PUs show all these features, and each feature can be present in a given PU to a certain degree. If a prototype perspective is adopted, it is not difficult to agree with Van Lawick (forthcoming) when she claims that the more features are shown by a PU, the more prototypical that PU will be. However, it is far from easy to draw a clear-cut line between phraseological and non-phraseological linguistic usage. Sinclair (2000: 13–14) makes this clear when he posits a cline with the so-called *open choice principle* at one end and the *idiom principle* at the other. According to the former, lexical units combine freely and the only rules they obey are those of grammar, whereas according to the latter lexical combination has rules and restrictions of its own.

Many classifications of PUs have been put forward in the literature on the basis of widely different criteria. For the practical purposes of our empirical work within the COVALT group, we decided to follow Corpas' (2003) threefold typology, according to which PUs can be divided up into collocations, idioms and utterances. Utterances can work as fully autonomous speech acts (e.g. *All that glitters is not gold*), whereas idioms and collocations cannot. Idioms can display a relatively high degree of non-compositionality (e.g. *to kick the bucket, a red herring, to spill the beans*), typically operate at phrase or clause level and are fixed in the language system. Collocations, on the other hand, are regarded as more peripheral to the whole category in that they are more compositional, more predictable from the meaning of their constituent items (e.g. *pay attention, lend support*). They typically operate at phrase level and are fixed in the use (or the norm), not the system, as they are the outcome of combinatory restrictions imposed by language use.

1.3 Methodology and results

The study which constitutes the point of departure for the present article (Marco 2009) focused on 23 pairs of source text + target text belonging to the English-Catalan component of COVALT. Some of the texts in that component had to be provisionally left out as the bilingual concordancer did not work smoothly on them and they needed re-editing. The source texts included in the study amounted to 571,909 words, and the target texts to 589,450. In order to study the way in which phraseological units are translated, 13 English lemmas denoting body parts (*arm, blood, body, ear, eye, face, foot, hair, hand, mouth, neck, nose, tongue*) were selected as search words, together with their Catalan counterparts (*braç, sang, cos, orella, ull, cara, peu, cabell / pèl, mà, boca, coll, nas, llengua*). Selection of lemmas was based upon two criteria. Firstly, according to cognitive theory, the body is the focal point of our experience as humans and is therefore often (metaphorically) projected upon more remote and more abstract domains of human experience. As a result, all languages display a fairly large number of PUs revolving around the body. And secondly, the selected lemmas show a high frequency of occurrence among lemmas denoting body parts and were accordingly chosen on the basis of their potential for phraseological productivity. The query matches yielded by AlfraCOVALT (a bilingual concordancing programme developed within the research group: see Guzman 2007) were then manually analysed in order to distinguish phraseological from non-phraseological occurrences. It must be borne in mind that, for the purposes of this particular study, we decided to concentrate on the first two types of PUs identified by Corpas (utterances and idioms) and to leave out collocations, for two reasons. First, collocations show a lower degree of fixedness than other phraseological units and, as a result, a higher frequency of occurrence, which would make the number of concordance lines to be dealt with virtually unmanageable. And second, as remarked above, collocations are generally regarded (e.g. Van Lawick 2006: 71–72) as less prototypical representatives of the *phraseological unit* class than the other types. Since the division between collocations and other kinds of PUs is not clear-cut either, it has been necessary to resort to several dictionaries, repertoires and even general corpora, both in English and Catalan. Since the corpus is not lemmatised, all forms of a given lemma were searched for (e.g. for the lemma *body* both *body* and *bodies* were entered as search words; for *orella*, both *orella* ('ear') and *orelles* ('ears') were entered, etc.) and all query matches were checked for phraseological status.

The PUs thus identified were copied onto an Excel file and assigned a technique label; i.e. the relationship between ST and TT segments was analysed and described in terms of the technique used. Eight techniques were identified:

a. PU → Similar PU;
b. PU → Different PU;
c. PU → Collocation;
d. PU → No PU;
e. Omission;
f. Direct copy (the ST segment has been translated more or less literally, but the result is not a phraseological unit in the target text. It is a calquing technique which gives rise to a certain degree of incoherence in the translation);
g. Collocation → PU;
h. No PU → PU.[2]

Some of these techniques (PU → Similar PU and PU → Different PU) were seen to imply preservation of the phraseological nature of the ST segment, whereas others resulted in either phraseological loss (PU → Collocation, PU → No PU, Omission and Direct copy) or phraseological gain (Collocation → PU and No PU → PU). Therefore, the techniques provided by the classification were arranged on a cline based on the phraseological loss / preservation / gain gradation, as shown in Figure 1.

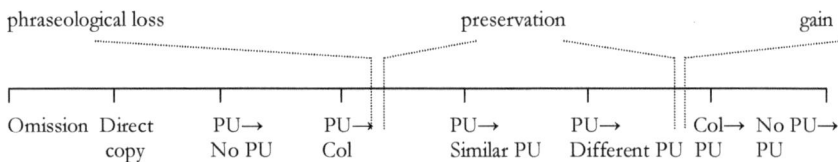

Figure 1. Distribution of translation techniques along the phraseological loss / preservation / gain cline.

When the relevant counts were made, the results showed that preservation-oriented techniques accounted for 394 cases (51.10%), whereas 167 occurrences (21.66%)

---

[2] For examples of techniques, see Marco (2009).

fell under techniques resulting in phraseological loss and 210 translation solutions (27.24%) led to phraseological gain. Thus, preservation features prominently in the translation of phraseology; even more than that, phraseological loss is (more than) compensated by phraseological gain, as a result of which the target texts in the corpus can be said to be more *phraseological* than their corresponding source texts.

1.4 Phraseology and normalisation

It was argued in a previous study (Marco 2009: 844) that phraseological usage in translated text can be regarded as an indicator of normalisation. Normalisation can be defined as the tendency of translated texts to be more *conventional* than originals, i.e. to replace source text segments implying a certain amount of creativity with target language segments adhering more closely to what is typical in that language and thus conforming to target reader's expectations.

Normalization was identified as a feature of translated text even before the advent of Corpus-Based Translation Studies. Toury's *law of growing standardisation* is but another way of referring to the same phenomenon. This author (1995: 267–268) claims that "in translation, source-text textemes tend to be converted into target-language (or target-culture) repertoremes". Textemes are textual elements and relations which characterise the source text and often give it its peculiar flavour; repertoremes, for their part, are elements and relations belonging to the habitual repertoire of the target language or culture; and the alleged replacement of ST textemes with TL repertoremes is a way of saying that translated texts tend to be more conventional than originals, to leave aside much of what is distinctive of those originals, either through translator's lack of awareness or because the distinctive features in question will not travel well.

With the advent of electronic corpora, normalisation remains one of the translation features under scrutiny. There is no space here to provide a thorough account of corpus-based studies of normalisation in translation, but a few of these studies will be mentioned by way of illustration. Kenny (2001) set out to examine some items involving creativity and how they fared in translation. She focused on three kinds of phenomena: creative *hapax legomena* (or word forms occurring only once in the corpus), forms peculiar to a particular author and unusual collocations. Kenny's findings are contradictory, as normalising techniques rank high with respect to the first phenomenon but not so high with respect to the other two. It is concluded that translators do often normalise, but they also deploy their skills in a creative way. Other studies, rather than being ambiguous, go against the assumptions underlying the normalisation hypothesis, as is the case of Mauranen (2000). Reporting on this study, she later claims that "[t]he results on patterns of lexical combination, mainly collocations, seem to point towards untypical combinatory tendencies in translations" (Mauranen 2005: 79): not only are lexical frequencies untypical in translations, but the collocational range of the lexical item under scrutiny (Finnish *haluta*) is wider in translated than in original Finnish, and its collocational patterns are also divergent. In an attempt to account for such divergence, the author claims that "it seems that translators utilize the resources of the target language by making relatively more use of what you *can do* than what you *typically* do" (2005: 80). However, Bernardini, in a very recent study (2007), reaches a somewhat different conclusion. Drawing on data provided by a small bi-directional corpus made up of "extracts from novels and short stories in original and translated English (source language: Italian)" and "similar extracts in original/translated Italian (source language: English)", she pursues a double aim: a) to determine whether translated texts are more *collocational* than original texts in the same language, and b) to elucidate whether any differences found can be attributed to the translation process. The author concludes by saying that "we can tentatively suggest that translated texts would seem to be more *collocational* than original texts in the same language, and that there is some evidence that this is a consequence of the translation process", even though "[i]t is difficult to tell what was the principal driving force behind these shifts [i.e. the shifts "leading to increased institutionalisation" referred to above]". Findings, then, are contradictory so far, as it is not at all clear that translated text tends to normalise in all cases.

Phraseological usage, on the other hand, as we have seen, consists by definition in the activation of a particular kind of typical segments: multi-word standardised units which, through frequency of use, have become part of the lexical repertoire. Thus, conventionality stands out as a common feature of both phraseology and the tendency to normalise. If this close link between phraseology and normalisation is accepted, the results shown in section 1.3 lend support to the normalisation hypothesis in the COVALT corpus, as the 27.24% of cases in which there is phraseological gain outnumber the 21.66% involving loss – though by not too wide a margin.

2 Research into the factors underlying the translation of phraseology: Aims, scope and methodology

As far as figures are concerned, that is how matters stand. But the next question is: why is that so? Corpus-based studies enable us to provide an account of a given state of affairs, but we need to go beyond description towards explanation. All kinds of factors, both textual and contextual, might be brought to bear on the translation of phraseology. Some of them may derive from the inherent translation difficulty of certain phraseological units, others may be sociocultural or even cognitive in nature. In the present study I intend to concentrate on two particular factors which are arguably of the utmost relevance: stylistic motivation (i.e. the degree of importance attached by translators to the phraseological units encountered in source texts and to the use of phraseology in their target texts) and translator expertise. In order to gauge the relevance of these (and other possible) factors, three translators of narrative works included in the English-Catalan component of COVALT were provided with questionnaires and interviewed, so that light might be thrown on the relationship between translator behaviour (as reflected in translation solutions) and textual and extratextual factors.

The three translators chosen were Jesús Cortés, Josep Franco and Víctor Oroval. They were chosen because their translations hold relatively different positions on the phraseological loss – preservation – gain cline. Cortés' only translation in the corpus (that of Melville's *Billy Budd, Sailor*) shows a higher percentage of techniques involving gain (56.25%) than the average (27.24%, as indicated above) and a correspondingly lower percentage of loss (12.50%) than the average (22.57%). Franco's percentages vary not only with regard to translations by other translators, but also from one another, so it is difficult to generalise. However, there is at least one translation (that of *Dr Jekyll and Mr Hyde*) in which techniques involving gain (8.77%) are remarkably lower than the average, whereas both loss and preservation stand at higher levels than the average. Oroval, for his part, is responsible for two of the translations under scrutiny, one of which (that of Conan Doyle's story *The*

Adventure of the Bruce-Partington Plans) shows no techniques implying phraseological gain (0%), preservation standing at a much higher level (75%) than the average, whereas the other translation (that of Barry Faville's *The Keeper*) shows closer percentages to the average – 22.73% for loss, 56.81% for preservation and 20.45% for gain.

Both Jesús Cortés (henceforward JC) and Josep Franco (henceforward JF) were contacted and sent the questionnaire via e-mail. They both agreed to be interviewed, and the interviews, which eventually took place in October 2009, were recorded. I then transcribed the interviews, though not thoroughly, as there were frequent digressions and remarks which could be regarded as irrelevant for the study. Víctor Oroval (henceforward VO) preferred to answer the questionnaire via e-mail.

An English translation of the questionnaire (in Catalan) that the three translators were requested to fill in is reproduced in the appendix. Part 1 of the questionnaire concentrates on the translator themselves – their expertise and the languages they translate from. Part 2 focuses on the translation of phraseology and attempts to elicit information on the stylistic relevance that phraseology holds for translators, the translation techniques they favour and the factors impinging on their decisions. Part 3 is a multiple choice exercise in which the translators are faced with excerpts from English texts containing at least one phraseological unit and two or three different translation solutions in Catalan for each excerpt. An English back-translation is provided of the translated segments matching source-text phraseological units. Moreover, source-text segments are labelled "PU" (phraseological unit), "No PU" (no phraseological unit) or "Col" (collocation), as the case may be, and target-text segments are classified on the basis of the translation technique used. It must be added that the translation options provided for each excerpt are variations on the corresponding segment of the published translation, and they are identical in everything except the segment involving phraseological usage either in the source or in the target text.

3 Data analysis and discussion

Let us start with the two factors that this paper set out to bring under scrutiny: stylistic motivation and translator expertise. Their importance is adequately confirmed by the answers provided by the translators. With regard to the former, the three translators regard phraseology as stylistically relevant. Two of them look at this device from the source text's perspective: JC claims that phraseology is important because it is in the source text (i.e. out of respect for it) and JF goes one step further and says that phraseological units (together with other stylistic devices) belong to the spirit of the text. VO, on the other hand, seems to look at stylistic relevance from the viewpoint of the target text, as he attributes it to the fact that phraseology enables us to *appropriate* texts, to make them our own. What may strike one as somewhat odd is that they do not establish a scale of stylistic motivation or relevance (e.g. 'some phraseological units are more stylistically motivated, and therefore more relevant, than others'), but seem to consider phraseology as an inherently relevant feature.

As to translator expertise, it must be stressed that the three translators show remarkable differences. JC has worked as a translator for 10 years, though not uninterruptedly, and has translated 8 or 9 literary works. JF's experience covers a period of about 20 years, as he has been a translator since the late eighties, and his output is by far the largest of the three: although he is not able to be more precise, he claims to have translated over 100 literary works. VO has translated 16 literary works over a similar period to that covered by JF's career, i.e. 20 years. Despite these differences concerning their individual careers, the three translators agree on the importance of expertise. However, JC qualifies his statement by saying that experience is useful but is only relatively helpful when you are dealing with an author that you have never translated before.

These are the two factors that the questionnaire was targeting, but, since the questions were open, several other factors came up in the translators' answers. They were all predictable as factors, but some of the emphases laid by particular translators on certain factors seem to point towards their priorities and even their underlying theories. In what follows those factors will be enumerated and referred to the translators' specific answers.

A group of factors is related to the translator's knowledge, skills and attitudes. JF (2, 6) claims that "knowledge of the source language and the translator's versatility when using the target language" are the main factors impinging upon preservation of source-text phraseological units.[3] For JC it is "stubbornness", here regarded not as a fault but as a virtue, akin to perseverance and opposed to lack of rigour. When looking for a phraseological equivalent, the translator may not be able to "reach far enough" in their search (JF, 3, 3). Translation solutions that show too much interventionism on the translator's part may be attributed to their ignorance of the language (VO, 3, 4). Finally, the three translators agree on showing an attitude of respect for the source text, for its spirit, which should discourage translators from overstepping certain limits (JF, 2, 8).

Another group of factors is related to cross-linguistic differences. Again, this is very conspicuous in the translators' answers. JC (2, 3) favours a "literal" approach, but is well aware that "sooner or later we will have to adapt, because the (target) language is different". However, it must be added that by literalness JC understands the option furnished by the dictionary, provided that it fits in with overall meaning. He trusts the dictionary ("the dictionary knows more than me", he claims) as long as the solution it provides is passed by his own filter. By literalness he does not mean word-for-word translation. JF, for his part, claims (2, 3) that "The best way [*to translate a PU*] would be to find an idiom which is a close parallel or has a very similar meaning, even though it may not always be easy to find one. Seeking parallels, but without taking it too far". Later on (2, 5) he emphasises the fact that sometimes it is impossible to find an equivalent idiom in the target language. When asked about the factors that make it difficult for a translator to preserve source-text phraseological units (2, 7), the three translators are unanimous in pointing the finger at the target language and, more particularly, at its specificity: "it is a language's personality, history and evolution that make it difficult to bring phraseological units across from one language to another" (JF, 2, 7); "those resources and references that belong to a specific language and culture" (VO, 2, 7).

A third group of factors is clearly situated at the target reader's pole, as it emphasises the target text's readability and comprehensibility. VO (2, 3) claims that the best way of translating phraseological units is "to try and reflect the original as

---

[3] References to the translators' answers (in brackets) are made up of two figures: the first indicates part number and the second, question number.

closely as possible, as long as the original meaning and effect are preserved, *in a comprehensible way*" [*VO's emphasis*]. In the multiple choice section of the questionnaire, JC uses *fluency* as one of his guiding criteria (3, 7; 3, 8): he explicitly argues that a given option must not constitute a *stumbling-block* for the reader. And JF puts forward *universality* (i.e. the fact that an idiom, or some other kind of expression, is widely used across the target language community) as a touchstone for deciding which translation solution is the most suitable one (3, 2; 3, 3; 3, 4). He insists on the need to avoid the danger of dialectalism or localism, and favours "universal" options because they can be understood in more "contexts".

Another factor frequently mentioned in the translators' answers and also situated at the target pole could be termed *stylistic consistency*. Phraseological usage is not independent of characters' speech or the overall tone of the narrator's discourse in the source text, nor must it be so in the target text. Therefore, issues of characterisation and register are brought to bear on the choice of phraseological solutions, or otherwise, in the target text. JF (2, 2) is very explicit about this: "The language level at which you want to set your expression, or, in more contemporary literature, the difference between narrator and characters, or between a first-person and a third-person narrator, or whether the narrator is omniscient or not – these are all issues which condition the use of phraseology very much".[4] JC (e.g. 3, 5, but also elsewhere in the multiple choice section) voices the need "to know what precedes this particular sentence and what kind of language is used by this character in order to determine whether the option fits in with the character". Stylistic consistency goes beyond the particular work under scrutiny and is even made to embrace the overall style of the author in question. Thus, JF chooses one option over another because "Baum does have a penchant for such expressions" (3, 6), or because "it is not unlikely that Twain should put that kind of language in the mouths of his characters" (3, 7).

Finally, another factor is mentioned which might be termed *expressivity*, a stylistic value often associated with phraseology. There is no space here to trace this connection; suffice it to say, then, that it is well documented in the literature on

---

[4]   What the translators mean by *language level* is something akin to *register*. It obviously has nothing to do with the usual meaning of *language level* as 'layer' (i.e. phonological, morphological, syntactic…). However, I was reluctant to translate the expressions as *register*, because the term exists in Catalan too and they did not use it.

phraseology (González Rey 1998; Ruiz 1998; Corpas 2000; Van Lawick 2006; Sabban 2007; Häcki Buhofer 2007). Other stylistic effects may be created through phraseology, but expressivity, as opposed to stylistic neutrality or even flatness, stands out as a singularly important one. None of the three translators interviewed mentions the term, but an identical or similar notion seems to underlie some of their remarks. JC, for instance, while reflecting on the two options provided for "saw before his mind's eye" (3, 8), argues that "had remembered" is "too limp, inadequate", whereas "had seen with the eyes of his imagination" is "more poetic, less cold". And JF, when asked about the contribution of phraseology to style, claims that the former "endows the text with character and personality". These terms are admittedly vague, but they might be regarded as the opposite of neutrality or flatness, which imply lack of character.

4 Conclusion

My starting-point in this article was the outcome of a previous study on the translation of phraseology in the English-Catalan component of the COVALT corpus. Assuming that some translation techniques imply phraseological loss, whereas others imply preservation or gain, it was found that cases of gain outnumbered cases of loss. Since phraseological units are often relatively difficult to translate, those findings enable the analyst to conjecture that translators attach a high degree of importance to phraseology. The aim of this article was to find out what factors impinge on the translation of phraseology, with special attention to two particular (previously hypothesised) ones: stylistic motivation and translator expertise. With that aim in view, a questionnaire was designed and administered to three translators some of whose translations are part of our corpus. Answers to the questionnaire not only confirmed the two factors just mentioned but helped to uncover others, which could be grouped under five different headings: the translator's knowledge, skills and attitudes; cross-linguistic differences; the target text's readability and comprehensibility; stylistic consistency; and expressivity (a stylistic value often associated with phraseology).

It remains to be seen to what extent the translators interviewed are representative of their universe, i.e. translators of works included in the English-Catalan component of COVALT. The six translations in the corpus for which they are responsible amount to a total of 165,355 words, out of the 589,450 which make up the translated component of COVALT under scrutiny here, which means that the three translators interviewed have authored 28.05% of this translated component. Whatever their degree of representativeness may be in statistical terms, it seems clear that this article's contribution to the study of the translation of phraseology lies in the opportunity it affords to gain insights into the factors conditioning translator behaviour which are based not on speculation but on the translators' statements. The empirical basis may not be broad enough, but the translators' answers are bound to be, if not conclusive, at least indicative.

References

Baker, Mona (1993): "Corpus Linguistics and Translation Studies – Implications and Applications." In: Baker, Mona / Francis, Gill / Tognini-Bonelli [eds.] (1993): *Text and Technology. In Honour of John Sinclair*. Amsterdam and Philadelphia: John Benjamins. 233–250.

―― (1995): "Corpora in Translation Studies: An Overview and Some Suggestions for Future Research". In: *Target* 7 (2), 223-243.

Bernardini, Silvia (2005): "Reviving old ideas: parallel and comparable analysis in translation studies – with an example from translation stylistics." In: Aijmer, Karin / Alvstad, Cecilia [eds.] (2005): *New Tendencies in Translation Studies*. Göteborg: University of Göteborg. 5–18.

―― (2007): "Collocations in Translated Language. Combining parallel, comparable and reference corpora." In: Davies, Matthew / Rayson, Paul / Hunston, Susan / Danielsson, Pernilla [eds.] (2007): *Proceedings of the Corpus Linguistics Conference* (Corpus Linguistics Conference, Birmingham, 27-30 July 2007). http://ucrel.lancs.ac.uk/publications/CL2007/paper/15_Paper.pdf. Visited 2 July 2009.

Corpas Pastor, Gloria (2000): "Fraseología y traducción." In: Salvador, Vicent / Piquer, Adolf [eds.] (2000): *El discurs prefabricat. Estudis de fraseologia teòrica i aplicada*. Castelló: Servei de Publicacions de la Universitat Jaume I. 107–138.

―― (2003): *Diez años de investigación en fraseología: análisis sintáctico-semánticos, contrastivos y traductológicos*. Madrid and Frankfurt am Main: Iberoamericana / Vervuert.

Fleischer, Wolfgang (1982): *Phraseologie der deutschen Gegenwartssprache*. Leipzig: Bibliographisches Institut.

González-Rey, M. (1998): "Estudio de la idiomaticidad en las unidades fraseológicas." In: Wotjak, Gerd [ed.] (1998): *Estudios de fraseología y fraseografía del español actual*. Madrid and Frankfurt am Main: Iberoamericana / Vervuert. 57–73.

Guzman, Josep R. (2007): "El uso de COVALT y AlfraCOVALT en el aprendizaje traductor." In: *Actas del XXIV Congreso Internacional de AESLA. Aprendizaje de lenguas, uso del lenguaje y modelación cognitiva: perspectivas aplicadas entre disciplinas*. Madrid: UNED. 1743–1749.

Häcki Buhofer, Annelies (2007): "Psycholinguistic aspects of phraseology: European tradition." In: Burger, Harald / Dobrovol'skij, Dmitrij / Kühn, Peter / Norrick, Neal R. [eds.] (2007): *Phraseologie: ein internationales Handbuch der zeitgenössischer Forschung / Phraseology: an international handbook of contemporary research*. Berlin: Walter de Gruyter. 836–853.

Kenny, Dorothy (2001): *Lexis and Creativity in Translation. A Corpus-based Approach*. Manchester: St. Jerome.

Marco, Josep (2009): "Normalisation and the Translation of Phraseology in the COVALT Corpus." In: *Meta* 54 (4), 842–856.

Mauranen, Anna (2000): "Strange Strings in Translated Language: A Study on Corpora." In: Olohan, Maeve [ed.] (2000): *Intercultural Faultlines. Research Models in Translation Studies 1: Textual and Cognitive Aspects*. Manchester: St. Jerome. 119–141.

—— (2005): "Contrasting languages and varieties with translational corpora." In: *Languages in Contrast* 5 (1), 73-92.

Mauranen, Anna / Kujamäki, Pekka [eds.] (2004): *Translation Universals: Do they Exist?* Amsterdam and Philadelphia: John Benjamins.

Ruiz Gurillo, Leonor (1998): "Una clasificación no discreta de las unidades fraseológicas del espanyol." In: Wotjak, Gerd [ed.] (1998): *Estudios de fraseología y fraseografía del español actual*. Madrid and Frankfurt am Main: Iberoamericana / Vervuert. 13–37.

Sabban, Annette (2007): "Culture-boundness and problems of cross-cultural phraseology." In: Burger, Harald / Dobrovol'skij, Dmitrij / Kühn, Peter / Norrick, Neal R. [eds.] (2007): *Phraseologie: ein internationales Handbuch der zeitgenössischer Forschung / Phraseology: an international handbook of contemporary research*. Berlin: Walter de Gruyter. 590–605.

Sinclair, John (2000): "The search for units of meaning." In: Corpas, Gloria [ed.] (2000): *Las lenguas de Europa: Estudios de fraseología, fraseografía y traducción*. Granada: Comares. 7–37.

Toury, Gideon (1995): *Descriptive Translation Studies and Beyond*. Amsterdam and Philadelphia: John Benjamins.

—— (2004): "Probabilistic explanations in translation studies: Welcome as they are, would they qualify as universals?" In: Mauranen, Anna / Kujamäki, Pekka [eds.] (2004): *Translation Universals: Do they Exist?* Amsterdam and Philadelphia: John Benjamins. 15–32.

Van Lawick, Heike (2006): *Metàfora, fraseologia i traducció. Aplicació als somatismes en una obra de Bertolt Brecht*. Aachen: Shaker Verlag.

—— (forthcoming): "Fonaments teòrics per a l'anàlisi traductològica d'unitats fraseològiques." In a collective volume by COVALT, in preparation.

Appendix: Questionnaire about the translation of phraseological units

PART 1. ABOUT THE TRANSLATOR
1. How long have you worked as a translator?
2. How many literary works have you translated (approximately)?
3. What languages do you translate from?

PART 2. ON THE TRANSLATION OF PHRASEOLOGICAL UNITS
1. Do you think that phraseological units are important from a stylistic viewpoint in a literary text?
2. How do phraseological units contribute to the style of a literary work?
3. What do you think is the best way of translating phraseological units?
4. Why?

5. Is it always possible to preserve in the target text the phraseological units encountered in the source text?
6. What factors do you think help the translator preserve source-text phraseological units?
7. What factors do you think make it difficult for the translator to preserve those phraseological units?
8. Do you think it is acceptable to insert a phraseological unit in the target text at a point where there was none in the source text?
9. Do you think the translator's experience influences the way in which they translate phraseological units?

PART 3. MULTIPLE CHOICE

Please indicate which you think is the best solution to each excerpt provided:

1. Then we sallied forth into the streets, arm in arm <PU>, continuing the topics of the day, or roaming far and wide until a late hour, seeking, amid the wild lights and shadows of the populous city, that infinity of mental excitement which quiet observation can afford. (E.A. Poe, *The Murders of the Rue Morgue*)
a) Llavors eixíem, agafats del braç [*'taken by the arm'*] <PU → Col>, a passejar per aquells carrers on continuàvem la conversa del dia i vaguejàvem per onsevulla fins molt tard, tot buscant a través dels estrafolaris llums i ombres de la populosa ciutat aquelles innombrables excitacions mentals que no poden ser aconseguides mitjançant la tranquil·la meditació.
b) Llavors eixíem a passejar de bracet [*very difficult to translate literally; 'bracet' is a diminutive of* braç, *meaning 'arm', and 'de' means 'of'*] <PU → Similar PU> per aquells carrers on continuàvem la conversa del dia i vaguejàvem per onsevulla fins molt tard, tot buscant a través dels estrafolaris llums i ombres de la populosa ciutat aquelles innombrables excitacions mentals que no poden ser aconseguides mitjançant la tranquil·la meditació.

2. "Mr. Utterson, sir, asking to see you," he called; and even as he did so, once more violently signed to the lawyer to give ear <PU>.
A voice answered from within: "Tell him I cannot see anyone," it said complainingly. (R. L. Stevenson, *The Strange Case of Dr Jekyll and Mr Hyde*)
a) —Senyor —digué, mentre tornava a fer un senyal al seu acompanyant, per indicar-li que escoltara amb atenció [*'to listen attentively'*] <PU → Col> —, el senyor Utterson voldria passar a veure'l.
—Dis-li que no puc veure ningú —respongué, des de dins, una veu esgarrada.
b) —Senyor —digué, mentre tornava a fer un senyal al seu acompanyant, per indicar-li que parara l'orella [*'to prick up his ear'*] <PU → Similar PU> —, el senyor Utterson voldria passar a veure'l.
—Dis-li que no puc veure ningú —respongué, des de dins, una veu esgarrada.

3. And one of the most curious things about them is that they can carry you to any place in the world in three steps, and each step will be made in the wink of an eye <PU> (Frank L. Baum, *The Wizard of Oz*)
a) I una de les coses més curioses que poden fer és traslladar qui les porta a qualsevol lloc del món en tres passes, i cada passa es pot fer en un breu instant [*'in a brief instant'*] <PU → No PU>
b) I una de les coses més curioses que poden fer és traslladar qui les porta a qualsevol lloc del món en tres passes, i cada passa es pot fer en un tres i no res [*very difficult to translate literally; it might be paraphrased as 'in no time'*] <PU → Different PU>
c) I una de les coses més curioses que poden fer és traslladar qui les porta a qualsevol lloc del món en tres passes, i cada passa es pot fer en un obrir i tancar d'ulls [*very similar to 'in the wink of an eye'; it could be paraphrased as 'while you open and close your eyes'*] <PU → Similar PU>

4. Little Jacky Gaffin was pinned down under the wreckage, and while the nurse <u>had her hands full</u> <PU> with the goat Hyacinth was laying into Jacky's legs with his belt like a small fury (Saki, *Tobermory*)
a) Jacky Gaffin es va quedar enganxat sota les restes de l'accident, i, mentre la mainadera <u>s'ocupava</u> [*'took care of', 'was busy with'*] <PU → No PU> del cabrot, Jacint, fet una petita fúria, començà a fuetejar amb el cinturó les cames de Jacky
b) Jacky Gaffin es va quedar enganxat sota les restes de l'accident, i, mentre la mainadera <u>amb prou feines donava l'abast</u> [*'could hardly cope with'*] <PU → Different PU> amb el cabrot, Jacint, fet una petita fúria, començà a fuetejar amb el cinturó les cames de Jacky
5. <u>I've had very little practice</u> <No PU> in this sort of thing, you see. Another time I shall do better. (Saki, *Tobermory*)
a) <u>No tinc la mà trencada</u> [*literally, 'my hand is not broken at this sort of thing',* having a broken hand meaning *'having a lot of practice or experience'*] <No PU → PU> en aquesta mena de coses, sabeu. La pròxima vegada ho faré millor.
b) <u>No hi tinc molta pràctica</u> [*'I haven't had much practice'*] <No PU → No PU>, en aquesta mena de coses, sabeu. La pròxima vegada ho faré millor.
6. "Really," said the Scarecrow, "you ought to <u>be ashamed of yourself</u> <No PU> for being such a humbug." (Frank L. Baum, *The Wizard of Oz*)
a) —La veritat —va dir l'Espantaocells— és que t'hauria de <u>caure la cara de vergonya</u> [*literally, 'your face should fall off out of shame'*] <No PU → PU> per ser tan farsant.
b) —La veritat —va dir l'Espantaocells— és que t'hauries d'<u>avergonyir</u> [*'should / ought to be ashamed'*] <No PU → PU> de ser tan farsant.
7. "You will allow me to say, and without apologies for my language, <u>damn the money</u> <PU>!" (Mark Twain, *The Man that Corrupted Hadleyburg*)
a) Em permetreu que diga, i sense disculpar-me pel meu llenguatge, <u>que al dimoni els diners</u> [*'to the devil with the money'*] <PU → Similar PU>!
b) Em permetreu que diga, i sense disculpar-me pel meu llenguatge, <u>que a fer la mà els diners</u> [*again, difficult to translate literally;* fer la mà *is slang for 'to masturbate', so a possible literal (and meaningless) translation into English could be 'let money jerk off'*] <PU → Different PU>!
8. For once more he <u>saw before his mind's eye</u> <PU>, as clear as transparency, the strange clauses of the will. (R. L. Stevenson, *The Strange Case of Dr Jekyll and Mr Hyde*)
a) I dubtava perquè, una vegada més, <u>havia recordat</u> [*'had remembered'*] <PU → No PU>, tan clares com la mateixa transparència, les estranyes clàusules del testament.
b) I dubtava perquè, una vegada més, <u>havia vist amb els ulls de la imaginació</u> [*'had seen with the eyes of imagination'*] <PU → No PU>, tan clares com la mateixa transparència, les estranyes clàusules del testament.
9. That is Madame de Maintenon, that one he called Mrs. Hemans. She begs Louis not to go on this expedition, but he <u>turns a deaf ear</u> <PU>. (Saki, *Tobermory*)
a) Aquella és Madame de Maintenon, de la qual ha dit que era la senyora Hemans. Li demana a Lluís que no participe en aquella expedició, però ell <u>es fa el desentès</u> [*'pretends not to hear', 'pays no attention'*] <PU → Different PU>.
b) Aquella és Madame de Maintenon, de la qual ha dit que era la senyora Hemans. Li demana a Lluís que no participe en aquella expedició, però ell <u>hi fa el sord</u> [*'pretends to be deaf'*] <PU → Similar PU>.
10. <u>chuckled</u> <No PU> Mr Fisher (Barry Faville, *The Keeper*)
a) va dir el senyor Fisher <u>rient per sota el nas</u> [*literally, 'laughing under his nose'*] <No PU → PU>
b) <u>va riure</u> [*'laughed'*] <No PU → No PU> el senyor Fisher

Source Language Influence Without the Effect of "Shining Through": Over-Representation of Generic Person Reference in Translations

Leena Kolehmainen
University of Eastern Finland, Joensuu

Abstract

This paper is a contribution to the study of translation universals. It is a corpus-based investigation of non-typical frequencies in translated texts, and it participates in the discussion concerning the reasons of over-representation. Its aim is to examine over-representation of generic person reference in German translations from Finnish, and to focus on reasons that may account for non-typical frequencies. The results show how cross-linguistic differences in grammatical devices that express person are reflected in German translations from Finnish. Hence, this paper supports previous studies in which researchers have observed a conspicuous correlation between over-representation and source language stimulus. However, unlike previous studies, the source language impact manifested in this study does not involve the deviating use of a target language item imitating the source language practices. The source language is not "shining through", but nevertheless, it is causing untypical frequencies of an item which already exists and is used in any case. In other words, what is preserved in translation is not a linguistic form echoing the source language form but the same semantic domain of generic person reference which is conveyed by structurally different means in the target language. The method of the study entails both a target-language oriented comparison of translated and non-translated texts and a parallel corpus analysis.

1 Introduction[1]

This article examines the over-representation of generic person reference in German translations from Finnish by focusing on the reasons for non-typical frequencies in translated texts.

Person is a linguistic category which has attracted a lot of attention in studies which have compared Finnish to other languages. In contrast to many (but not all) Indo-

---

[1] I thank the two anonymous reviewers for their constructive comments and valuable suggestions.

European languages, Finnish is a so-called pro drop language in which 1st and 2nd person pronominal subjects are optional. In addition, explicit reference to a person can be absent on other occasions, as well. The most conspicuous feature noticed by several researchers is the general tendency in Finnish to avoid direct reference both to the speaker and to the addressee (cf. e.g. Hakulinen 1987; Yli-Vakkuri 2005), due to which there are significant cross-linguistic differences between Finnish and Germanic languages in the use of deictic forms that refer to discourse participants. For example, recent contrastive German-Finnish studies show that in Finnish advertising brochures (Vesalainen 2001), enterprise websites (Ylönen 2003; 2007), linguistic book reviews (Piitulainen 2003) and obituaries (Piitulainen 1993) the reader is addressed less often than in comparable German texts. A further typical feature of the same Finnish texts concerns the means of speaker deixis: the sender does not typically refer to him- or herself directly by using 1st person forms, as in German texts, but appears in a more distanced 3rd person form, instead.

The ways and forms of addressing the co-participant and referring to oneself are closely connected with politeness. Therefore, cross-linguistic differences in the grammar and conventions of person reference are especially important from the point of view of translation. However, the study of person reference in translation is intriguing, per se, and contributes to the investigation of properties of translated texts, in general. Previous research shows, for example, that the frequency of personal pronouns is higher in Finnish translated texts than in Finnish original ones: in the studies by Mauranen & Tiittula (2005) and Mauranen (2006) the 1st and 2nd person singular pronouns *minä* 'I' and *sinä* 'you' tended to show higher frequencies in texts translated from English and German than in original Finnish texts. This over-representation resulted from classic source language influence, due to which translators chose to insert pronominal subjects in contexts in which their use is optional (cf. the pro drop-feature mentioned above).

The results mentioned above concern Finnish as a target language. This article, however, is more concerned with how Finnish as a source language can open-up new perspectives on this discussion. The subject of the study is one particular German pronoun with person reference, the pronoun *man* ('one') which refers to people in general. *Man* is an intriguing pronoun because its frequency is notably higher in texts translated from Finnish than in original non-translated German ones. This study focuses on the reasons for over-representation, thus providing the contemporary discussion about non-typical frequencies in translated texts with new data. In addition, this paper contributes to the cross-linguistic study of person in German-Finnish comparison.

This study combines a target-language oriented comparison of translated and non-translated texts with a parallel corpus analysis. In addition, its results are complemented by the use of additional monolingual non-translated reference corpora in the target language. As a whole, the methodology in this paper conforms to the requirements recently expressed by some translation scholars, according to which only such a corpus composition can simultaneously reveal overall trends in translations and provide explanations for them (Bernardini 2010).

Table 1. Finnish and German texts of the *FinDe* corpus which are used in this study.

a) German original texts	Tokens
Literary prose	
Grass, Günter: Unkenrufe. Eine Erzählung. First published 1992.	60,422
Hein, Christoph: Der Tangospieler. Erzählung. First published 1989.	48,925
Strauß, Botho 1994: Niemand anderes. First published 1987.	50,555
	In sum 159,902
b) German target texts	
Literary prose	
Haavikko, Paavo: Fleurs mittlere Reife. Roman. Aus dem Finnischen von Gisbert Jänicke. 1994.	31,081
Idström, Annika: Mein Bruder Sebastian. Roman. Deutsch von Gabriele Schrey-Vasara. 1993.	47,915
Tuuri, Antti: Winterkrieg. Roman. Aus dem Finnischen von Peter Uhlmann. 1992.	53,267
Non-fiction	
Nikula, Riitta: Bebaute Landschaft. Finnlands Architektur im Überblick. Deutsche Fassung Carl-August von Willebrand. 1993.	44,191
Tarkka, Pekka: Weder Stalin noch Hitler. Finnland während des zweiten Weltkrieges. Aus dem Finnischen von Carl-August von Willebrand. 1991.	21,781
	In sum 198,235
c) Finnish original texts	
Haavikko, Paavo: Fleurin koulusyksy. 1992.	22,813
Idström, Annika: Veljeni Sebastian. 1985.	34,547
Tuuri, Antti: Talvisota. 1989.	43,143
	In sum 100,503

The Finnish-German corpus, which forms the heart of this study, comprises currently available literary and non-fiction texts in the Finnish-German *FinDe* corpus (presently under major reconstruction and extension) which is a bi-directional corpus consisting of Finnish and German original texts and their translations into the other language (cf. Kolehmainen & Stahl 2007). All texts were published in the 1980s–1990s and they are full, unabridged texts, not text fragments. The matching text pairs have been aligned. All translators are native speakers of the respective language. Except for two texts which were translated by the same translator, all remaining texts were translated by different translators. The quantitative corpus analysis is carried out mainly with the help of *WordSmith Tools* (cf. http://www.lexically.net/wordsmith/), the parallel text analysis with the help of TUSTEP (Tübinger System von Textverarbeitungs-Programmen, cf. http://www.tustep.uni-tuebingen.de/). Table 1 above presents the Finnish-German texts to be studied.

2 Generic person reference in German and Finnish, and the prediction for translation

Linguistic means to refer to people in general are quite different in German and Finnish. The typical, unmarked way in German involves the pronoun *man* which occurs in North-Germanic languages as well (e.g. in Swedish and Norwegian, cf. Altenberg 2005; Johansson 2003) and whose equivalent in English is the pronoun *one*, in French *on*:

(1) Sprich   lauter,   sagte   **man** [...]. (*FinDe* corpus)
     speak   louder   said   one
     'Speak louder, someone suggested.'

Most German grammars present *man* in the category of indefinite pronouns (cf. e.g. Dudengrammatik 2005: 327). Building upon Haspelmath (1997), the Internet grammar "grammis" of the Institute for German Language in Mannheim provides a completely new solution and forms an entirely new category of generic pronouns for it. The point of reference of *man* can be a single unspecific person in general or a group of unspecific persons in general in which the speaker can include him-/herself (cf. e.g. Marschall 1996; Dudengrammatik 2005: 327).

Finnish lacks a direct counterpart for German *man*. As a whole, it lacks a stylistically neutral pronominal device to express a generic person reference. The 2nd person singular pronoun *sinä* 'you', which can refer to people in general, is a rather marked way of expressing generic person reference, and its primary domain of use is colloquial discourse (VISK 2004: §1395; Laitinen 1995; 2006). Besides, its nearest counterpart in German is not *man*, but the corresponding 2nd person pronoun *du* 'you' which can also be used as an expression of generic person reference (cf. Zifonun et al. 1997: 318). The stylistically neutral way of generic person reference in Finnish does not involve the use of pronouns. I will discuss this in Section 5.

Due to the lack of a direct pronominal counterpart, one is tempted to claim that the German *man* is a "unique" item in comparison with Finnish. *Unique item* is a term[2] suggested by Tirkkonen-Condit (2002; 2004; 2005), who defines it as a target-language-specific element having no straight-forward or direct counterpart in the source language. On the basis of her quantitative corpus analysis, she formulates a hypothesis according to which unique items tend to occur less frequently in translated texts than in non-translated original texts in the same language. In other words, the unique items hypothesis predicts target-language-specific elements are under-represented in translations. According to Tirkkonen-Condit (2004), this peculiar behavior results from cognitive matters. Because a straight-forward counterpart is absent in the source language, the source text does not provide any direct stimulus for the element in the target language and it does not spring to translator's mind when (s)he is producing the target text. In previous studies, researchers have investigated items representing different linguistic levels, morphological (Tirkkonen-Condit 2004; 2005), lexical (Kujamäki 2004; Mäkisalo 2007) and syntactic unique items (Eskola 2002; 2004; Mauranen & Tiittula 2005; Mauranen 2006), and found strong evidence in favor for the hypothesis.

Since Finnish lacks a straight-forward pronominal counterpart, the unique items hypothesis predicts German *man* will have lower frequencies in texts translated from Finnish than in non-translated German ones. However, the data in the next section show that German *man* does not follow this prediction. Instead, it behaves in the opposite way in texts translated from Finnish and is over-represented. The reason for its untypical frequency is revealed in the parallel text analysis in Section 5 which shows that *man* does have regular counterparts in Finnish which, however,

---

2   The term has been criticised by Chesterman (2007; 2010), who recommends it be replaced. His own suggestion is *target-language-specific item* (Chesterman 2010). Because the term *unique item* has already been established and the term proposed by Chesterman is not unambiguous either (it resembles the notion of culture specific items in translation without being its synonym), I am not going to reject the original term.

represent a completely different linguistic level. In other words, it turns out that *man* is not a unique item after all.

3 Over-representation of German *man* in translations from Finnish

Table 2 contains the frequencies of *man* in the texts chosen from the *FinDe* corpus. The German translated texts entail three texts representing literary prose and two texts representing non-fiction. The original German text part is smaller, consisting only of three literary texts. The individual texts were listed in Table 1 above. The figures in Table 2 show that the frequency of *man* is notably higher in German texts translated from Finnish than in German original ones. In other words, German *man* is over-represented in translations. The comparison is based on relative frequency per one thousand words. Whereas in translations the pronoun *man* has 4.3 appearances per one thousand words, in original German literary texts it has 2.7.

Table 2. Frequencies of *man* in German texts of *FinDe* corpus.

Data	*man* total	F per 1000 words
German literary prose and non-fiction translated from Finnish (5 books) (198,235 tokens)	847	4.3
Original German literary prose (3 books) (159,902 tokens)	426	2.7

This result was checked with the help of four other corpora at varying sizes representing non-translated German texts from different genres. Table 3 summarizes their results and confirms that *man* is, in general, more frequent in German texts translated from Finnish. In all the reference corpora, which were compiled from the corpora of the Institute for German Language in Mannheim (cf. http://www.ids-mannheim.de/), the frequency of *man* is lower than in texts translated from Finnish. In the first subcorpus, consisting of 11 original German non-fictional books published in the late 1990s and in the early 2000s the frequency of *man* is 2.3 per one thousand words. The second subcorpus shows a rather similar frequency, 2.2 appearances per one thousand words. This second corpus comprises 52 original German literary texts (novels, short stories, one detective story, one medical novel) representing the 1990s and the early 2000s, as well. In the third and the smallest subcorpus, involving original German trivial literature (12 books) published 1960–1974 and in 1990, the frequency of *man* is lower than in the previous corpora, 1.6. The lowest frequency of *man*, 1.5, is in German newspaper texts which form the last reference corpus in Table 3. The newspaper subcorpus covers one annual volume of *Mannheimer Morgen* (2008).³

Table 3. Frequencies of *man* in four control corpora.

Data	*man* total	F per 1000 words
Original German non-fictional prose (11 books) (571,032 tokens)	1,311	2.3
Original German literary prose (52 books) (3,494,141 tokens)	7,644	2.2
Original German trivial literatur (12 books) (297,217 tokens)	473	1.6
Newspapers: *Mannheimer Morgen* 2008 (19,796,457 tokens)	28,865	1.5

The over-representation of *man* in translations from Finnish relates to several previous works in which translations have been shown to over-represent particular linguistic items. These previous studies show us how the over-representation can lead to varying effects – or to varyingly interpretable effects – in translation. For example, in Laviosa's (1996) study high frequency lexical items were even more frequent in translations than in comparable non-translated texts in the same language. In addition, these high frequency items accounted for a larger amount of the tokens in the corpus, i.e. they occurred more often in translated than in non-translated texts. According to Laviosa, these characteristics indicate a general tendency towards simplification in translation. Ebeling (1998), for his part, discovered a feature in translations which he characterized as semantic despecification and which was caused by an over-representation of particular items. He focused, among others, on Norwegian translations of English presentative constructions (e.g. *There is a waiting room along the hall*) in which verbs of existence are used more often than in corresponding Norwegian constructions which in turn favor other verbs belonging to other semantic fields. Ebeling's results show that the translators do not always follow the target language norms but tend to over-use

---

3 Newspapers do not of course entail only non-translated texts but also translations.

verbs of existence in translated Norwegian presentative constructions. Finally, in Olohan's and Baker's (2000) study, the optional reporting *that* was found to be over-represented in English translations compared with non-translated English texts. The authors interpreted the over-use as explicitation.

It is a difficult task to characterize the over-representation of *man* with regard to any tendency claimed so far to be typical for translations in general. It is particularly challenging to evaluate the result with respect to the so-called T-universals, which characterize universal differences between translations and comparable non-translated texts (cf. Chesterman 2004): what kind of effect does the over-representation of a particular pronoun with generic person reference have in comparison with German original texts? Because the data in the present study are language-pair specific, considerations along the lines of S-universals and differences between translations and their source texts (cf. Chesterman 2004) seem more approachable. Previous studies discussing source language impact in over-representation are of special interest. Interestingly, their results are partially contradictory. In some research settings the researchers observe a conspicuous correlation between over-representation and source language stimuli. This is the case, for example, in Ebeling's (1998) paper presented above and in Eskola's (2002; 2004) study, in which the author examined (among others) two particular infinitive constructions in Finnish translations from English and Russian and in comparable Finnish original texts. One type of her infinitive constructions consisted of target-language-specific, unique constructions that have no obvious counterparts in either source language. The other type entailed infinitive constructions with direct equivalents both in English and in Russian. Compared with Finnish non-translated texts, the target-language-specific syntactic structures were under-represented in translations, and those with direct source language equivalents were over-represented. In other studies, however, the over-representation occurs regardless of the fact that the source language lacks a direct equivalent. For example, in the seminal paper by Baker (1993) on universal features of translation, the author mentioned "exaggeration" of features of the target language as one possible characteristic of translated language in general. She illustrated the feature with Toury's (1980: 130) results on Hebrew binomials[4], which according to Toury are a

---

4 Binomials are "relatively fixed conjoint phrases having two members" (Quirk et al. 1985: 971), e.g. *through thick and thin, law and order, day and night, hit and run, come and go*.

typical feature in Hebrew writing. The binomials tended to occur more frequently in translated than in non-translated Hebrew texts, although they replaced non-binomials of source texts which, in other words, did not provide any direct stimuli for them. A similar tendency was discovered by Halverson (2007), who noticed an over-use of the English progressive construction *be V-ing* in English translations from Norwegian, in which a corresponding grammatical construction does not exist and a direct counterpart is missing.

Hence, previous studies on over-representation form a partly inconsistent background against which it is fascinating to reflect upon the reasons for over-use of the German pronoun *man*. The following discussion focuses on the role of source language impact. In the first step, I will investigate the distribution of *man* in the individual target texts. Second, I will compare German *man* with its source expressions.

4 Distribution of *man* in individual German target texts: text-specific differences

The data summarized in Table 4 allows us to conclude that the over-representation of *man* is a text-specific feature and does not necessarily concern all translations from Finnish. The figures indicate notable differences between individual target texts translated from Finnish. For example, whereas the translation of Haavikko's text has 9.2 appearances of *man*, the translations of Idström's has only 2.4. In addition, in the latter text *man* is not over-represented at all and displays similar or even lower frequencies as in the original German texts (cf. Tables 2, 3 and 5). The small size of the available German corpus translated from Finnish is of course a slight weakness in this study. The frequencies are distorted by one translation, Haavikko, but nevertheless, the average frequency of *man* is still noticeably higher in German translations than in original writings.

Table 4. Frequencies of *man* in the individual target texts of *FinDe* corpus.

German target texts (tokens)	man total	F per 1000 words
Literary prose		
• Haavikko (31,081)	287	9.2
• Idström (47,915)	115	2.4
• Tuuri (53,267)	265	5.0
Non-fiction		
• Nikula (44,191)	115	2.6
• Tarkka (21,781)	65	3.0
Tokens in sum: 198,235	847	4.3

Table 5 shows that a similar text-specific variation in the frequency of *man* occurs in original German narrative prose, as well. However, the scale of variation is clearly smaller, 1.4–4.1, whereas in translated texts it is 2.4–9.2.

Table 5. Frequencies of *man* in the individual German original texts of *FinDe* corpus.

German original texts (tokens)	man total	F per 1000 words
Literary prose		
• Grass (60,422 tokens)	153	2.5
• Hein (48,925 tokens)	68	1.4
• Strauß (50,555 tokens)	205	4.1
Tokens in sum: 159,902	426	2.7

The quantitative data in Table 4 can be interpreted in two ways. On the one hand, it suggests that the varying frequency of *man* in the individual target texts is a result of individual translator styles in the same way as it is an author-specific feature in original German narrative prose (cf. Table 5). In order to be able to test this hypothesis and to exclude the possibility of source language influence on over-representation, we would, however, need a whole set of new tools and additional translations from the same translators. On the other hand, the data propose that there might be something occurring in the source texts which triggers an unusual amount of *man* in part of the translations, and that it is worthwhile examining the source texts. This will be done in the next section, in which I will compare German *man* with its Finnish source expressions. The parallel text comparison will be restricted to the literary texts, to the translation of Haavikko's novel, in which *man* shows the highest frequency (9.2), to the translation of Idström's novel, with the lowest proportion of *man* appearances (2.4), and to the translation of Tuuri's novel, in which the frequency of *man* lies between these two ends (5.0).

5 Cross-linguistic comparison: German *man* and its Finnish sources

Table 6 summarizes the results of the cross-linguistic comparison by presenting the Finnish source expressions for German *man* in the three narrative text pairs chosen for the comparison. In the following sections, I will present the types of source expressions in turn and illustrate them with the help of examples taken from the corpus texts. What follows is an in-depth German-Finnish cross-linguistic analysis. Readers primarily interested in conclusions may want to skip the cross-linguistic comparison in Sections 5.1–5.4 and proceed directly to Section 5.5, in which the results will be related to the discussion of over-representation in general.

Table 6. Finnish source expressions for German *man* in three narrative text pairs.

	P. Haavikko: Fi.: *Fleurin koulusykvy* Ge.: *Fleurs mittlere Reife*		A. Idström: Fi.: *Veljeni Sebastian* Ge.: *Mein Bruder Sebastian*		A. Tuuri: Fi.: *Talvisota* Ge.: *Winterkrieg*	
	Σ	%	Σ	%	Σ	%
Zero person	153	53	59	51	60	23
Passive	75	26	30	26	123	46
Diverse nonfinite constructions	25	9	9	8	27	10
Explicit subject	8	3	9	8	21	8
Diverse other constructions	24	8	7	6	27	10
Ø	2	1	1	1	7	3
Total	287	100	115	100	265	100

5.1 Zero person and the passive

The comparison reveals that in most cases German *man* can be traced back to two particular construction types in Finnish source texts, either to so-called zero person clauses or to passive clauses which will be presented below, in turn. This result is fascinating because these two source constructions do not have any syntactic subjects. In other words, what is at play here is the fact that the two source constructions with null subjects give rise to the over-use of a particular subject in the target text. In the translation of Haavikko's novel, these two constructions cover 79% of the Finnish sources for German *man*, in the translation of Idström's text 77%, and in the translation of Tuuri's novel 69%.

Zero person clauses represent a particular impersonal construction type in Finnish. The verb is always inflected in the 3rd person singular, and the subject is in most cases missing, cf. (2). The meaning of the clauses is generic: they refer to people in general in the same way as their German translation equivalent, the pronoun *man*, does. In the following examples, the German translations marked with the sign ➔ follow their Finnish sources:

(2) Voi   vain   toivoa   että [...].
     can   only   hope   that
     'One can only hope that'

➔ **Man** kann nur hoffen, daß [...].
     one can only hope   that
     'One can only hope that'

Section 2 above stressed that Finnish does not possess a stylistically neutral generic pronoun and that the main resource to refer to people in general involves the use of rather different devices. This is exactly the domain where zero person clauses like (2) are needed: they are the main means to express generic person reference in Finnish.

Zero person is a term suggested by Laitinen (1995). In previous studies, the construction was labeled, among others, as "Missing person sentences" (Hakulinen & Karttunen 1973). Both characterizations refer to the fact that the possible reference to a human participant has been left out. The missing person can be a nominative subject, cf. (2), or genitive subject required by necessive verbs and particular necessive constructions, cf. (3). In addition, the person "normally" expressed in other cases and grammatical functions can be omitted, as well. For example, an experiencer participant in the elative case, cf. (4), or a possessor participant in the ablative case (cf. *require something of someone*), cf. (5), can be missing. (VISK 2004: §1358–§1361) The character # signals possible places where the missing person reference can be inserted:

(3) Olen 11 vuotta, se # täytyy muistaa.
    I am 11 years, that must remember.
    'I am 11 years old, one should remember it.'

➔ Ich bin elf, das muß **man** bedenken.
    I am eleven that must one consider.
    'I am eleven, one should consider that.'

(4) Jälkeenpäin ajatellen # tuntui uhkarohkealta, että [...].
    afterwards considering felt reckless that
    'Considering it afterwards, it felt reckless that'

➔ Überlegt **man** es sich im nachhinein, dann erscheint es tollkühn, daß [...].
    considers one it REFL afterwards then seems it reckless that
    'If one considers it afterwards, then it seems reckless that'

(5) Jokaista vastoinkäymistä seuraa hyvityksen mahdollisuus,
    'Every setback is followed by the possibility of reconciliation,'

    vaatii # älykkyyttä huomata se.
    demands intelligence notice it
    'it requires intelligence to notice it.'

➔ Jedem Fehlschlag folgt die Möglichkeit, ihn wieder auszugleichen.
    'Every failure is followed by the possibility to reconcile it.'

    Man braucht Intelligenz, um sie zu erkennen.
    one needs intelligence in order it to notice
    'One needs intelligence to notice it.'

Typical contexts in which zero person occurs comprise, among others, the use of modal verbs (2), including necessive verbs (3) and necessive constructions, diverse experiencer constructions (4) and conditional subordinate clauses, cf. (6) (VISK 2004: §1347–1361):

(6) Jos # hänelle puhui hän ei vastannut [...].
    if to him talked he not answered
    'If you talked to him he did not answer'

➔ Wenn **man** ihn ansprach, gab er keine Antwort.
    if one him talked gave he no answer
    'If you talked to him he gave no answer.'

Zero person is a strategy used to present individual and personal experience as typical for humans in general. By fading out any person reference, it opens a place for people in general to identify with the situation in question (Laitinen 1995; 2006).

Passive clauses constitute the second major source for German *man*. The Finnish passive differs from the Indo-European passive in some important respects. First of all, as example (7) shows, its structure is synthetic and its formation involves derivation, whereby a particular suffixal morpheme is added to the verb root. Second, it is an impersonal subjectless construction. But there are similarities as well: the Finnish passive shares its function with its Indo-European counterparts by backgrounding the agent participant and fading out its identity. Although the agent is left unexpressed and its identity remains unknown, the Finnish passive always presumes a human agent or a group of them (VISK 2004: §1313–§1326; Helasvuo & Laitinen 2006). In this respect, the function of the Finnish passive resembles its German translation equivalent *man*, which refers to an animated, indefinite human participant or to a plurality of them.

(7) Puhu   kovempaa, minulle sanottiin [...].
    speak   louder   to me   tell.PASS.PAST[5]
    'I was told to speak louder.'

→ Sprich   lauter,   sagte   **man** [...].
    speak   louder   said   one
    'Speak louder, someone suggested.' (= Ex. (1))

In colloquial Finnish, the passive is also used as an alternative verb form for the 1st person plural, in which case it can optionally be combined with the subject pronoun *me* 'we' (VISK 2004: §1315, §1326). In narrative prose, authors exploit this particular passive function in order to create an illusion of spoken language (cf. Nevalainen 2003; Schwitalla & Tiittula 2009). Example (8), taken from the corpus of this study, illustrates this passive function and its German translation equivalent, the pronoun *man*. In this example, the Finnish 1st person plural *me* 'we' alternates with two verbs in the passive. The interpretation of both passive forms is expressly 'we'. In the corresponding German example, this 'we'-interpretation becomes evident in the translation of the first Finnish passive form, *wir* 'we'. The second Finnish passive is translated with *man*. Simultaneously, the translator has taken a slightly different perspective: whereas in Finnish the particular group of persons considers whether it has to go somewhere, in the German translation it is

---

5   The grammatical abbreviations are explained in the Appendix.

considering whether it is going to be sent somewhere by an unknown group of persons referred to by *man*:

(8) Seinäjoella **me** jouduimme viikon päivät odottelemaan,
 in Seinäjoki we had to a week wait
 'We had to wait a week in Seinäjoki'

 eikä sinä aikana oikein **tiedetty** varmasti,
 not during which time really know.PASS.PAST certainly
 'during which time we did not really certainly know'

 jouduttaisiinko mihinkään lähtemäänkään.
 have-to.PASS.PAST.QUESTIONPART anywhere go
 'whether we would have to go anywhere.'

→ In Seinäjoki blieben **wir** eine Woche und warteten.
 in Seinäjoki stayed we a week and waited
 'We stayed a week in Seinäjoki and waited.'

 Wir wußten die ganze Zeit nicht genau,
 we knew the whole time not exactly
 'The whole time we did not know exactly.'

 ob **man** uns überhaupt irgendwohin schicken würde.
 whether one us at all somewhere send would
 'whether they were going to send us somewhere at all.'

The fact that both the Finnish zero person and the passive can be translated with *man* in German is explained by their common features: all three activate the domain of indefinite and general person reference by pointing to a human participant or a group of them whose identity remains unknown. In addition, the point of reference for all three can include the speaker and the addressee.

There is one remarkable difference between the zero person and the passive, which is most probably reflected in the results presented in Table 6 above. Zero person implies a single indefinite human participant, but the passive implies always plurality. These semantic features might be the reason for the fact that the individual text pairs display significant differences in the distribution of the two source expressions. In the two first novels by Haavikko and Idström, the zero person constitutes the major source for German *man* (53% resp. 51%) and the passive plays a smaller role (26% resp. 26%). In the third novel by Tuuri, the distribution between these two constructions is opposite: the passive (46%) clearly dominates, and the zero person (23%) stands in its shade. The varying distribution of the source expressions seems to indicate that the zero person and the passive are generally used differently in the source texts. In this paper it is not possible to pursue this idea any further, but it is certainly compatible with the narrative structure of the three books and with the semantic properties of the zero person and the passive. Both Idström's and Tuuri's novel has a single person as the narrator, Haavikko's novel, in turn, consists of four chapters, each with a different individual as the narrator. In Tuuri's novel, however, the narrator belongs to a particular group consisting of several persons. He is a soldier who moves and acts together with his troop, whereby he does not only mediate his own personal thoughts and experiences but relates them to the whole group in general. It is possible that this circumstance in Tuuri's novel affects the use of the passive referring to several human participants and explains the role of the passive as a dominant source expression for German *man*.

5.2 Diverse nonfinite constructions

The third category "Diverse nonfinite constructions" in Table 6 is a label for diverse infinitive, participial and nominalized constructions that function as Finnish source expressions for German *man*. Compared with the zero person and the passive, their role is notably smaller, varying between 8–10% in the three novels.

These nonfinite constructions (to be presented in more detail below) are condensed synthetic structures derived from their verb stems with the help of particular suffixes, and they can be characterized as "packed" (Eskola 2004: 88) or – using a computer metaphor – "zipped" structures that compress information into a tighter package than in finite clauses. Their level of redundancy is thus lower. They could, alternatively, be realized as independent clauses with finite verbs – either as main or subordinate clauses, depending on the particular construction and context. Stylistically, they have been regarded as a representative of a more static nominal style than corresponding finite structures which have been claimed to be more dynamic. Järventausta & Schröder (1995: 74–86) provide an extensive summary of their discussion in previous and contemporary prescriptive language planning in Finland and state that they have been regarded as structures, which cognitively burden the working memory and complicate comprehension. Puurtinen (1995), who compared their use in original and translated Finnish children's literature, strove for an operationalization of their claimed cognitive complexity. The results of her experimental tests indicate that the nonfinite constructions can only be partly regarded as a resource that increases cognitive complexity and reduces the level of readability and speakability (the suitability to be read aloud). This result was clearest for non-fluent child readers, whereas the test groups consisting of adults failed to support the claimed difficulty of nonfinite constructions.

Examples in the following discussion show that, when translated into German, the Finnish nonfinite constructions are replaced by German finite clauses with the pronoun *man* as their subject. Hence, the nonfinite Finnish constructions become, in a sense, "unzipped" in German target texts. In many cases, German possesses equivalent nonfinite constructions that represent a similar nominal style. The overview in Järventausta & Schröder (1995: 59–73) shows that infinitives, participles and nominalizations are and have been subject to prescriptive language planning and negative criticism in Germany as well, especially when they appear as parts of NPs or when they bring along their own inherited arguments that contribute to an extended NP-structure which has been judged to reduce comprehensibility. However, Järventausta & Schröder (ibid.) stress that a straightforward consideration of nonfinite constructions as linguistic forms that complicate communication is problematic. Their assumed complexity has not been operationalized and tested in German, to my knowledge not even to this day, and above all, their textual functions have not been taken into account when discussing context-free examples. In addition, Järventausta & Schröder (ibid.) emphasize that meaning and linguistic form always go hand in hand. If one changes the form, the meaning is changed as well, and vice versa. In other words, finite paraphrases are not complete synonyms for their corresponding nonfinite constructions and have other functions in texts.

Because finite clauses tend to include more redundancy than nonfinite clauses and express the relationship between clauses more clearly, one might be tempted to regard the finite translations as a clarifying or explicating strategy. However, the arguments presented by Järventausta & Schröder (1995) and the only partly conclusive results of Puurtinen's study (1995) lead one unavoidably to the conclusion that there are cogent reasons to be cautious when characterizing the shift from Finnish nonfinite constructions into "unzipped" finite translations with *man* in German. In addition, a global characterization of finite translations as a clarifying strategy or as explicitation is not possible for stylistic reasons, either: the nonfinite German constructions are not adequate translations in all contexts causing, among others, stylistic breaches in narrative texts, when the aim is, for example, to create the illusion of spoken discourse.

The following examples will illustrate the Finnish nonfinite source constructions and their German translations with finite clauses with *man* as their respective subjects. I will first present the Finnish infinitive constructions. After that I will turn to the participial and nominalized constructions.

The Finnish system of infinitive verb forms is quite complex and involves several different types with distinct semantic, morphological and syntactic properties. The infinitives cannot be inflected in person categories but they can receive case endings. Yet, their case paradigm is incomplete. In addition, particular infinitive forms can be combined with possessive suffixes that indicate the agent participant. The function as independent predicates is excluded but infinitive verbs can form a part of a complex predicate. Alternatively, they can function as autonomous constituents of clauses or form a part of a NP-constituent.

The Finnish and German infinitive systems differ from each other significantly, due to which only a part of Finnish infinitives have an infinitive equivalent in German. Such cases include, among others, the so called *MA*-infinitives in the abessive case, whose matching pair in German are *ohne etwas zu tun*-infinitives (e.g. *ohne etwas zu sagen* 'without saying something'), cf. (9), *MA*-infinitives in the illative case having *um etwas zu tun*-infinitive constructions as their German counterpart (e.g. *um etwas zu verkünden* 'in order to declare something'), cf. (10), and plain *A*-infinitives as subjects of copula verbs with equivalent infinitive verb forms in the subject function in German (*es ist besser, etwas zu tun* 'it is better to do something'), cf. (11). (For an overview of equivalence relations between German and Finnish infinitives on the system level cf. Tarvainen 1985: 152–172). In the following examples, these matching German infinitive constructions have not been chosen. Instead, the Finnish infinitives have been translated with finite clauses with *man* functioning as their subject.

(9) [...] niin voi jo nopeasti kertoa että kaikki on hyvin,
'so one can quickly tell that everything is fine'

sitä   sanomatta.
it   say.MA-INF-ABES
'without saying it.'

➔ [...] und schon kann man schnell [...] mitteilen, daß alles in Ordnung ist,
'and one can quickly tell that everything is fine'

ohne daß **man** es sagt.
without that one it says
'without saying it.'

(10) Koivut näyttävät syöpäläisiltä jotka
'The birches look like vermin which'

on istutettu metsiköksi **julistamaan** sitä että [...].
have plant.PASS.PAST as a forest declare.MA-INF-ILL it that
'have been planted into a forest shape in order to declare that ...'

➔ Die Birken sehen aus wie Ungeziefer, das man in Form von Wald gepflanzt hat,
'The birches look like vermin which one has planted into a forest shape'

womit **man** verkünden will, daß [...].
by way of which one declare want that
'by way of which one wants to declare that ...'

(11) Eikö olisi parempi **tehdä** lapsenlapsista ihmisinä vanhoja eikä
not were better do.A-INF from grandchildren as-people old and-not

päinvastoin?
vice versa
'Would it not be better to create old people from grandchildren and not vice versa?'

➔ Wäre es nicht besser, **man** machte aus Enkelkindern die alten
were it not better one would-do of grandchildren the old

Menschen, und nicht umgekehrt?
people and not vice versa
'Would it not be better to create old people from grandchildren and not vice versa?'

Finnish infinitive constructions lacking infinitive counterparts in German comprise among others *MA*-infinitives in the adessive case, cf. (12), and E-infinitives in the inessive case, cf. (13). Tarvainen (1985: 160, 169) points out that they can be translated into German with diverse subordinate clauses. The following examples show such cases in which *man* occupies the subject function.

(12) Yhtä hyvin **pääsee** paaviksi **viemällä** raamatun
as well gets to pope bring.MA-INF-ADE bible

käsikirjoituksen [...] Vatikaaniin.
manuscript to Vatican
'One might even make it to the Pope by bringing a bible manuscript to Vatican.'

➔ Genausogut wird man Papst, wenn **man** ein Bibelmanuskript in
as well become one pope when one a biblemanuscript to

den Vatikan bringt.
the Vatican brings
'One might even make it to the Pope if one brings a biblemanuscript to Vatican.'

(13)   [...] kuin kiikarin   lävitse   väärin päin **katsoessa**.
      like   binoculars.GEN through backwards look.E-INF-INE
      'like when looking backwards through binoculars'

→   [...] wie wenn **man** verkehrtherum durchs Fernglas schaut.
     like   when one backwards   through binoculars looks
     'like when one looks backwards through binoculars.'

The participles for their part as the Finnish source for *man* comprise present and past participles both in the active and in the passive form. Compared with their infinitive systems, Finnish and German participles show substantially more similarities (Tarvainen 1985: 172). This fact is evident in the Finnish and German example pairs of this study: except for one frozen idiomatic expression, all other Finnish participles translated with finite clauses with *man* possess direct participial equivalents in German. Alternatively, they have adjectival or infinitive counterparts in German.

For example, past participles occurring as premodifiers of nouns and partly inheriting their arguments from the verb are also possible in German (cf. e.g. Tarvainen 1985: 183). In the following German translation, the information compressed in the Finnish participial construction has been unpacked to a German finite subordinate relative clause with *man* as its subject.

(14)   [...] mutta ne suomalaiset olivat olleet
      'but those Finns had been'

     rannikon   **ruotsalaispitäjistä**   **juuri**   **rintamalle**   **tuotua joukkoa.**
     coast.GEN   from Swedish parishes recently to the front   brought group'
     'a group recently brought from the Swedish parishes on the coast.'

→   Das waren aber Einheiten aus den schwedischen Gemeinden an der Küste,
     'But they were units from Swedish parishes on the coast'

     die   **man** gerade   an die   Front   gebracht hatte.
     which one   recently at the front   brought   had
     'which had been recently brought to the front.'

Another recurrent participial construction serving as a source for *man* is the present participle in the passive that functions in the predicative role, cf. (15), or as a premodifier, cf. (16). Finnish present participles in the passive have a modal meaning of possibility, desirability or obligation, thus expressing what can be done, what should be done or what has to be done (VISK 2004: §524). Equivalent modalities can be expressed in German by using different kinds of constructions. For example, verbal adjectives derived with the suffix *-bar* (expressing possibility, e.g. *erkennbar* 'recognizable') and infinitive constructions with the particle *zu* (expressing obligation or necessity, e.g. *etwas ist zu verdrängen und zu vergessen* 'something is to be rejected and forgotten') represent a similar nominal style as the Finnish participles and can occur as premodifiers of nouns as well (cf. e.g. Tarvainen 1985: 180–181). Instead of these possible translation equivalents, in the following examples the translator has preferred finite clauses with the indefinite pronoun *man* as their respective subjects.

(15) Vaimoni   on   tunnistettavissa   sieraimistaan.
      my wife   is   recognize.PAST-PARTIC.PASS   by her nostrils
      'My wife is recognizable by her nostrils.'

→ Meine   Frau   erkennt   **man** an ihren Nasenflügeln.
   my   wife   recognizes   one   at her   nostrils
   'One can recognize my wife by her nostrils'

(16) Se oli   ollut   **häivytettävä**   ja
      it had   been   reject.PAST-PARTIC.PASS   and

      unohdettava   asia.
      forget.PAST-PARTIC.PASS   matter
      'It had been a matter best to reject and forget.'

→ Es   war   etwas,   was   **man**   besser   verdrängte   und   vergaß.
   it   was   something   that   one   best   rejected   and   forgot
   'It was something best rejected and forgotten.'

So-called referative participial constructions constitute a special type of participial structures in Finnish. They are a special resource which enables an alternative expression for *että*-clauses ('that') functioning as objects of certain verbs (VISK 2004: §538). In German, infinitives (*accusativus cum infinitivo*-constructions) serve in the same function and can occupy the position of an accusative object as well (Tarvainen 1985: 186–190; Zifonun et al. 1997: 1386–1392). However, in the following example pair a finite clause with *man*-subject appears as a counterpart for the Finnish referative participial construction. There are actually two *man* pronouns in this German translation. The first one is a translation of a Finnish zero person construction. The second one, which I am concentrating on, is the German translation of the Finnish referative construction, highlighted with bold.

(17) [...] lapsenhan   sitä   kuvittelee   **tuntevansa** [...].
      child   PARTICLE   imagine   know.REF-PARTIC
      'One imagines knowing a child'

→ [...] man glaubt   ja   immer,   **man**   kenne   ein   Kind [...].
   one   believes   PARTICLE   always   one   knows   a   child
   'One believes one knows a child'

Finally, nominalizations with the suffix *-minen* were included in the category "Diverse nonfinite constructions", cf. (18). *-minen* is the most productive nominalizing suffix in Finnish. Verbal nouns suffixed with it are *Nomen actionis* expressing activities, achievements or states, referred to by their verb stems. From all possible *Nomen actionis* in Finnish, the *-minen*-nouns are those keenest to inherit the arguments of their verb stems and rarely lexicalized. (VISK 2004: §223–§225, §227) Compared with the use of the same verbs as finite predicates in active clauses, the verbal nouns are claimed to be more difficult to comprehend, especially when combined with several inherited arguments and their possible modifiers (Hakulinen & Karlsson [1979] 1995: 395). In German, a corresponding strategy is available. It involves either derivation with the suffix *-ung* or direct conversion of infinitives into nouns (e.g. *verbessern* 'to improve' > *Verbesserung* 'improvement' / *Verbessern* 'improving'). Both strategies are highly productive. (Cf. Fleischer & Barz 1995: 172–177, 211–212) However, the presence of a structurally and stylistically equivalent nominal strategy does not mean that it is should be chosen in the translation. In the following example pair, for instance, two *Nomen actionis* (*turvautuminen* 'resorting', *tarrautuminen* 'clinging') are combined with a *Nomen acti* (pako '*escape*') in the Finnish source. In German, the corresponding co-ordinated finite verbs have different government properties (*bauen auf* 'resort to', *sich klammern an* 'cling to', (*irgendwohin*) *fliehen* 'escape (somewhere)'). Besides, the second verb is reflexive. These circumstances complicate the use of a similar nominalization strategy in German, and actually, it would have made the clause rather heavy. Instead, the translator replaces the verbal nouns with an active finite clause inserting *man* as its subject.

(18) Epäpätevän henkilön elämän ja työskentelyn täytyy olla alusta loppuun
'From beginning to end the life and work of an unqualified person must be'

sietämätöntä **muihin turvautumista, tarrautumista** ja – pakoa.
unbearable to others resorting clinging and escape
'an unbearable resorting and clinging to others and – escape.'

→ Das Leben und die Arbeit einer unqualifizierten Person muß von Anfang bis Ende bedeuten, daß
'From beginning to end, the life and work of an unqualified person must mean that'

man in unerträglicher Weise auf andere baut, sich an andere klammert
one in unbearable way on others resort REFL at others cling
und – flieht.
and – escapes
'one in an unbearable way resorts to others, clings to others and – escapes.'

5.3 Explicit subject

"Explicit subject" in Table 6 is a label for two smaller groups that account for 3–8% of source expressions which German *man* can be traced back to. In both types an explicit subject is present in the Finnish source text, and the translation involves a partial shift in perspective either by replacing the Finnish explicit subject with *man* or by downgrading the Finnish subject to an object function and by inserting *man* into the subject slot.

In examples (19) and (20) Finnish source texts have explicit subjects, which in both cases are particular human participants, 1st person singular in (19) and 2nd person singular in (20). In each example verbal person marking signals the person subject and enables the omission of the overt pronominal subjects. In the German translations, these explicit participants have been replaced by *man*. Simultaneously, the situation is regarded from a more general perspective. Øverås (1998) examines similar cases in which explicit source text items have been replaced by ambiguous target text items and characterizes them as implicitation.

(19) Sebastian oli oikeassa, vaaran **aistin** joka askeleella [...].
 Sebastian was right danger.OBJ sense.1SG every step
 'Sebastian was right, I could sense the danger in every step'

→ Sebastian hatte recht, **man** witterte die Gefahr auf Schritt und Tritt [...].
 Sebastian was right one sensed the danger on step and step
 'Sebastian was right, one could sense the danger step by step.'

(20) Älä puhu isille rumasti.
 do not.2SG talk to daddy nasty
 'Do not talk nasty to daddy.'

→ So spricht **man** nicht zu Vati!
 so talks one not to daddy
 'One does not talk so to daddy.'

The second group covers cases of cross-linguistic "conversion" with subject-to-object-shift: the source text subject is expressed as an object in the target text, and the pronoun *man* occupies the subject position. This shift often seems to concern Finnish perception verbs with stimulus subjects like *kuulua* 'be heard', cf. (21), and *näkyä* 'be visible', cf. (22) (cf. Viberg 2008). No human experiencer participant is present. German lacks corresponding verbs of perception with stimulus subjects, due to which the translator is forced to find other solutions. In examples (21) and (22), the translation equivalents are perception verbs which receive experiencer subjects (cf. Viberg 2008). The human experiencer subject is represented by the pronoun *man*. There is a small perspective difference between the source and the target: whereas in Finnish a rustle is heard and breasts can be seen, in the German translation *people in general* hear the rustle and see the breasts.

(21) **Kuului** heikko rasahdus [...].
    be heard.PAST.3SG week rustle
    'A week rustle was heard.'

➔   *Man* hörte ein schwaches Knacken [...]
    one heard a week rustle
    'One could hear a week rustle.'

(22) Rintasi **näkyvät**, sanoin.
    your breasts be visible.3PL said.1SG
    'Your breasts can be seen, I said.'

➔   "*Man* sieht deinen Busen", sagte ich.
    one sees your breast said I
    'One can see your breasts, I said.'

5.4 Diverse other constructions and Ø

German *man* can of course have several other Finnish source expressions or no overt source at all. These cases are presented separately in Table 6 but are dealt with together in this section.

The category "Diverse other constructions" covers 6–10% of the Finnish source expressions for *man*. The category members are heterogeneous and do not have anything in common. Example (23) illustrates one of them. In this example, the Finnish verb *hymyillä* 'smile' occurs with an adessive phrase expressing the instrument. In German *lächeln* 'smile' does not allow an instrument as its partner. Consequently, the translator has to arrive at another solution:

(23) Liisa seisoi [...] lumen keskellä [...]
    'Liisa stood in the middle of snow'

    ja hymyili **keltaisilla hampaillaan.**
    and smiled with yellow teeth
    'and smiled with her yellow teeth.'

➔   Liisa stand mitten im Schnee [...]
    'Liisa stood in the middle of snow'

    und lächelte, **man sah** ihre gelblichen Zähne.
    and smiled one saw her yellowish teeth
    'and smiled, one could see her yellowish teeth.'

1–3% of all *man* occurrences cannot be traced back to any apparent linguistic expression in the Finnish source text. The symbol Ø in Table 6 refers to such cases which seem to explicate particular circumstances. In the following example, the added *man*-clause expresses evidentiality and explicates how the narrator has received his information and arrived at his conclusion.

(24) Ne eivät olleet ensimmäistä kertaa hevosta jokiavannosta nostamassa.
 they were not first time horse from river-ice-hole lifting
 'It was not the first time they were lifting a horse from an ice-hole in a river.'

→ **Man sah**, daß sie das nicht zum ersten Mal machten.
 one saw that they it not for first time did
 'One could see that they did not do it for the first time.'

With regard to the role of source language impact on over-representation, these cases do not offer any relevant aspects, so they are not discussed any further.

5.5 Source language impact

Table 6 above and the discussion in Sections 5.1–5.4 showed that German *man* can, in most cases, be traced back to two particular Finnish source constructions, to the Finnish impersonal passive and to the Finnish impersonal zero person construction. Depending on the individual text, their common share varied between 69–79%. Furthermore, in 8–10% of cases, the source for *man* was a particular translation strategy in which diverse Finnish nonfinite constructions, infinitives, participles and nominalizations were translated with German finite constructions with *man* occupying the subject slot. The other translation strategy that covered 3–8% of source expressions involved a partial perspective shift, either by replacing an explicit Finnish subject with the indefinite *man* or by downgrading an explicit Finnish subject to object function in the target text and by inserting *man* to the subject position. Finally, German *man* could have diverse other Finnish source expressions that shared no common denominator (6–10% of all cases) or no overt source expression at all (1–3% of all cases).

In Section 2, it was concluded that *man* conforms to the definition of unique items of the unique items hypothesis suggested by Tirkkonen-Condit (2002; 2004; 2005) by having no straight-forward and direct pronominal counterpart in the Finnish source language. However, the cross-linguistic comparison in the previous sections revealed that *man* does have a regular counterpart in Finnish, actually there are no fewer than two of them, the Finnish passive and the Finnish zero person construction functioning as sources for *man* in translations. In other words, it seems that *man* is not a unique item at all. This explains, of course, why it does not behave like the unique items hypothesis predicts and is over-represented in translations. In fact, German *man* has proven to be an item which does not have a straight-forward and direct counterpart in Finnish representing the same linguistic level, but it does have counterparts with rather different structural properties which nevertheless activate the same cognitive-semantic domain of indefinite-generic person reference.

The most important results of the cross-linguistic comparison are the reasons for *man*'s over-representation. The notably higher frequency of *man* in German translations results mainly from the two source constructions, the passive and the zero person, owing to which translators tend to insert *man* more frequently than in the original German texts. Hence, the reason for over-representation is classic source language impact, a process in which "phenomena pertaining to the make-up of the source text tend to be transferred to the target text" (Toury 1995: 275). However, as opposed to previous studies (cf. e.g. Ebeling 1998; Eskola 2004; Nilsson 2004), the source language impact manifested in the present study does not involve the use of an item imitating the source language model in the target text. The source language stimuli, the passive and the zero person, are structurally quite different from German *man*. Semantically they do share properties. The Finnish impersonal passive implies a group of animated, human agents whose identity remains unknown. The impersonal zero person construction, in turn, creates an open reference to people in general. Hence, both constructions activate the domain of indefinite and generic person reference which is the main function of their translation equivalent, German *man*, as well. In other words, what is preserved in translation is not a linguistic form echoing the source language form but the same indefinite-generic person reference which is conveyed by a structurally different item in the target language.[6]

---

[6] German *man* is of course not the only translation option for the Finnish passive and the zero person. How else these constructions are translated and what are the frequencies of the different translation options are questions to be answered in a future study.

6 Conclusion

This paper examined the over-representation of generic person reference in translations and focused on the reasons leading to a non-typical frequency. The analysis concentrated on the German pronoun *man* 'one, people in general', which displays notably higher frequencies in texts translated from Finnish than in the original non-translated German texts. The results showed how cross-linguistic differences in the grammatical devices expressing person are reflected into German translations from Finnish and cause an untypical frequency of generic person reference. The cross-linguistic comparison revealed that German *man* can, in most cases, be traced back to two particular Finnish source constructions, to the Finnish impersonal passive and to the Finnish impersonal zero person construction. Hence, the over-representation of *man* is a result of classic source language impact.

Teich (2003: 145–146) characterizes the source language influence as a "shining through" effect: the target language is oriented towards the source language which "shines through" in the translation. Toury (1995: 275) reminds us, however, that the source language impact, the "law of interference" in his terms, can manifest itself in multiple ways, in the form of negative or positive transfer. With regard to the results of this study, this is an important distinction: in this study, the source language influence did not lead to the use of a linguistic form imitating the source language form or to the use of a form or a combination which would deviate from the usual practices of the target language. Instead, the translation involved the transfer of the semantic domain of indefinite-generic person reference, which was encoded by a structurally completely different item in the target text. In other words, the source language is not "shining through", but nevertheless, it is causing untypical frequencies.

As a whole, the present study supports previous studies in which the researchers have observed a conspicuous correlation between over-representation and source language stimulus. In addition, the results of this study may point to new possibilities and directions in the study of cross-linguistic influence in translation: the source language influence does not necessarily involve a "shining through" of a linguistic form, but it can manifest itself in other ways as well.

References

Altenberg, Bengt (2005): "The generic person in English and Swedish. A contrastive study of *one* and *man*." In: *Languages in Contrast* 5: 1, 93–120.

Baker, Mona (1993): "Corpus linguistics and translation studies. Implications and applications." In: Baker, Mona / Francis, Gill / Tognini Bonelli, Elena [eds.]: *Text and technology. In honour of John Sinclair*. Amsterdam and Philadelphia: John Benjamins. 233–250.

Bernardini, Silvia (2010): "Parallel corpora and the search for translation norms/universals." Plenary talk given at the symposium "MATS 2010: Methodological Advances in corpus-based Translation Studies". Ghent, 8–9 January, 2010.

Chesterman, Andrew (2004): "Beyond the particular." In: Mauranen, Anna/ Kujamäki, Pekka [eds.]: *Translation universals: Do they exist?* Amsterdam and Philadelphia: John Benjamins. 33–49.

——— (2007): "What is a unique item?" In: Gambier, Yves / Shlesinger, Miriam / Stolze, Radegundis [eds.]: *Doubts and directions in translation studies: selected contributions from the EST Congress, Lisbon 2004*. Amsterdam and Philadelphia: John Benjamins. 3–13.

——— (2010): "Response and discussion." Plenary talk given at the symposium "MATS 2010: Methodological Advances in corpus-based Translation Studies". Ghent, 8–9 January, 2010.

Dudengrammatik = *Duden, die Grammatik* (2005). 7., völlig neu erarbeitete und erweiterte Auflage. Ed. by Duden editors. Duden Band 4. Mannheim: Dudenverlag.

Ebeling, Jarle (1998): "Contrastive linguistics, translation, and parallel corpora." In: *Meta: Translators' Journal* 43, 602–615. Available at: http://www.erudit.org/revue/meta/1998/v43/n4/002692ar.pdf.

Eskola, Sari (2002): *Syntetisoivat rakenteet käännössuomessa. Suomennetun kaunokirjallisuuden ominaispiirteiden tarkastelua korpusmenetelmillä*. Joensuu: University of Joensuu.

——— (2004): "Untypical frequencies in translated language: A corpus-based study on a literary corpus of translated and non-translated Finnish." In: Mauranen, Anna / Kujamäki, Pekka [eds.]: *Translation universals. Do they exist?* Amsterdam and Philadelphia: John Benjamins. 83–99.

Fleischer, Wolfgang / Barz, Irmhild (1995): *Wortbildung der deutschen Gegenwartssprache*. Unter Mitarbeit von Marianne Schröder. 2., durchgesehene und ergänzte Auflage. Tübingen: Niemeyer.

Grammis. Das grammatische Informationssystem des IDS. Last update 21.11.2007. Available at: http://hypermedia.ids-mannheim.de/index.html.

Hakulinen, Auli (1987): "Avoiding personal reference in Finnish." In: Verschueren, J. /Bertucelli-Papi, M. [eds.]: *The Pragmatic Perspective*. Amsterdam: Benjamins. 141–153.

Hakulinen, Auli / Karttunen, Lauri (1973): "Missing persons: on generic sentences in Finnish." In: *Papers from the Ninth Regional Meeting of the Chicago Linguistic society*, 157–171.

Halverson, Sandra (2007): "Investigating gravitational pull in translation: the case of the English progressive construction." In: Jääskeläinen, Riitta / Puurtinen, Tiina / Stotesbury, Hilkka [eds.]: *Text, Processes, and Corpora: Research Inspired by Sonja Tirkkonen-Condit*. Joensuu: University of Joensuu. 175–196.

Haspelmath, Martin (1997): *Indefinite pronouns*. Oxford: Oxford University Press.

Järventausta, Marja / Schröder, Hartmut (1995): *Nominalstil und Fachkommunikation. Analyse komplexer Nominalphrasen in deutsch- und finnischsprachigen philologischen Fachtexten*. Frankfurt a.M.: Peter Lang.

Johansson, Stig (2003): "Viewing languages through multilingual corpora, with special reference to the generic person in English, German, and Norwegian." In: *Languages in Contrast* 4:2, 261–280.

Kolehmainen, Leena / Stahl, Peter (2007): "Das zweisprachige FinDe-Korpus." In: *FinDe. Arbeiten mit dem finnisch-deutschen Kontrastkorpus 3*. OPUS: Online-Publikations-Server der Universität Würzburg. Available at: http://www.opus-bayern.de/uni-wuerzburg/volltexte/2007/2537/.

Kujamäki, Pekka (2004): "What happens to 'unique items' in learner's translations? 'Theories' and 'concepts' as a challenge for novices' views on 'good translation'." In: Mauranen, Anna & Kujamäki, Pekka [eds.]: *Translation universals. Do they exist?* Amsterdam and Philadelphia: John Benjamins. 188–204.

Laitinen, Lea (1995): "Nollapersoona." In: *Virittäjä* 99, 337–358.

―― (2006): "Zero person in Finnish. A grammatical resource for construing human reference". In: Helasvuo, Marja-Liisa / Campbell, Lyle [eds.]: *Grammar from the Human perspective. Case, space and person in Finnish*. Amsterdam and Philadelphia: John Benjamins. 209–231.

Laviosa, Sara (1996): "The English comparable corpus (ECC): A resource and a methodology for the empirical study of translation." Unpublished PhD thesis, University of Manchester.

Mäkisalo, Jukka (2007): "A quantitative approach to compounds in translated Finnish: The unique item hypothesis." In: Jääskeläinen, Riitta / Puurtinen, Tiina / Stotesbury, Hilkka [eds.]: *Text, Processes, and Corpora: Research Inspired by Sonja Tirkkonen-Condit*. Joensuu: University of Joensuu. 197–210.

Marschall, Gottfried R. (1996): "Was bezeichnet *man*? Das indefiniteste 'Indefinitpronomen' und seine Verwandten." In: Pérennec, Marie-Hélène [ed.]: *Pro-Formen des Deutschen*. Tübingen: Stauffenburg. 87–98.

Mauranen, Anna (2006): "Genre, käännös ja korpus. Elämäntaito-oppaat tarkastelussa." In: Mäntynen, Anne et al. [eds.]: *Genre – tekstilaji*. Helsinki: SKS. 214–239.

Mauranen, Anna / Tiittula, Liisa (2005): "MINÄ käännössuomessa ja supisuomessa." In: Mauranen, Anna / Jantunen, Jarmo H. [eds.]: *Käännössuomeksi. Tutkimuksia suomennosten kielestä*. Tampere: Tampere University Press. 35–69.

Nevalainen, Sampo (2003): "Käännöskirjallisuuden puhekielisyyksistä – kaksinkertaista illuusiota?" In: *Virittäjä* 1/2003, 2–26.

Nilsson, Per-Ola (2004): "Translation-specific lexicogrammar? Characteristic lexical and collocational patterning in Swedish texts translated from English." In: Mauranen, Anna / Kujamäki, Pekka [eds.]: *Translation universals. Do they exist?* Amsterdam and Philadelphia: John Benjamins. 129–141.

Olohan, Maeve & Baker, Mona (2000): "Reporting that in translated English. Evidence for subconscious processes of explicitation?" In: *Across Languages and Cultures* 1 (2), 141–158.

Øverås, Linn (1998): "In search of the third code: an investigation of norms in literary translation." In: *Meta: Translators' Journal* XLIII (4), 1–20. Available at: http://www.erudit.org/revue/meta/1998/v43/n4/003775ar.pdf.

Piitulainen, Marja-Leena (1993): "Die Textstruktur der finnischen und deutschsprachigen Todesanzeigen." In: Schröder, Harmut [ed.]: *Fachtextpragmatik*. Tübingen: Narr. 141–186.

―― (2003): Zur Personenreferenz in deutschen und finnischen sprachwissenschaftlichen Rezensionen. In: Barz, Irmhild / Lerchner, Gotthard / Schröder, Marianne [eds.]: *Sprachstil – Zugänge und Anwendungen. Festschrift für Ulla Fix zum 60. Geburtstag*. Heidelberg: Winter. 219–229.

Puurtinen, Tiina (1995): *Linguistic acceptability in translated children's literature.* Joensuu: University of Joensuu.

Quirk, Randolph / Greenbaum, Sidney / Leech, Geoffrey / Svartvik, Jan (1985): *A comprehensive grammar of English language.* London and New York: Longman.

Schwitalla, Johannes / Tiittula, Liisa (2009): *Mündlichkeit in literarischen Erzählungen. Sprach- und Dialoggestaltung in modernen deutschen und finnischen Romanen und deren Übersetzungen.* Tübingen: Stauffenburg.

Tarvainen, Kalevi (1985): *Kielioppia kontrastiivisesti. Suomesta saksaksi.* Jyväskylä: University of Jyväskylä.

Teich, Elke (2003): *Cross-linguistic variation in system and text.* Berlin and New York: Mouton de Gruyter.

Tiittula, Liisa (1995): "Kulturelle Unterschiede im mündlichen und schriftlichen Gebrauch von Sprache." In: Raible, Wolfgang [ed.]: *Kulturelle Perspektiven auf Schrift und Schreibprozesse. Elf Aufsätze zum Thema Mündlichkeit und Schriftlichkeit.* Tübingen: Narr. 233–257.

Tirkkonen-Condit, Sonja (2002): "Translationese – a myth or an empirical fact? A study into the linguistic identifiability of translated language." In: *Target* 14:2, 207–220.

—— (2004): "Unique items – over- or under-represented?" In: Mauranen, Anna / Kujamäki, Pekka [eds.]: *Translation universals. Do they exist?* Amsterdam and Philadelphia: John Benjamins. 184–177.

—— (2005): "Häviävätkö uniikkiainekset käännössuomesta?" In: Mauranen, Anna / Jantunen, Jarmo H. [eds.]: *Käännössuomeksi. Tutkimuksia suomennosten kielestä.* Tampere: Tampere University Press. 123–137.

Toury, Gideon (1980): *In search of a theory of translation.* Tel Aviv: Tel Aviv University.

—— (1995): *Descriptive Translation Studies and beyond.* Amsterdam and Philadelphia: John Benjamins.

Vesalainen, Marjo (2001): *Prospektwerbung: vergleichende rhetorische und sprachwissenschaftliche Untersuchungen an deutschen und finnischen Werbematerialien.* Frankfurt a.M.: Peter Lang.

Viberg, Åke (2008): "Swedish verbs of perception from a typological and contrastive perspective." In: de los Ángeles Gómez Gonzáles, Maria / Mackenzie, J. Lachlan / Gonzáles Álvarez, Elsa M. [eds.]: *Languages and cultures in contrast and comparison.* Amsterdam and Philadelphia: John Benjamins. 123–172.

VISK = Hakulinen, Auli / Vilkuna, Maria / Korhonen, Riitta/ Koivisto, Vesa/ Heinonen, Tarja Riitta / Alho, Irja (2004): *Iso suomen kielioppi.* Helsinki: SKS. Electronic version, available at: http://scripta.kotus.fi/visk.

Yli-Vakkuri, Valma (2005): "Politeness in Finland: Evasion at All Costs." In: Hickey, Leo / Stewart, Miranda [eds.]: *Politeness in Europe.* Clevedon: Multilingual Matters. 189–202.

Ylönen, Sabine (2003): " WEBVERTISING deutsch/finnisch – Kulturgebundene Unterschiede in der Wirtschaftskommunikation mit neuen Medien." In: Piitulainen, Marja-Leena/ Reuter, Ewald [eds.]: *Internationale Wirtschaftskommunikation auf Deutsch.* Frankfurt a.M.: Peter Lang. 217–252.

—— (2007): "Culture specific differences in business communication with new media?" In: Muráth, Judith / Oláh-Hubai, Ágnes [eds.]: *Interdisciplinary Aspects of Translation and Interpreting.* Wien: Praesens Verlag. 337–366.

Zifonun, Gisela / Hoffmann, Ludger / Strecker, Bruno (1997): *Grammatik der deutschen Sprache.* Berlin and New York: Walter de Gruyter.

Appendix: Grammatical abbreviations in the examples

1	= 1ˢᵗ person	OBJ	= grammatical object
2	= 2ⁿᵈ person	PARTIC	= participle
3	= 3ʳᵈ person	PARTICLE	= pragmatic particle
A-INF	= A-infititive	PASS	= passive
E-INF-INE	= E-infinitive in the inessive case	PAST	= past tense
		PL	= plural
GEN	= genitive	QUESTIONPART	= enclitic question particle
MA-INF-ABES	= MA-infinitive in the abessive case	REFL	= reflexive pronoun
MA-INF-ADE	= MA-infinitive in the adessive case	REF-PARTIC	= referative participial construction
MA-INF-ILL	= MA-infinitive in the illative case	SG	= singular

English Gatecrashers in Finnish: Directly Translated English Idioms as Novelties of Finnish

Esa Penttilä and Pirkko Muikku-Werner
University of Eastern Finland, Joensuu

Abstract

In this article, we will discuss a phenomenon that we have recently come across on internet discussion groups and various other informal contexts. At least in these contexts, it seems that the number of idiomatic expressions that have been translated word-for-word from English into Finnish is on the increase. These novel creations are of various types, and in this article we will classify them into four different categories depending on how easy it is to understand them and how well they have been adapted to the Finnish usage. The classification is based on Cacciari (1993), who originally used it for classifying idioms in one's native tongue, but here it is applied to the translation idioms under discussion. The original classification has been refined by adding a further criterion (adaption) to it. Although the phenomenon seems to concern laypersons' language use only, Abu-Ssaydeh's (2004) survey results indicate that it is also common in professional translation circles – at least in some contexts – and therefore it deserves further discussion in translation studies as well. At the moment, the main source language of this type of translation in the Finnish contexts seems to be English, but the phenomenon is possible from other source languages as well.

1 The properties of idioms

Idioms are multiword expressions that have been defined in various ways in the literature. One of the most cited traditional idiom definitions is listed in sense 3.a. in *Oxford English Dictionary*, where idiom is defined as follows:

> 3.a. A form of expression, grammatical construction, phrase, etc., peculiar to a language; a peculiarity of phraseology approved by the usage of a language, and often having a signification other than its grammatical or logical use.

This definition contains two somewhat independent properties that are usually related to idioms (see e.g. Grant & Bauer 2004: 39). First of all, idioms clearly have a language-related or culture-specific nature, which means that an idiomatic way of expressing oneself equals to the way native speakers express themselves. An idiom is a way of expression that native speakers have internalized and use naturally. This aspect of idiomaticity can be seen in the first part of the *OED* definition and resembles what Pawley and Syder (1983: 191) have referred to by the term "nativelike selection". This property is also closely related to Sinclair's (1987: 320) "idiom principle", which means that although linguistic structure could in theory be organized in infinitely many ways, native speakers often have at their disposal "a large number of semi-preconstructed phrases that constitute single choices, even though they might appear to be analysable into segments". For example, in everyday English native speakers say *commit a crime* rather than *perform an act punishable by law*, although the latter would be just as correct from the grammatical point of view.

The second property that has usually been related to idioms can be seen in the latter part of the *OED* definition, where idioms are viewed as multiword units with non-compositional semantics whose meaning cannot be arrived at by combining the meanings that their individual parts have in isolation from one another. For example, *kick the bucket* 'to die' has nothing to do with kicking or buckets, when it is used in its idiomatic sense. The property of non-compositional meaning could be regarded as the primary criterion for idiom, and it is used in various forms in basically all idiom definitions in the literature (see e.g. Makkai 1972; Nunberg et al. 1994; Fernando 1996; Valero-Garcés 1997; Moon 1998; Langlotz 2006).

In addition to the two above-mentioned features, there are various other properties that may be related to idioms as well, such as syntactic frozenness, proverbiality, colloquial nature or pragmatic restrictedness (see e.g. Barkema 1996; Penttilä 2006), but from the point of view of idiom translation and contrastive linguistics the two most important idiom characteristics are their culture-specificity and semantic non-compositionality, and these two properties are the ones on which we will base our discussion in the following pages. We will also delimit our discussion to the relationship between English and Finnish, because our main aim is to discuss newly translated idiomatic expressions that have their origin in English, since at the moment the number of such expressions seems to be increasing in Finnish. In general, of course idiom translation can occur between any language pair whatsoever.

2 Idioms in different languages

The fact that idioms are culture-specific and semantically non-compositional may at times cause problems for their translation from one language to another. The culture-relatedness may show itself, for example, in figurative idioms which contain culture-specific references that may be very difficult to translate to another culture with no relevant knowledge and experience. For example, the idea of *carrying coals to Newcastle* 'do something pointless because there is no need for it' might not open up to someone outside Britain who does not know about the historic importance of coal industry to the economy of Newcastle upon Tyne (although in this case the interpretation is alleviated by the fact that the idiom follows the same pattern as some other more or less synonymous phrases: *taking owls to Athens, selling sand to Sahara* or *bringing ice to the Eskimos*). The non-compositional meaning, on the other hand, has consequences for the formal realization of translated idioms: word-for-word translation from one language to another can easily become totally incomprehensible. For example, *potkaista sankoa/ämpäriä* 'lit. to kick the bucket', a direct translation of the English *kick the bucket*, would not be understandable to a Finnish speaker, even though Finnish contains a semantically and structurally fairly similar expression *potkaista tyhjää* 'lit. kick the void (space)', which even shares the verb with the word-for-word translation. Or maybe the problem is that Finnish already has a similar-appearing idiom with this meaning, and therefore there is no need for yet another similar phrase. These problems are real for both trained translators and laymen, who may sometimes have difficulties of even recognizing idioms in a foreign language let alone understanding their meanings (Baker 1992: 65–67).

Languages and cultures do not exist in a vacuum but are in constant contact with each other, which is why they share material with one another, including idiomatic expressions (see e.g. Parkkinen 2005). Especially in the areas of religion, literature and art, and other spheres of life where we share common, supranational culture, idioms and other phraseological units have always been borrowed between languages. This has led to cross-linguistic idioms which exist in more or less equivalent linguistic form in various languages. For example, in the so-called western Judeo-Christian world there are numerous translated idioms that derive from the Bible. Examples of these include the English *a double-edged/two-edged sword* 'something that has both a good and a bad side to it' and its Finnish counterpart *kaksiteräinen miekka* 'lit. a double-edged sword' or *in a lion's den* 'in a dangerous or difficult situation' and its counterpart *leijonan luolassa* 'lit. in a lion's den'. Other corresponding shared idioms come from antiquity, such as the Latin saying *alea jacta est* 'lit. the die is cast, meaning an important and unalterable decision about the future has been made', which has been translated directly into English as *the die is cast* and into Finnish as *arpa on heitetty* 'lit. the die is cast', or from culturally widespread works of art, such as those of Shakespeare, Molière or Goethe.

The examples above contain translated idioms that have retained their form and meaning when they have been translated into target language. Sometimes culturally shared idioms, however, exist in different languages in a slightly different form, since they have been adapted to those specific cultures (see e.g. Penttilä et al. 1998). Good examples of this exist between English and Finnish. For example, *have goose pimples* 'have small raised spots on your skin' takes the form *olla kananlihalla* 'lit. to have chicken pimples' in Finnish, which is natural, since in the traditional Finnish culture chickens have had a much more important role than geese, and rather than plucking geese Finns have plucked chickens. Similarly, the English expression *a storm in a teacup* 'something that people make unnecessary fuss about' takes that form *myrsky vesilasissa* 'lit. a storm in a water glass' in Finnish because, contrary to the British culture, the status of tea as a refreshment has been fairly insignificant in Finland. Of course, we do not at this point aim to suggest that these idioms have been translated into Finnish from English, but they are given here as examples of a multicultural pool of figurative idioms that are shared by several languages in various forms, some of which are most certainly translations. It is most likely that, if these particular idioms are translation idioms in Finnish, their origin is in some other language than English, for example, Swedish or German. However, since our main point in this article is not to discuss the possible origin of such conventionalized Finnish idioms, we will not explore this question any further.

3 Novel English-based translation idioms in Finnish

Idioms have been translated from different languages into Finnish presumably for as long as Finnish language has existed. For example, the texts of Mikael Agricola, the Father of Written Finnish, are full of translated idioms, which is only natural, since most of his texts were translations. Naturally, the primary source language for idioms that have been translated into Finnish has varied at different times mainly depending on the strength of cultural ties that Finnish speakers have had with speakers of other languages. The long shared history between Finland and Sweden is reflected in loan translations, and the close ties that Finland had with Germany at the first half of the twentieth century influenced the repertoire of Finnish idioms as well. Since the Second World War, the strongest influence upon Finnish has come from the English-speaking popular culture, because Finnish culture has not been able to escape the global "rule" of English any more than any other western European society has. In the Finnish context, English has for some time at least humorously been referred to as the third domestic language – in addition to Finnish and Swedish, which are the two official languages of Finland (see e.g. Leppänen et al. 2008). In the near future, English influence does not seem to be diminishing in any way, rather on the contrary, although especially in some subcultures other languages have also began to play an important role as well. For example, the rise of Japanese popular culture in Finland in recent years may reflect on idioms used by, for example, certain youth groups (see e.g. Valaskivi 2009: 59).

One aspect of English influence on Finnish can be seen in the phenomenon that we have recently noticed to be on the increase: at least, in certain registers Finnish seems to import new expressions that have their origins in English and are translated directly, i.e. word-for-word, into Finnish. Expressions like these are often figurative, but they are not institutionalized in Finnish and cannot, for example, be found in monolingual or bilingual phraseological dictionaries such as Wirén (2007) or Muikku-Werner et al. (2008). If one comes across them in dictionary format, it is mainly in humorous contexts (see e.g. Westlake et al. 2004; 2008). However, in the actual usage of Finnish speakers these idioms are used in informal contexts, where the colloquial expression is the suitable mode of usage. Another interesting feature of these expressions is that in many cases their understanding seems to require knowledge of English, and, moreover, familiarity with the meaning of the original idiom. In that sense, many of them are semantically opaque for ordinary Finnish speakers, even though their figuration might offer an aid that helps in deciphering their meaning (about the motivation behind idiom meaning, see e.g. Langacker 1991; Gibbs 1994; Geeraerts 1995; Hamblin and Gibbs 1999; Nenonen 2002). In the following, we will offer examples of these newly-invented English-derived idioms in Finnish and discuss their semantic nature.

We will base our classification in Cacciari's (1993) categorization of idioms, where the main point is that idiom meanings vary in degree from totally opaque to totally transparent ones. For our purposes we have modified the original classification to some extent, the main distinction being that we talk about translation idioms instead of idioms in general. Cacciari's (1993: 39) classification has the following four classes: 1) totally opaque idioms, 2) retrospectively transparent idioms, 3) directly transparent idioms, and 4) figuratively transparent idioms. The first of these classes contains idioms whose meaning cannot be deduced from their parts – even the figurative image does not help. The second class contains idioms whose meaning may appear opaque at first but becomes transparent once the recipient learns the connection between the literal and figurative meanings of the parts or the situational origin of the expression. The third category includes idioms whose parts have meanings that help in understanding the idiomatic meaning either by analogy or by mapping the metaphorical meaning with the final meaning. This resembles Geeraerts's (1995) notion of isomorphism, which refers to idiom meanings that can be arrived at on the basis of the meanings their individual components carry in other contexts. Cacciari's (1993: 39) fourth and final idiom type contains expressions that could be described as "idioms composed of other idioms, or parts that appear in other idioms or as metaphorical vehicles". Since Cacciari does not give examples, it is unclear how the last two classes differ from one another, and therefore – from our point of view – we can treat them as similar.

Although Cacciari's (1993) classification concerns idioms in one's native language only, we apply it to idioms that are borrowed or translated from another language. However, when translation enters the picture, the picture becomes more complicated and further dimensions need to be accounted for. One aspect that is involved in translated idioms is their degree of adaptation, in other words, the degree to which they have been adjusted to the principles of target language. By this, we do not simply mean how well the novel creation conforms to the grammatical principles of the target language – after all, strictly defined, traditional idioms can also be ungrammatical, or "extragrammatical", as Fillmore et al. (1988: 505) call them – but rather to what extent it has become part of the nativelike fluent articulation of the target language in the sense of Pawley and Syder's (1983) nativelike selection and Sinclair's (1987) idiom principle mentioned above. When we add this property of adaptation to the characteristics that translated idioms may have, we get a classification that slightly differs from Cacciari's (1993). The first three categories are based on her categories (with the last two of them combined), but the fourth class is a new one. Our categories of translated idioms can be labeled as follows:

1) totally opaque translation idioms,
2) retrospectively transparent translation idioms,
3) directly or figuratively transparent translation idioms, and
4) directly or figuratively transparent adapted translation idioms.

As the names suggest, it is only the last class of translation idioms in our analysis that contains expressions that have been fully adapted to the Finnish idiom, so to speak, whereas this adjustment process in all the other classes is still somewhat incomplete. This means that, although we have combined Cacciari's last two classes into one, we have further redivided this combined class into two on the basis of a self-developed criterion of adaptation.

Usually one would expect that when idioms are translated from one language to another, this mainly concerns expressions that tend to be closer to the transparent end of the above-mentioned scale. After all, transparent idioms could most likely be understood even by speakers who do not know either the original expression or even the language from which the idiom has originated. However, this does not seem to be the rule in any way. We have noticed that in present-day Finnish usage there exist – at least in some contexts – directly translated English-derived idioms that are only very vaguely transparent, if at all. In the following, we will give examples of such novel creations and discuss their characteristics in more detail. Since the discussion is qualitative and not quantitative, we will not even try to give any estimation about the possible frequencies of the various idiom types. This will be left for a possible future study. Our database consists of the internet at large, and we have gathered our examples by googling. The examples come from various blogs, forums, discussion groups and such, although we have occasionally come across similar examples also in newspaper and television contexts. The method for collecting the examples was simple. We searched English idiom dictionaries for commonly used idioms that have no word-for-word counterparts in Finnish. Then we randomly picked some of them, translated them word-for-word into Finnish, and googled them. Practically always it was possible to find instances of such word-for-word translations on the net. However, when we tried to google various adaptations of the phrases, it became clear that only in certain cases such transformed variants could be found; we used this as an indicator of the degree to which the idiom had been adapted to Finnish, although one has to admit that this is not a foolproof method.

3.1 Totally opaque translation idioms

Kick the bucket 'to die' is probably the most often cited idiomatic expression in idiom literature, and it can be regarded as opaque in meaning. There are some explanations about the possible origins of the phrase, but they do not make the idiom in any way semantically transparent. Besides, as Hendrickson (1997: 384) points out, since there are various diverging theories about the etymology the phrase, it must in the end be marked "of uncertain origin". This means that the phrase is opaque even to native speakers of English, let alone to non-natives. Nevertheless, instances of word-for-word translations of this idiom can be found in the Finnish data, as examples (1)–(3) indicate.

(1) Sitten toinen, joka *potkaisi ämpäriä* jo 1988 oli kommunisti [...]
 (http://kemppinen.blogspot.com/2009/03/likaisen-tyon-tekija.html)
 'Then the other, who *kicked the bucket* already in 1988, was a communist'

(2) [...] Ismo on hengissä, asuu Venäjällä ja soittelee kotio päin perinnön perässä kun joku *potkaisee ämpäriä...* (http://www.murha.info/phpbb2/viewtopic.php?f=7&t=112&start=60)
 'Ismo is alive, lives in Russia and rings home for his inheritance when someone *kicks the bucket*'

(3) Ja toivon mukaan jatkuu siihen asti, että jompikumpi meistä *potkaisee sankoa* ja heittää lusikkansa nurkkaan. (http://foorumit.fffin.com/showthread.php?p=84643)
 'And hopefully this continues until one of us *kicks the bucket* and throws the spoon into the corner'

The phrase *potkaista ämpäriä/sankoa* is translated word-for-word from English, and it does not have an idiomatic meaning in Finnish. Literally of course it is possible to kick the bucket in Finnish just as well as it is in English, but there is no connection with this wording and dying, and therefore the phrase clearly is an expression that no Finnish speaker would understand without knowing the original English idiom – or without a context that would support the proper interpretation of the phrase. For example, in (2) the adjoined mention of inheritance offers a clue to the meaning of the phrase, while in (3) the accompanied Finnish idiom *heittää lusikka nurkkaan* 'lit. throw the spoon to the corner' carries the same idiomatic meaning as *kick the bucket* thus explaining its content. Of course there is no reason why one would need to translate *kick the bucket* into Finnish, since Finnish already has numerous idiomatic expressions that refer to dying. A few examples have already been mentioned earlier, and some others include *heittää veivinsä* 'lit. to throw one's crank' and *siirtyä manan majoille* 'lit. to move the cabins of Hades'. With these idioms, it is not easy to see whether they have been adapted to idiomatic Finnish or not, since Finnish, like any language, contains totally opaque traditional idioms whose holistic meaning cannot be distributed over their parts. However, there is at least one indicator that could be used as a criterion. If an idiom is used creatively, in other words, if it can exist as different lexical variants, if it can be complemented, if its parts can be modified etc., then it clearly has been adapted to the target language. This does not seem to occur with *potkaista ämpäriä/sankoa*, although the phrase clearly has two lexical variants. However, *ämpäri* and *sanko* are both full semantic synonyms with no real stylistic differences, and in this sense they are not creative variants of each other. As far as we can tell, totally opaque translation idioms do not seem to be used creatively in Finnish, but this is something that definitely needs further investigation.

3.2 Retrospectively transparent translation idioms

In addition to totally opaque expressions, the newly created English-derived Finnish translation idioms also contain expression that are superficially opaque but can eventually be regarded as slightly transparent. For example, the English idiom *spill the beans* 'to reveal a secret' is an instantiation of this class. For a native Finnish speaker, it probably would not mean a thing, but after one thinks more closely about the figuration behind the expression, one might be able to see the connection between the literal and figurative meanings of the parts of the expression, although it might require further explanation. Or, at least, that is what we think, but this is of course only speculation at this point, and the validity of this claim needs to be separately tested before it can be confirmed. Examples (4) and (5) show how the idiom is used in Finnish contexts.

(4) Oli miten oli, Empire Online *kaataa pavut* Abramsin isännöimästä raakileversionäytöksestä.
(http://forum.starwreck.com/viewtopic.php?f=7&t=2444&start=15)
'However, Empire Online *spills the beans* on the raw version presentation hosted by Abrams'

(5) Pitäneekö minunkin jossain vaiheessa *kaataa pavut* pöydälle niistä yhtyeistäni, jotka jäivät arvaamatta?
(http://www.ntfa.net/forums/index.php?showtopic=1318&mode=threaded&pid=2370)
'Should I at some point *spill the beans* on the table about those of my bands, which were not guessed?'

What is interesting here is not only the fact that the idiom is translated word-for-word from English but that it is, in addition, extended and incorporated into a wider context, which shows an aim to make it a natural part of Finnish usage. In (4), the idiom is followed by the topic of the revealed secret in the elative case (*Abramsin isännöimästä raakileversionäytökse* + *stä*). This creative extension could be regarded as a step towards adapting the idiom into Finnish, since elative would be the natural case for expressing the topic in this context; if the idiom were replaced by its literal Finnish counterpart, *paljastaa salaisuus* 'to reveal a secret', the topic would be in the elative case. However, the case suffix could also be regarded as still being influenced by the source language and not totally adapted to Finnish. After all, in English the possible topic would be included in this idiom by adding a prepositional object with either the preposition *on* or *about*, and both of these prepositions are commonly translated into Finnish with the elative case. Another, and somewhat clearer, indicator of the fact that the idiom is only partially adapted to Finnish is that so far we have not been able to find a single example of this idiom where the object of the verb phrase would take the partitive form *papuja* 'beans', which is a natural for an object in Finnish; whenever beans are in the partitive, the phrase carries its literal meaning.[1]

In (5), the idiom also combines with the topic, but here there is a further modification included as well, since the phrase contains a spatial expression in the

---

[1] One has to admit that in Finnish there is also a meaning difference between the partitive object and the so-called total object, which may take the nominative, genitive, or (with pronouns) partitive case. The total object forms a bounded whole, and would in this case refer to the whole secret, whereas the partitive object indicates unboundedness and would in this case mean that only part of the secret is revealed, while another part of it still remains hidden (see *VISK* 2004: §925). The definite article in English also indicates the totality. In any case, the fact that the idiom only exists in this total object form in Finnish shows that its use is to some extent restricted.

allative case *pöydä + lle* 'on the table', which expresses the space, or surface, onto which the beans are spilled. This formulation may also derive from the source language, since English allows a similar addition; it is possible to spill the beans *on the table* or *on the floor* with the figurative, idiomatic sense of the expression retained. So, the addition in both English and Finnish could be regarded as a mere figurative addition that enforces the visual image behind the expression thus making its interpretation easier. There is, however, another interpretation that is possible for the complemented idiom in (5). The phrase *kaataa pavut pöydälle* could be regarded as a combination of two different English idioms that are semantically related: *to spill the beans* and *to lay one's cards on the table* 'to tell the truth about one's feelings and plans'. The latter of these explanations can be justified by the fact that Finnish actually has a similar idiom *paljastaa korttinsa* 'lit. to reveal one's cards', but this phrase never mentions the space to which the cards are placed when they are shown to others. Of course Finnish speakers in practice often reveal their cards by laying them on the table, but there are also other ways in which one can reveal one's cards. So, it is possible that the mention of space comes from English, in which case the translation would involve two idioms instead of one. Nevertheless, independent of which interpretation one gives to example (5), the idiomatic phrase can still be regarded as an expression that is not totally adapted to the target language. It may have begun to take steps towards nativelike Finnish usage, but its creative elements may be considered as deriving from the source language, and therefore the expression is still fairly unadapted. However, whether this conclusion applies to other retrospectively transparent translation idioms requires further analysis.

3.3 Directly or figuratively transparent translation idioms

Among idioms that have been directly translated from English into Finnish, it is possible also to find expressions that can very easily be interpreted because of their obvious figurative motivation. In this sense, they are different from the above listed examples; they cause no difficulties for understanding. However, they are expressions which are not conventionally used in Finnish and could be replaced by a Finnish expression that a native speaker would more plausibly use – in many cases, this replacement would be a Finnish idiom. For example, the English phrase *not my cup of tea* 'something that one is not enthusiastic about or interested in' can be found in Finnish contexts.

(6) Helikoptereilla susia metsästävät hullut kreationistit *eivät ole koskaan olleet minun kuppini teetä.* (http://keronen.blogspot.com/2008/11/barack-obama-ei-ole-rotu.html)
'Mad creationists who hunt wolves with helicopters *have never been my cup of tea*'

(7) Juu ei, ei ole *minun kuppini teetä* tämä suomalainen teennäinen versio. (http://www.viisukuppila.fi/phpBB3/televisio/topic108-990.html?sid=6bf4d218d9ee06584312cfc8a64c4a76)
'Yeah, no, it is *not my cup of tea*, this Finnish artificial version'

This novel translation is interesting in the sense that, although the formulation does not exactly break the principles of Finnish grammar, the phrase in this form would not be regarded as natural for a native Finnish speaker. First of all, when the word teacup consists of two separate words, *kuppi teetä* 'cup of tea', it is conventionally without a possessive suffix, and the context is very general with no reference to the owner of the cup. In this way, the expression would be used, for example, when someone orders a cup of tea in a cafeteria. However, when a Finnish speaker talks about a cup of tea that belongs to someone, for example, my cup of tea, the expression would normally be formed as a compound and the possessive suffix would be added to the end of the whole compound. The formulation would then be *minun tee+kuppi+ni* 'I+GEN tea+cup+POSS' instead of *minun kuppi+ni tee+tä* 'I+GEN cup+POSS tea+PART' as in the translated idiom. This indicates that the phrase has not yet been adapted to the idiomatic reality of Finnish. Of course, there is a possibility that this formulation in the future becomes the norm in Finnish, but that remains to be seen. At present a more idiomatic way of expressing the same idea would probably be to use a corresponding Finnish idiom *ei minun heiniäni* 'lit. not my hay', which would be natural and idiomatic in this context.

Other similar newly-created English-derived Finnish translation idioms include, for example, *go off on a tangent* 'to say/think something that is not directly connected to what was said/thought before', instantiated in example (8).

(8) Olet oikeassa että *se* [luennolla käytetty esimerkki] *lähti tangentilla* eri suuntaan kuin oli tarkoitettu, mutta toisaalta [...] (http://www.gemilo.com/yritysblogi/pysyvassa-hoitosuhteessa/)
'You're right about *it* [an example presented at a lecture] *going off on a tangent* to a different direction than it was meant, but then again'

It could to some extent be interpretable to Finnish speakers who have no knowledge of English or of the original idiom, but the correct interpretation would certainly require further thinking and even rethinking. This is suggested, for example, by the fact that example (8) does not simply contain the translated idiom but the phrase is accompanied by an explanatory complement that helps its interpretation. Since the topic does not merely go off on a tangent but also takes to the direction that is different from the originally intended one, this slightly redundant addition emphasizes how the phrase should be understood. Because the phrase seems to be used in a frozen format, this implies that the expression has not yet been adapted to the Finnish idiomatic usage.

3.4 Directly or figuratively transparent adapted translation idioms

Some novel idiom translations clearly require no further explanations. They are expressions that contain such a vivid figurative image that they can easily be understood. They are often so commonly used that they are understood in the whole western world. In this sense, they may have been incorporated into the Finnish way of speaking to a greater extent than some of the earlier examples we have given. One common source for such idioms is the language of sport, since English plays a significant role in Finnish television broadcasts; athletes are often interviewed in English, and sports broadcasts can be regarded as an environment that is tolerant to foreign language use (Koskela 2008: 332). Moreover, many of the idioms used by sports commentators are strongly figurative. As an example of this, we can take the English idiom *have a monkey on one's back/get a monkey off one's back* 'have/put an end to a serious problem that makes your life difficult', which contains such a vivid metaphorical image that its meaning is likely to be grasped by anyone, although one might still argue that it is not totally transparent. The phrase does not have a word-for-word counterpart in Finnish, but its word-for-word translation has recently become widely used especially in sport-related language. It could be that it is so common at present that at least some of its Finnish users do not even realize that it has been originally translated from English. In its basic form, presented in example (9), the phrase can be heard in broadcasted sports interviews or found on the pages of newspaper sports sections.

(9) Jotain on tehtävä myös silloin, kun pelaajalla tai joukkueella *on apina selässä*.
    (http://www.salibandy.net/liitto/salibandylehti/arkisto/0501.pdf)
    'Something must be done also when a player or a team *has a monkey on its back*'

As an indicator of how well the phrase has been adapted to the Finnish usage we find its alternative wordings that can be found in various sources. The word *selkä* 'back' can be replaced by more or less synonymous alternatives such as *hartiat* 'shoulders' (10) or *niska* 'neck' (11).

(10) Germanin ja Miettisen maalit kyllä lämmittää. Kummallakin *on ollut apina harteilla*, mutta nyt näyttää kyllä hyvältä.
    (http://www.vaihtoaitio.net/viewtopic.php?f=149&t=2742&start=15)
    'German's and Miettinen's goals gladden one's heart. Both *have had a monkey on their shoulders*, but now it looks good'

(11) Kähkösellä *on* tosiaan isohko *apina niskassa* ja jopa liikkuminen on jotenkin kankeampaa kuin normaalisti (johtuisiko apinan painosta).
    (http://keskustelu.jatkoaika.com/showthread.php?t=48036&page=2)
    'Kähkönen really *has* a fairly large *monkey on his neck* and even his moving has been clumsier than usual (could it be the monkey's weight)'

Moreover, example (11) illustrates a further modification – and adaption – of the idiom, since the object in the phrase, *apina* 'monkey', has been premodified by an adjectival phrase *isohko* 'a fairly large'.

In addition to this, there are even more extensive modifications that occur with this idiom. In fact, it seems that the phrase can be fairly freely modified in the way that is possible for fully adapted native idioms (about the flexibility of idioms, see Fellbaum 2007). In this way, it seems to be fairly deeply rooted into the Finnish way of expression, although it definitely has not existed in Finnish for long. For example, in (12) the verb *olla* 'have' has been changed into *kasvaa* 'grows' and in (13) the whole structure of the idiom has been changed at the same time as its figurative image has been slightly renewed by changing the verb.

(12) Shanahanin *selässä apina vain kasvaa*; sen verran tiukasti koitettiin jatkoajallakin miehelle pedata 500. maalia. (http://keskustelu.jatkoaika.com/showthread.php?t=9919&page=2)
    '*In Shanahan's back the monkey just keeps growing*, so intensively they tried to help his 500th goal during overtime'

(13) Voi olla, että vasta siitä jatkoaikamaalista *jonkunmoinen apina selästä tipahti*.
    (http://keskustelu.jatkoaika.fi/showthread.php?t=34500&page=4)
    'It could be that it was only because of that overtime goal that *some sort of a monkey fell off the back*'

Expressions such as these are idioms that are naturally and creatively used by native Finnish speakers, especially in certain contexts. And since they are not used only in their frozen, idiomatic form, but could be modified in a creative fashion, it is obvious that they have to a large extent been absorbed to native, idiomatic Finnish and are not regarded as mere fixed borrowings from a foreign language. In that sense, they are at least well on their way to become truly adapted idiomatic loans in Finnish. One would even assume that they could be used by professional translators. Although translator training makes students aware of the hazards of transfer from the source language, and in this way teaches them consciously to avoid translated idioms in the first three of our categories – unless they either do not do not recognize the idiom or strive for a special effect such as foreignization – there should be no problem in producing translated novel idioms of this last type, especially in cases where there is no corresponding Finnish idiom that would carry as vivid an image as the word-for-word translation does.

4 Conclusion

The phenomenon that we have been discussing in this article, i.e. translating idioms word-for-word from English into Finnish, seems to be on the increase. At least, that is what we intuitively feel after having recently come across it so often in the media and especially on the internet. We can think of various reasons for this. English is a widely spread language and is constantly gaining a stronger international foothold both in the media and in the professional life, and therefore contacts between English and Finnish become more and more common in everyday life as well. Since Finns learn English and encounter it in so many circumstances, they may become so familiar with English expressions that they sometimes do not even realize they are translating these phrases into their native tongue – especially if they have to express themselves under stress or in a situation in which they do not consciously concentrate on their enunciation.

Sometimes people do direct translation consciously. They wish to express themselves humorously or wittily, trying to show off their skills, and therefore they include English-derived word-for-word translated idioms into their expression. This could also be used for an ingroup effect; those who know enough English to appreciate the translated idioms are included in one's ingroup, whereas those who do not understand the point are excluded from it. This could be related to the phenomenon of style shifting (see e.g. Auer 2007). After all, style shifting has relevance for speaker identity. In this respect, the notions of genre, domain and discourse community deserve to be mentioned, although it is not possible to discuss them in detail here. Especially those idioms which have not yet been adapted to Finnish, i.e. our first two or three classes, may form a linguistic resource for individuals and groups who share a multilingual discourse world. To be able to fully participate in this world, one has to know both Finnish and English. In a way, this resembles code shifting, and although the final product is in Finnish, one needs to know English to be able to understand it completely. It may be that this phenomenon is regular, for example, in certain subcultures or for regular users of certain genres, but that is something that deserves further discussion somewhere else. Naturally, other language besides English may also function as sources for the translation idioms discussed here.

Direct idiom translation may be based on mere fun with no ulterior motives. Creating novel Finnish expressions based on fixed English phrases is something that can be done simply to amuse our fellow speakers. This is one possible origin for wordplay and it may be used to enrich one's expression. It does not necessarily require highly developed English skills. On the contrary, word-for-word translation could be easier for someone who does not know idiomatic English. Those who are familiar with the original idioms and their meanings easily fail to notice the meanings that could be arrived at by combining the separate, distributed meanings of the idiom parts, whereas people who do not know the holistic meaning of the idiom, might make such interpretations by default. Naturally, this partly depends on the transparency of the expression as well.

As a consequence of this type of word-for-word translation of foreign idioms, we get new idiomatic expressions that become part of the Finnish idiom repertoire after a while. After all, it is one of the reasons for using idioms that they have expressive strength; they create vivid images in people's minds and provide color to our eloquence, thus adding an extra dimension to our language. Since this is possible with idioms of any language, it is also possible with English idioms: the felicity of a certain English idiom could be so applicable that its translation into Finnish brings an apt addition to the target language. This is one way of extending the idiomatic vocabulary of a language. In contact situations it is not only single words but also multiword expressions that are borrowed, and this is something that happens independent of possible institutional endeavors to prevent it. For example, the idiom *pitkässä juoksussa* 'lit. in the long run, meaning later in the future', which has been translated word-for-word from English into Finnish, has during the last few decades become part of the Finnish native repository of commonly-used idioms despite the efforts of the Finnish Language Office to recommend that the phrase not be used.

It may seem that the phenomenon we have discussed here does not concern professional translators, who only sarcastically sneer at it, but this may be an illusion. At least, Abu-Ssaydeh's (2004: 128) study has shown that – at least in certain contexts – literal translation of English idioms "forms a dominant strategy", even in cases where the word-for-word translation may be awkward or even incomprehensible in the target language. Besides, as Baker (1992: 65–67) points out, even professional translators may at times fail to recognize a source language idiom and therefore translate it word-for-word as an expression that makes no sense in the context. To minimize this possibility, the phenomenon deserves to be recognized by professional translators. Moreover, since translation is one way of introducing new expressions to a language, professional translators should certainly be aware of the phenomenon. They should be sensitive to the fact that source language idioms could provide a possible source of linguistic enrichment as well. Occasionally, they might even exploit this source consciously to introduce new items into their own native language. So, although the phenomenon would at first appear somewhat irrelevant from the perspective of translation studies, we firmly believe that it deserves to be explored further in the future.

References

Abu-Ssaydeh, Abdul-Fattah (2004): "Translation of English idioms into Arabic." In: *Babel* 50:2, 114–131.
Auer, Peter [ed.] (2007): *Style and Social Identities: Alternative Approaches to Linguistic Heterogeneity.* Berlin and New York: Mouton de Gruyter.
Baker, Mona (1992): *In Other Words: A Coursebook on Translation.* London & New York: Routledge.
Barkema, Henk (1996): "Idiomaticity and Terminology: A Multi-Dimensional Descriptive Model." In: *Studia Linguistica* 50 (2), 125–160.

Cacciari, Cristina (1993): "The place of idioms in a literal and metaphorical world." In: Cacciari, Cristina / Tabossi, Patrizia [eds.] (1993): *Idioms: Processing, Structure, and Interpretation*. Hillsdale: Lawrence Erlbaum. 27–55

Fellbaum, Christiane [ed.] (2007): *Idioms and Collocations: Corpus-based Linguistic and Lexicographic Studies*. London: Continuum.

Geeraerts, Dirk (1995): "Specialization and reinterpretation in idioms." In: Everaert, Martin / van der Linden, Eri-Jan / Schenk, André / Schreuder, Rob [eds.] (1995): *Idioms: Structural and Psychological Perspectives*. Hillsdale: Lawrence Erlbaum. 57–73.

Grant, Lynn and Laurie Bauer (2004): "Criteria for re-defining idioms: Are we barking up the wrong tree?" In: *Applied Linguistics* 25/1, 38–61.

Fernando, Chitra (1996): *Idioms and Idiomaticity*. Oxford: Oxford University Press.

Fillmore, Charles J. / Kay, Paul / O'Connor, Mary Catherine (1988): "Regularity and idiomaticity in grammatical constructions: The case of *let alone*." In: *Language*, 64 (3), 501–538.

Gibbs, Raymond W., Jr. (1994): *The Poetics of Mind*. Cambridge: Cambridge University Press.

Hamblin, Jennifer L. / Gibbs, Raymond W., Jr. (1999): "Why you can't kick the bucket as you slowly die: Verbs in idiom comprehension." In: *Journal of Psycholinguistics Research*, Vol. 28, No. 1, 25–39.

Hendrickson, Robert (1997): *The Facts on File Encyclopedia of Word and Phrase Origins*. Revised and expanded edition. New York: Facts On File.

Koskela, Heidi (2008): "That was smooth and fast: Kannanotot englanninkielisissä urheiluhaastatteluissa" [Comments in English sports interviews]. In: Leppänen, Sirpa / Nikula, Tarja / Kääntä, Leila [eds.] (2008): *Kolmas kotimainen: Lähikuvia englannin käytöstä suomesta Suomessa* [The third domestic language: Close-ups of the usage of English in Finland]. Helsinki: SKS. 323–354.

Langacker, Ronald (1991): *Concept, Image, and Symbol: The Cognitive Basis of Grammar*. Berlin: Mouton de Gruyter.

Langlotz, Andreas (2006): *Idiomatic Creativity*. Amsterdam and Philadelphia: John Benjamins.

Leppänen, Sirpa / Nikula, Tarja / Kääntä, Leila [eds.] (2008): *Kolmas kotimainen: Lähikuvia englannin käytöstä suomesta Suomessa* [The third domestic language: Close-ups of the usage of English in Finland]. Helsinki: SKS.

Makkai, Adam (1972): *Idiom Structure in English*. The Hague: Mouton.

Moon, Rosamund (1998): *Fixed Expressions and Idioms in English: A Corpus-Based Approach*. Oxford: Clarendon Press.

Muikku-Werner, Pirkko / Jantunen, Jarmo Harri / Kokko, Ossi (2008): *Suurella sydämellä ihan sikana: Suomen kielen kuvaileva fraasisanakirja* [With all one's heart and at full blast: The descriptive phrasal dictionary of Finnish]. Jyväskylä: Gummerus.

Nenonen, Marja (2002): *Idiomit ja leksikko: Lausekeidiomien syntaktisia, semanttisia ja morfologisia pürteitä suomen kielessä* [Idioms and the lexicon: Syntactic, semantic and morphological features of phrasal idioms in Finnish]. Joensuu: University of Joensuu. (University of Joensuu Publications in the Humanities. 29.)

Nunberg, Geoffrey / Sag, Ivan A. / Wasow, Thomas (1994): "Idioms." In: *Language*, 70 (3), 491–538.

Oxford English Dictionary (2010): Oxford: Oxford University Press. Available online at: http://dictionary.oed.com/. Visited 18 March, 2010.

Parkkinen, Jukka (2005): *Aasinsilta ajan hermolla* [Asses' Bridge attuned to the times] Helsinki: WSOY.

Pawley, Andrew / Syder, Frances Hodgetts (1983): "Two puzzles for linguistic theory: Nativelike selection and nativelike fluency." In: Richards, J.C. / Schmidt, R. W. [eds.] (1983): *Language and Communication*. London: Longman. 191–226.

Penttilä, Esa (2006): *It Takes an Age to Do a Chomsky: Idiomaticity and Verb Phrase Constructions in English*. Unpublished PhD Thesis. Department of English, University of Joensuu.

Penttilä, Esa / Nenonen, Marja / Niemi, Jussi (1998): "Cultural and biological basis of idioms: A crosslinguistic study." In: Niemi, Jussi / Odlin, Terence / Heikkinen, Janne [eds.] (1998): *Language Contact, Variation, and Change*. Joensuu: University of Joensuu, Faculty of Humanities. (Studies in Languages. 32.) 234–245.

Sinclair, John (1987): "Collocation: A progress report." In: Steele, R. / Threadgold, T. [eds.] (1987): *Language Topics: Essays in Honour of Michael Holiday*. Amsterdam and Philadelphia: John Benjamins. 319–331.

Valaskivi, Katja (2009): *Pokemonin perilliset: Japanilainen populaarikulttuuri Suomessa* [Heir's of Pokemon: Japanese Popular Culture in Finland]. Tampere: Juvenes Print – Tampereen yliopistopaino Oy.

Valero-Garcés, Carmen (1997): "Contrastive idiomatology: Equivalence and translatability of English and Spanish Idioms." In: *PSiCL*, Vol. 32, 29–38.

VISK = Hakulinen, Auli / Vilkuna, Maria / Korhonen, Riitta / Koivisto, Vesa / Heinonen, Tarja Riitta / Alho, Irja (2004): *Iso suomen kielioppi* [Big Finnish grammar]. Helsinki: SKS. Available online at: http://scripta.kotus.fi/visk/.

Westlake, Paul / Partti, Krista / Pitkänen, Eeva-Liisa (2004): *Parempi pyy pivossa kuin two in the bush*. Helsinki: WSOY.

—— (2008): *Se ei ole minun cup of tea*. Helsinki: WSOY.

Wirén, Veijo (2007): *Suomi-englanti idiomi- ja fraasisanakirja* [Finnish-English Idiom and Phrasal Dictionary]. Helsinki: Art House.

TRANSÜD. Arbeiten zur Theorie und Praxis des Übersetzens und Dolmetschens

Die Bände 1 bis 5 sind bei der Peter Lang GmbH erschienen und dort zu beziehen.

Bd. 6 Przemysław Chojnowski: Zur Strategie und Poetik des Übersetzens. Eine Untersuchung der Anthologien zur polnischen Lyrik von Karl Dedecius. 300 Seiten. ISBN 978-3-86596-013-9

Bd. 7 Belén Santana López: Wie wird *das Komische* übersetzt? *Das Komische* als Kulturspezifikum bei der Übersetzung spanischer Gegenwartsliteratur. 456 Seiten. ISBN 978-3-86596-006-1

Bd. 8 Larisa Schippel (Hg.): Übersetzungsqualität: Kritik – Kriterien – Bewertungshandeln. 194 Seiten. ISBN 978-3-86596-075-7

Bd. 9 Anne-Kathrin D. Ende: Dolmetschen im Kommunikationsmarkt. Gezeigt am Beispiel Sachsen. 228 Seiten. ISBN 978-3-86596-073-3

Bd. 10 Sigrun Döring: Kulturspezifika im Film: Probleme ihrer Translation. 156 Seiten. ISBN 978-3-86596-100-6

Bd. 11 Hartwig Kalverkämper: „Textqualität". Die Evaluation von Kommunikationsprozessen seit der antiken Rhetorik bis zur Translationswissenschaft. ISBN 978-3-86596-110-5

Bd. 12 Yvonne Griesel: Die Inszenierung als Translat. Möglichkeiten und Grenzen der Theaterübertitelung. 362 Seiten. ISBN 978-3-86596-119-8

Bd. 13 Hans J. Vermeer: Ausgewählte Vorträge zur Translation und anderen Themen. Selected Papers on Translation and other Subjects. 286 Seiten. ISBN 978-3-86596-145-7

Bd. 14 Erich Prunč: Entwicklungslinien der Translationswissenschaft. Von den Asymmetrien der Sprachen zu den Asymmetrien der Macht. 442 Seiten. ISBN 978-3-86596-146-4 (vergriffen, siehe Band 43 der Reihe)

Bd. 15 Valentyna Ostapenko: Vernetzung von Fachtextsorten. Textsorten der Normung in der technischen Harmonisierung. 128 Seiten. ISBN 978-3-86596-155-6

Bd. 16 Larisa Schippel (Hg.): TRANSLATIONSKULTUR – ein innovatives und produktives Konzept. 340 Seiten. ISBN 978-3-86596-158-7

Bd. 17 Hartwig Kalverkämper/Larisa Schippel (Hg.): Simultandolmetschen in Erstbewährung: Der Nürnberger Prozess 1945. Mit einer orientierenden Einführung von Klaus Kastner und einer kommentierten fotografischen Dokumentation von Theodoros Radisoglou sowie mit einer dolmetsch-wissenschaftlichen Analyse von Katrin Rumprecht. 344 Seiten. ISBN 978-3-86596-161-7

Frank & Timme

TRANSÜD. Arbeiten zur Theorie und Praxis des Übersetzens und Dolmetschens

Bd. 18   Regina Bouchehri: Filmtitel im interkulturellen Transfer. 174 Seiten.
ISBN 978-3-86596-180-8

Bd. 19   Michael Krenz/Markus Ramlow: Maschinelle Übersetzung und XML im Übersetzungsprozess. Prozesse der Translation und Lokalisierung im Wandel. Zwei Beiträge, hg. von Uta Seewald-Heeg. 368 Seiten. ISBN 978-3-86596-184-6

Bd. 20   Hartwig Kalverkämper/Larisa Schippel (Hg.): Translation zwischen Text und Welt – Translationswissenschaft als historische Disziplin zwischen Moderne und Zukunft. 700 Seiten. ISBN 978-3-86596-202-7

Bd. 21   Nadja Grbić/Sonja Pöllabauer: Kommunaldolmetschen/Community Interpreting. Probleme – Perspektiven – Potenziale. Forschungsbeiträge aus Österreich. 380 Seiten. ISBN 978-3-86596-194-5

Bd. 22   Agnès Welu: Neuübersetzungen ins Französische – eine kulturhistorische Übersetzungskritik. Eichendorffs *Aus dem Leben eines Taugenichts*. 506 Seiten. ISBN 978-3-86596-193-8

Bd. 23   Martin Slawek: Interkulturell kompetente Geschäftskorrespondenz als Garant für den Geschäftserfolg. Linguistische Analysen und fachkommunikative Ratschläge für die Geschäftsbeziehungen nach Lateinamerika (Kolumbien). 206 Seiten. ISBN 978-3-86596-206-5

Bd. 24   Julia Richter: Kohärenz und Übersetzungskritik. Lucian Boias Analyse des rumänischen Geschichtsdiskurses in deutscher Übersetzung. 142 Seiten. ISBN 978-3-86596-221-8

Bd. 25   Anna Kucharska: Simultandolmetschen in defizitären Situationen. Strategien der translatorischen Optimierung. 170 Seiten. ISBN 978-3-86596-244-7

Bd. 26   Katarzyna Lukas: Das Weltbild und die literarische Konvention als Übersetzungsdeterminanten. Adam Mickiewicz in deutschsprachigen Übertragungen. 402 Seiten. ISBN 978-3-86596-238-6

Bd. 27   Markus Ramlow: Die maschinelle Simulierbarkeit des Humanübersetzens. Evaluation von Mensch-Maschine-Interaktion und der Translatqualität der Technik. 364 Seiten. ISBN 978-3-86596-260-7

Bd. 28   Ruth Levin: Der Beitrag des Prager Strukturalismus zur Translationswissenschaft. Linguistik und Semiotik der literarischen Übersetzung. 154 Seiten. ISBN 978-3-86596-262-1

Bd. 29   Iris Holl: Textología contrastiva, derecho comparado y traducción jurídica. Las sentencias de divorcio alemanas y españolas. 526 Seiten. ISBN 978-3-86596-324-6

TRANSÜD. Arbeiten zur Theorie und Praxis des Übersetzens und Dolmetschens

Bd. 30 Christina Korak: Remote Interpreting via Skype. Anwendungsmöglichkeiten von VoIP-Software im Bereich Community Interpreting – Communicate everywhere? 202 Seiten. ISBN 978-3-86596-318-5

Bd. 31 Gemma Andújar/Jenny Brumme (eds.): Construir, deconstruir y reconstruir. Mímesis y traducción de la oralidad y la afectividad. 224 Seiten. ISBN 978-3-86596-234-8

Bd. 32 Christiane Nord: Funktionsgerechtigkeit und Loyalität. Theorie, Methode und Didaktik des funktionalen Übersetzens. 338 Seiten. ISBN 978-3-86596-330-7

Bd. 33 Christiane Nord: Funktionsgerechtigkeit und Loyalität. Die Übersetzung literarischer und religiöser Texte aus funktionaler Sicht. 304 Seiten. ISBN 978-3-86596-331-4

Bd. 34 Małgorzata Stanek: Dolmetschen bei der Polizei. Zur Problematik des Einsatzes unqualifizierter Dolmetscher. 262 Seiten. ISBN 978-3-86596-332-1

Bd. 35 Dorota Karolina Bereza: Die Neuübersetzung. Eine Hinführung zur Dynamik literarischer Translationskultur. 108 Seiten. ISBN 978-3-86596-255-3

Bd. 36 Montserrat Cunillera/Hildegard Resinger (eds.): Implicación emocional y oralidad en la traducción literaria. 230 Seiten. ISBN 978-3-86596-339-0

Bd. 37 Ewa Krauss: Roman Ingardens „Schematisierte Ansichten" und das Problem der Übersetzung. 226 Seiten. ISBN 978-3-86596-315-4

Bd. 38 Miriam Leibbrand: Grundlagen einer hermeneutischen Dolmetschforschung. 324 Seiten. ISBN 978-3-86596-343-7

Bd. 39 Pekka Kujamäki/Leena Kolehmainen/Esa Penttilä/Hannu Kemppanen (eds.): Beyond Borders – Translations Moving Languages, Literatures and Cultures. 272 Seiten. ISBN 978-3-86596-356-7

Bd. 40 Gisela Thome: Übersetzen als interlinguales und interkulturelles Sprachhandeln. Theorien – Methodologie – Ausbildung. 622 Seiten. ISBN 978-3-86596-352-9

Bd. 41 Radegundis Stolze: The Translator's Approach – Introduction to Translational Hermeneutics. Theory and Examples from Practice. 304 Seiten. ISBN 978-3-86596-373-4

Bd. 42 Silvia Roiss/Carlos Fortea Gil/María Ángeles Recio Ariza/Belén Santana López/ Petra Zimmermann González/Iris Holl (eds.): En las vertientes de la traducción e interpretación del/al alemán. 582 Seiten. ISBN 978-3-86596-326-0

Frank & Timme

TRANSÜD. Arbeiten zur Theorie und Praxis des Übersetzens und Dolmetschens

Bd. 43 Erich Prunč: Entwicklungslinien der Translationswissenschaft. 3., erweiterte und verbesserte Auflage (1. Aufl. 2007. ISBN 978-3-86596-146-4). 528 Seiten. ISBN 978-3-86596-422-9

Bd. 44 Mehmet Tahir Öncü: Die Rechtsübersetzung im Spannungsfeld von Rechtsvergleich und Rechtssprachvergleich. Zur deutschen und türkischen Strafgesetzgebung. 380 Seiten. ISBN 978-3-86596-424-3

Bd. 45 Hartwig Kalverkämper/Larisa Schippel (Hg.): „Vom Altern der Texte". Bausteine für eine Geschichte des interkulturellen Wissenstransfers. 456 Seiten. ISBN 978-3-86596-251-5

Bd. 46 Hannu Kemppanen/Marja Jänis/Alexandra Belikova (eds.): Domestication and Foreignization in Translation Studies. 240 Seiten. 978-3-86596-470-0

Bd. 47 Sergey Tyulenev: Translation and the Westernization of Eighteenth-Century Russia. A Social-Systemic Perspective. 272 Seiten. ISBN 978-3-86596-472-4

Bd. 48 Martin B. Fischer/Maria Wirf Naro (eds.): Translating Fictional Dialogue for Children and Young People. 422 Seiten. ISBN 978-3-86596-467-0

Bd. 49 Martina Behr: Evaluation und Stimmung. Ein neuer Blick auf Qualität im (Simultan-)Dolmetschen. 356 Seiten. ISBN 978-3-86596-485-4

Bd. 50 Anna Gopenko: Traduire le sublime. Les débats de l'Église orthodoxe russe sur la langue liturgique. 228 Seiten. ISBN 978-3-86596-486-1

Bd. 51 Lavinia Heller: Translationswissenschaftliche Begriffsbildung und das Problem der performativen Unauffälligkeit von Translation. 332 Seiten. ISBN 978-3-86596-470-0

Bd. 52 Claudia Dathe/Renata Makarska/Schamma Schahadat (Hg.): Zwischentexte. Literarisches Übersetzen in Theorie und Praxis. 300 Seiten. ISBN 978-3-86596-442-7

Bd. 53 Regina Bouchehri: Translation von Medien-Titeln. Der interkulturelle Transfer von Titeln in Literatur, Theater, Film und Bildender Kunst. 334 Seiten. ISBN 978-3-86596-400-7

Bd. 54 Nilgin Tanış Polat: Raum im (Hör-)Film. Zur Wahrnehmung und Repräsentation von räumlichen Informationen in deutschen und türkischen Audiodeskriptionstexten. 138 Seiten. ISBN 978-3-86596-508-0

Bd. 55 Eva Parra Membrives/Ángeles García Calderón (eds.): Traducción, mediación, adaptación. Reflexiones en torno al proceso de comunicación entre culturas. 336 Seiten. ISBN 978-3-86596-499-1

Frank & Timme

TRANSÜD. Arbeiten zur Theorie und Praxis des Übersetzens und Dolmetschens

Bd. 56 Yvonne Sanz López: Videospiele übersetzen – Probleme und Optimierung. 126 Seiten. ISBN 978-3-86596-541-7

Bd. 57 Irina Bondas: Theaterdolmetschen – Phänomen, Funktionen, Perspektiven. 240 Seiten. ISBN 978-3-86596-540-0

Bd. 58 Dinah Krenzler-Behm: Authentische Aufträge in der Übersetzerausbildung. Ein Leitfaden für die Translationsdidaktik. 480 Seiten. ISBN 978-3-86596-498-4

Bd. 59 Anne-Kathrin Ende/Susann Herold/Annette Weilandt (Hg.): Alles hängt mit allem zusammen. Translatologische Interdependenzen. Festschrift für Peter A. Schmitt. 544 Seiten. ISBN 978-3-86596-504-2

Bd. 60 Saskia Weber: Kurz- und Kosenamen in russischen Romanen und ihre deutschen Übersetzungen. 256 Seiten. ISBN 978-3-7329-0002-2

Bd. 61 Silke Jansen/Martina Schrader-Kniffki (eds.): La traducción a través de los tiempos, espacios y disciplinas. 366 Seiten. ISBN 978-3-86596-524-0

Bd. 62 Annika Schmidt-Glenewinkel: Kinder als Dolmetscher in der Arzt-Patienten-Interaktion. 130 Seiten. ISBN 978-3-7329-0010-7

Bd. 63 Klaus-Dieter Baumann/Hartwig Kalverkämper (Hg.): Theorie und Praxis des Dolmetschens und Übersetzens in fachlichen Kontexten. 756 Seiten. ISBN 978-3-7329-0016-9

Bd. 64 Silvia Ruzzenenti: «Präzise, doch ungenau» – Tradurre il saggio. Un approccio olistico al *poetischer Essay* di Durs Grünbein. 406 Seiten. ISBN 978-3-7329-0026-8

Bd. 65 Margarita Zoe Giannoutsou: Kirchendolmetschen – Interpretieren oder Transformieren? 498 Seiten mit CD. ISBN 978-3-7329-0067-1

Bd. 66 Andreas F. Kelletat/Aleksey Tashinskiy (Hg.): Übersetzer als Entdecker. Ihr Leben und Werk als Gegenstand translationswissenschaftlicher und literaturgeschichtlicher Forschung. 376 Seiten. ISBN 978-3-7329-0060-2

Bd. 67 Ulrike Spieler: Übersetzer zwischen Identität, Professionalität und Kulturalität: Heinrich Enrique Beck. 340 Seiten. ISBN 978-3-7329-0107-4

Bd. 68 Carmen Klaus: Translationsqualität und Crowdsourced Translation. Untertitelung und ihre Bewertung – am Beispiel des audiovisuellen Mediums TEDTalk. 180 Seiten. ISBN 979-3-7329-0031-1

Bd. 69 Susanne J. Jekat/Heike Elisabeth Jüngst/Klaus Schubert/Claudia Villiger (Hg.): Sprache barrierefrei gestalten. Perspektiven aus der Angewandten Linguistik. 276 Seiten. ISBN 978-3-7329-0023-7

Frank & Timme

TRANSÜD. Arbeiten zur Theorie und Praxis des Übersetzens und Dolmetschens

Bd. 70   Radegundis Stolze: Hermeneutische Übersetzungskompetenz. Grundlagen und Didaktik. 402 Seiten. ISBN 978-3-7329-0122-7

Bd. 71   María Teresa Sánchez Nieto (ed.): Corpus-based Translation and Interpreting Studies: From description to application / Estudios traductológicos basados en corpus: de la descripción a la aplicación. 268 Seiten. ISBN 978-3-7329-0084-8

Bd. 72   Karin Maksymski/Silke Gutermuth/Silvia Hansen-Schirra (eds.): Translation and Comprehensibility. 296 Seiten. ISBN 978-3-7329-0022-0

Bd. 73   Hildegard Spraul: Landeskunde Russland für Übersetzer. Sprache und Werte im Wandel. Ein Studienbuch. 360 Seiten. ISBN 978-3-7329-0109-8

Bd. 74   Ralph Krüger: The Interface between Scientific and Technical Translation Studies and Cognitive Linguistics. With Particular Emphasis on Explicitation and Implicitation as Indicators of Translational Text-Context Interaction. 482 Seiten. ISBN 978-3-7329-0136-4

Bd. 75   Erin Boggs: Interpreting U.S. Public Diplomacy Speeches. 154 Seiten. ISBN 978-3-7329-0150-0

Bd. 76   Nathalie Mälzer (Hg.): Comics – Übersetzungen und Adaptionen. 404 Seiten. ISBN 978-3-7329-0131-9

Bd. 77   Sophie Beese: Das (zweite) andere Geschlecht – der Diskurs „Frau" im Wandel. Simone de Beauvoirs *Le deuxième sexe* in deutscher Erst- und Neuübersetzung. 264 Seiten. ISBN 978-3-7329-0141-8

Bd. 78   Xenia Wenzel: Die Übersetzbarkeit philosophischer Diskurse. Eine Übersetzungskritik an den beiden englischen Übersetzungen von Heideggers *Sein und Zeit*. 162 Seiten. ISBN 978-3-7329-0199-9

Bd. 79   María-José Varela Salinas/Bernd Meyer (eds.): Translating and Interpreting Healthcare Discourses/Traducir e interpretar en el ámbito sanitario. 266 Seiten. ISBN 978-3-86596-367-3

Bd. 80   Susanne Hagemann: Einführung in das translationswissenschaftliche Arbeiten. Ein Lehr- und Übungsbuch. 360 Seiten. ISBN 978-3-7329-0125-8

Bd. 81   Anja Maibaum: Spielfilm-Synchronisation. Eine translationskritische Analyse am Beispiel amerikanischer Historienfilme über den Zweiten Weltkrieg. 144 Seiten mit CD. ISBN 978-3-7329-0220-0

Bd. 82   Sybille Schellheimer: La función evocadora de la fraseología en la oralidad ficcional y su traducción. 356 Seiten. ISBN 978-3-7329-0232-3

Frank & Timme

TRANSÜD. Arbeiten zur Theorie und Praxis des Übersetzens und Dolmetschens

Bd. 83 Franziska Heidrich: Kommunikationsoptimierung im Fachübersetzungsprozess. 276 Seiten. ISBN 978-3-7329-0262-0

Bd. 84 Cristina Plaza Lara: Integración de la competencia instrumental-profesional en el aula de traducción. 222 Seiten mit CD. ISBN 978-3-7329-0309-2

Bd. 85 Andreas F. Kelletat/Aleksey Tashinskiy/Julija Boguna (Hg.): Übersetzerforschung. Neue Beiträge zur Literatur- und Kulturgeschichte des Übersetzens. 366 Seiten. ISBN 978-3-7329-0234-7

Bd. 86 Heidrun Witte: Blickwechsel. Interkulturelle Wahrnehmung im translatorischen Handeln. 274 Seiten. ISBN 978-3-7329-0333-7

Bd. 87 Susanne Hagemann/Julia Neu/Stephan Walter (Hg.): Translationslehre und Bologna-Prozess: Unterwegs zwischen Einheit und Vielfalt / Translation/Interpreting Teaching and the Bologna Process: Pathways between Unity and Diversity. 434 Seiten. ISBN 978-3-7329-0311-5

Bd. 88 Ursula Wienen/Laura Sergo/Tinka Reichmann/Ivonne Gutiérrez Aristizábal (Hg.): Translation und Ökonomie. 274 Seiten. ISBN 978-3-7329-0203-3

Bd. 89 Daniela Eichmeyer: Luftqualität in Dolmetschkabinen als Einflussfaktor auf die Dolmetschqualität. Interdisziplinäre Erkenntnisse und translationspraktische Konsequenzen. 144 Seiten. ISBN 978-3-7329-0362-7

Bd. 90 Alexander Künzli: Die Untertitelung – von der Produktion zur Rezeption. 264 Seiten. ISBN 978-3-7329-0393-1

Bd. 91 Christiane Nord: Traducir, una actividad con propósito. Introducción a los enfoques funcionalistas. 228 Seiten. ISBN 978-3-7329-0410-5

Bd. 92 Fabjan Hafner/Wolfgang Pöckl (Hg.): „… übersetzt von Peter Handke" – Philologische und translationswissenschaftliche Analysen. 294 Seiten. ISBN 978-3-7329-0443-3

Bd. 93 Elisabeth Gibbels: Lexikon der deutschen Übersetzerinnen 1200–1850. 216 Seiten. ISBN 978-3-7329-0422-8

Bd. 94 Encarnación Postigo Pinazo: Optimización de las competencias del traductor e intérprete. Nuevas tecnologías – procesos cognitivos – estrategias. 194 Seiten. ISBN 978-3-7329-0392-4

Bd. 95 Marta Estévez Grossi: Lingüística Migratoria e Interpretación en los Servicios Públicos. La comunidad gallega en Alemania. 574 Seiten. ISBN 978-3-7329-0411-2